Companion to the
Revised Common Lectionary

6. Mining the Meaning

Year A

Already published

Companion to the Revised Common Lectionary

1: Intercessions

2: All Age Worship Year A

3: All Age Worship Year B

4: All Age Worship Year C

5: Before We Worship

Henry McKeating

Companion to the Revised Common Lectionary

6. Mining the Meaning

Help in Sermon Preparation

Year A

EPWORTH PRESS

British Library Cataloguing in Publication data

*A catalogue record of this book is available
from the British Library*

0 7162 0548 3

*First Published 2001
by Epworth Press
20 Ivatt Way
Peterborough, PE3 7PG*

*Typeset by Regent Typesetting, London
Printed and bound in Great Britain by
Biddles Ltd, Guildford and King's Lynn*

Contents

General Introduction to Mining the Meaning: help in sermon preparation, Year A

For almost twenty years Epworth Press has offered *Companions to the Lectionary* as an aid to preachers and worship leaders. The majority of the material has been prayers in various styles and for different purposes.

The *Companion to the Revised Common Lectionary* (from 1998) has already broken new ground with material for All Age Worship for Years A, B and C, but now Epworth offers aids to reflection and thought for those who will be preaching on the appointed lections.

The three volumes in the *Mining the Meaning* series, of which this is the first, will follow the Lectionary for the Principal Service for the day, as it is set out in the *Methodist Worship Book* (1999). This is virtually identical to the ecumenical *Revised Common Lectionary*, authorized for use in a number of major denominations. We offer this series, like its predecessors, to all who are called and appointed to preach.

The comments in this book are mainly based on the RSV translation, although the Lectionary itself is based on the NRSV (Anglicized) translation of the Bible.

Mining the Meaning volumes for Year B and C of the Lectionary are in preparation.

Gerald M. Burt
Editorial Secretary

Introduction

Preachers who became familiar with JLG 1 with its clearly stated 'themes' for each week got used to looking for uniting elements in the three readings, Old Testament, Epistle and Gospel; and even when JLG 2 appeared, in which no explicit themes were printed, it was evident that the lectionary makers had been working on the same principles as those who designed JLG 1, and 'spot the theme' became a regular game in places where preachers came together. In some quarters the idea got around that this was the one proper way to use a lectionary, i.e. to find one unifying theme which would enable the preacher to expound all three readings in a coherent way. Preachers who assume this will already have found RCL disconcerting. The incorporation of unifying themes, which relate all the readings for a given week to each other, has not been a major preoccupation of its makers.

The normal pattern of the lectionary is that a Gospel is followed through 'continuously', i.e. systematically, one Sunday's Gospel generally (though not invariably) taking up where last Sunday's left off. Alongside this go the readings from the Epistle, which are also treated 'continuously'. A moment's reflection will lead to the conclusion that on this system any thematic connections between Epistle and Gospel are likely to be fortuitous. Normally, the Old Testament readings are not continuous, and have evidently been chosen with an eye to a thematic connection with one of the New Testament readings, usually the Gospel. At certain periods of the liturgical year, however, an alternative set of Old Testament readings is offered, which *are* 'continuous'. At such periods the preacher has the option of following systematically through part of the Old Testament, though in this case the thematic connection of the Old Testament and New Testament readings is forfeited.

All this faces the preacher with a number of policy decisions. Preachers who occupy the same pulpit on most Sundays may wish to take their congregations systematically through an Epistle, or systematically through a Gospel, but they cannot do both at the same time. If they systemically follow a Gospel they will generally find a helpful thematic link in the Old Testament reading. At some periods of the year they also have the option of going systematically through a portion of the Old Testament, but as already stated, they will not in that case usually find any thematic link between the Old Testament reading and the New Testament ones. More occasional preachers can give themselves a freer hand and take each Sunday's lections as they come. If they set a high value on continuity from week to week they can only do so by getting together with the other occupants of the pulpit and devising a common policy. This is worthwhile, but very time consuming if it is to be done effectively.

Despondent footnote on continuity of preaching

The makers of RCL have given a high priority to continuity from week to week. Personally, I think this is a pity. Discussing this issue of continuity at a day conference I was told emphatically by one contributor that 'The days of continuity in preaching are gone.' Many even of our most loyal worshippers, it was said, though they may still worship regularly, do so less frequently than formerly. Their pattern is regularly every fortnight, or regularly every month, not every week. Continuity from week to week in the preaching is worthless if the congregation are not there to hear the follow-up. Whether this is true or not, and I believe it is, the preacher's primary aim, in constructing a sermon, should surely be to produce something which stands on its own feet and communicates a worthwhile message even to a listener who has not heard what preceded it the previous Sunday, and will not be there next Sunday to hear what follows. This is without prejudice to the hope that a listener who did hear last week's exploration of Romans 7 will be in a better position to appreciate the fullness of this week's exposition of Romans 8.

Given the characteristics of RCL, as described above, and the fact that its makers evidently did not set a high value on closely relating the three scripture readings, the preacher needs to resist the temptation, which some users of the previous JLG lectionaries may feel, to have something to say about all three readings. On most Sundays there is a sharp choice to be made: either one preaches from the Gospel – perhaps together with its associated Old Testament lesson – or from the Epistle. Relatively rarely is it possible to do both. The attempt to do both, when there is no genuine thematic connection between Epistle and Gospel, can only result in muddled, untidy and badly structured sermons which are likely to confuse the hearers more than they help them.

Perhaps the truth is that RCL is not really a preachers' lectionary at all. Those of us who have been brought up in the traditions of non-conformity naturally assume that Bible readings are there to be expounded. For the makers of RCL I suspect that the readings are there primarily to speak for themselves. If in public worship we *read* our way steadily through a Gospel (or any other book of the Bible), then in their minds that is what matters. We don't have to *preach* our way through it. Once we realize that what our instincts are leading us to do with the lectionary is something for which it was not primarily designed, we shall probably relate to it more happily. If nothing else, it will reduce unrealistic expectations and reassure us that if we find it difficult it is not entirely our fault.

FIRST SUNDAY OF ADVENT

Isaiah 2.1–5; Romans 13.11–14; Matthew 24.36–44

There is no attempt by the lectionary to make the Advent readings in any way 'continuous'. What holds them together is the Advent theme. Thematic links between the Old Testament, Epistle and Gospel readings are therefore strong at this point in the liturgical year.

Isaiah 2.1–5

In its original context this oracle concerns 'Judah and Jerusalem'. It has a strong element of nationalism, but it does have a universal reference. And it refers emphatically to this world. Though it relates to the future, it is not strictly an eschatological future. The prophet is not envisaging the end of the world or the last judgement. What we have here is a hopeful prediction that all nations will come to respect the God of Israel and his Law and his word. They will accept the Lord as arbitrator in their conflicts (though the mechanics of this process are not spelled out). The result will be universal peace.

Biblical faith is rooted in the past, but it is future orientated. The prophets believed that if people took God seriously then things could change, and change for the better. And they thought that this would not only make their society a better society, but the world a better world. This is something Christians ought not to lose sight of. Maybe someday the last trump will sound and God will make us a new heaven and a new earth, but in the meantime it is part of the biblical faith that we should try to make better the earth we have, and the way to make it better is by obedience to God and his Law and his word. The Advent hope relates to two futures: there is the eschatological future of which our Gospel and Epistle speak, and there is the future 'in the time of this mortal life', to which our prophetic reading addresses itself.

Romans 13.11–14

The epistle begins by directing our attention to what we usually call the 'second coming', to the salvation which is 'nearer to us now than when we first believed'. The perspective is therefore overtly eschatological in a sense in which that of our prophetic lection is not. Yet having established that perspective, St Paul immediately goes on to draw conclusions which relate to the present life of the Christian, and particularly to the *moral* life. If we take seriously the judgement of God then this has profound implications for the way we conduct ourselves. God's verdict on us, whether it be delivered soon or in the far future of eternity, is a verdict on what we do and what we are *now*. The day of judgement is in that sense always *today*.

It is worth noting that the specific sins against which St Paul warns his readers in this passage are not refined or subtle ones. Quarrelling and jealousy may not surprise us. They happen, regrettably, even among Christians, and even in the church, but the mention of debauchery, licentiousness and drunken orgies is unexpected. Perhaps we flatter our congregations by concentrating too much on the subtle sins. Maybe they are not as free of the grosser ones as we imagine. St Paul, at any rate, thinks it worth talking about moral basics.

Matthew 24.36–44

The thinking in the Gospel passage is closely parallel to that in the Epistle. It focuses on the coming of the Son of man, and it stresses the unexpectedness of that coming. We do not know when it will happen. Remarkably, it asserts that even the Son himself does not know. The fact that we are ignorant of the timing is not due to a divine oversight. It is that very ignorance that is meant to 'keep us on our toes'. Ignorance means unexpectedness, and unexpectedness means that we must be always prepared. It could be anytime; therefore it could be now. As it is for St Paul, therefore, the implications of the coming are implications for present behaviour. The Christian is to live every day and every hour as one accountable to God. The keynote, both in the Gospel and in the Epistle, is urgency.

SECOND SUNDAY OF ADVENT

Isaiah 11.1–10; Romans 15.4–13; Matthew 3.1–12

Isaiah 11.1–10

This is one of the classic 'messianic' prophecies of the Old Testament. Verses 1–5 are in fact a description of the ideal just ruler, as the people of Old Testament times envisaged him. His wisdom and righteousness are emphasized, as is his power, his ability to enforce his judgements. But from the outset it is made clear that these virtues are not ones that inhere in him as a man, they are given him by God, through the agency of his spirit. Some may find unexpected the statement in v. 3, 'He shall not judge by what his eyes see, or decide by what his ears hear'. Surely, what is required of a just judge is precisely that he *should* 'judge by what his eyes see', i.e. he should give judgement according to the evidence presented. But in an Ancient Near Eastern court, where bribery and corruption were rife, the evidence presented was all too often a pack of lies, and the wise and effective judge was the one who could see *through* the evidence presented and discern the truth.

In one sense what is being offered here is a mundane ideal. Not all kings or judges met this standard, but the ideal is not one which is out of this world. There was always hope in the mind of the unjustly accused that the judge in his case might be such a one.

What makes the reading relevant to Advent is that the ruler thus described is a ruler from the messianic royal house, 'a shoot from the stump of Jesse'. In these first five verses the prophet leaves us in doubt as to whether he expects his ideal ruler to be someone soon to emerge, a recently anointed prince, perhaps, who might turn out to be better than his predecessors, or whether he is more disillusioned with human government, and is looking for his ideal to the far future. But the rest of the passage, vv. 6–9, shifts the perspective decisively into the distance, into a far-off non-violent world where even the lions have become vegetarian.

Can we really apply any of this to our Christian messiah? The wisdom, and the ability to see to the heart of a question, to the question behind the question, is certainly characteristic of the earthly Jesus. That the earthly Jesus was filled with the divine spirit is made clear enough in the New Testament. So far the prophecy could be seen as predictive of his coming and of his earthly ministry. But the emphasis on the messiah's work of judgement recalls the other aspect of Advent. There *is* an element of judgement in the work of the earthly Jesus, at some points a strong element, but his work as judge is much more strongly associated with his coming in glory.

Romans 15.4–13

This reading links with the Old Testament one in that Rom. 15.12 directly quotes Isa. 11.10 (though in its Septuagint* form). For Paul a central element in the good news is that the salvation originally offered to the Jews is now offered to everyone. Christ came as a Jew, 'became a servant to the circumcised', to show that he was the One promised from of old to God's people. But even the old promises also included a promise of his rule over the gentiles. From the start, God's messiah was meant for everybody. In Paul's own ministry this was happening: gentiles were accepting the message. The first Christians had an overwhelming sense that the old promises of scripture were meant *for them* and for their time. They saw them coming true before their very eyes. As in our Old Testament reading from the previous week, what began as a nationalistic vision quickly expands to transcend nationalism.

* The Septuagint is a Greek translation of the Old Testament. This is the Bible with which Paul would be most familiar.

Matthew 3.1–12

Matthew's account of John the Baptist picks up the judgement theme from Isaiah 11. Not only has John himself an uncompromising message of judgement, but the messiah whom he announces, 'he who is coming after me', is also portrayed here exclusively as judge (v. 12). John baptizes with the water of repentance: the messiah will baptize with fire. The Gospel reading also links with the Epistle. Already here in the message of John the Baptist the Jews are warned not to rely on their Jewishness to give them privileges in the eyes of God. 'God is able from these stones to raise up children to Abraham.' In the ministry of Paul to the gentiles God was doing exactly that. Judgement is for everybody. The call to repentance is for everybody. The good news of salvation is for everybody.

THIRD SUNDAY OF ADVENT

Isaiah 35.1–10; James 5.7–10; Matthew 11.2–11

Isaiah 35.1–10

Isaiah 35 in its original context is a prophecy of the return from exile. Even in its time it was a highly coloured and not entirely realistic prediction, though in the circumstances the prophet's euphoria was no doubt forgivable. The theme of judgement appears only in v. 4, and there the judgement is for Israel's enemies. For God's own people the message of this chapter is unadulterated good news. It is doubtless selected by the lectionary makers because its prediction in vv. 5 and 6 of the healing of the blind, the deaf, the lame and the dumb is picked up in the Gospel for the day.

James 5.7–10

This Epistle is presumably chosen because it mentions the prophets, which is appropriate to the third Sunday in Advent, but unusually the apostle points to them not as predictors of the coming messiah but as examples of suffering and patience. This is a topic well worth exploring, as there are plentiful examples of prophetic suffering and patience in the Old Testament. Jeremiah, Hosea and Isaiah all spring to mind. (There is also no shortage of examples of prophetic *im*patience, but perhaps we had better keep quiet about those.) On second thoughts, perhaps the twin themes of patience *and* impatience in the prophets could profitably be explored together. What are the situations in which prophets are patient, and what are the ones in which they feel that a holy impatience is called for? Such an exploration would need to appeal to readings from the prophets very different from the Old Testament lesson appointed for this Sunday. It might be married, too, with gospel readings illustrating the patience and impatience of Christ.

Patience is certainly the theme of our Epistle. The topic was no doubt a pressing one for the apostle James and his contemporaries because the much awaited return of Christ had not taken place. Our own perspective is bound to be different, and after 2000 years' wait most of us are no longer in a hurry for it to happen. But we do get impatient about the way so many things in the world stubbornly do not improve, and some of them actually get worse. We have had the Christian gospel now for a long time, and two thousand Advents have

5

announced the coming of a Saviour to make the world a better place. And is it a better place? When are we going to se the evidence? (The hymn, 'Thy kingdom come, O God' expresses this impatience very sharply.)

Matthew 11.2–11

This reading begins with the impatience of John the Baptist. Has he got it right, he asks himself? *Is* this Jesus of Nazareth the one expected? His questions suggest that he was looking for more from Jesus than he thought Jesus had so far delivered. In reply Jesus points to the healings he is doing. The list picks up the one in Isaiah 35 but goes beyond it. Jesus is actually doing *more* than the prophet foretold, at least in this place. What John thought about Jesus is followed by what Jesus thought about John. Jesus is glowing in his praise. Not only is Jesus himself fulfilling the prophecies, John is fulfilling them too, for he is the one predicted in Mal. 3.1: 'Behold, I send my messenger…' Jesus sums up: 'Among those born of woman there has arisen no one greater than John the Baptist.' It is hard to imagine higher praise. And yet – 'He who is least in the kingdom of heaven is greater than he.' How do we explain this? Possibly by going back to our observation on the Gospel reading for Advent 2, that John, with all his merits, has no good news. His message is of judgement and only judgement. However important it may be in Advent to allow the word of judgement its full scope, it must not be the last word: another Word must ultimately take precedence.

FOURTH SUNDAY OF ADVENT

Isaiah 7.10–16; Romans 1.1–7; Matthew 1.18–25

Isaiah 7.10–16

The lection contains the famous Immanuel prophecy, which is picked up in the Gospel reading. As Isa. 7.16 makes very clear, the prophet is thinking of his country's immediate difficulties, political and military, viz. the threat of attack from its neighbours, Syria and Northern Israel. The child whose birth the prophet has in mind is not himself a saviour; he, and the propitious name he is to bear, will simply be a sign of a salvation shortly to be revealed. Before the child is much more than a toddler the Lord himself will save, by removing the threat of attack. St Matthew would have thought all this irrelevant. For him, the Old Testament was a book of oracles, the significance of which for his own time had nothing to do with what they might have meant earlier. He would have said that what the prophet Isaiah meant by the words of the Immanuel prophecy was quite beside the point. What matters is what the Holy Spirit meant by them, and he has no doubt about what that is.

Perhaps the preacher had better just swallow hard and accept St Matthew's line. However disposed we are to engage in scholarly nit-picking, to speak of original historical contexts or to dispute such questions as the true meaning of the word translated 'virgin', two thousand years of Christian tradition have seen these words as a prophecy of the coming of Jesus Christ. If we wish to stand within that tradition we had better respect what it tells us.

Romans 1.1–7

The opening of the letter to the Romans presents us with the key elements of the gospel in a nutshell, as those elements were understood by the first generation of Christians. Jesus is the Son of God, shown to be such by the Spirit and by his resurrection from the dead. But the proof is not merely retrospective. His coming was foretold by the prophets and witnessed by the scriptural record. Christ's Davidic ancestry is an important part of the evidence. Nearly all the Advent themes are thus put together. No direct word is said of judgement, but it is stressed that the response required is 'the obedience of faith' (v. 5), and that the gospel is for 'all the nations'.

Matthew 1.18–25

The story of the annunciation to Mary, which is so important in St Luke's account of the nativity, has no place in St Matthew's. What we have here instead is an annunciation to Joseph. The annunciation to Mary is marked by her simple and ready acceptance of what she is told: 'Behold, the handmaid of the Lord'. Joseph's acceptance is equally willing. He offers no arguments, and on waking he simply does what the angel has told him to do. He just doesn't sing a song about it. Both the parents of Jesus thus exhibit 'the obedience of faith' of which Paul speaks in our Epistle.

CHRISTMAS DAY

Isaiah 52.7–10; Hebrews 1.1–4 (5–12); John 1.1–14

The Christmas Day readings are the same for all three years. There are, nevertheless, three sets of readings offered. Of these, set III seems to be given priority, since the lectionary states that whatever others are or are not used, the lections of set III must be read. It is these readings, therefore, which will be commented on here.

Isaiah 52.7–10

As with some of the Old Testament readings earlier in Advent, these words from the book of Isaiah originally expressed the joy felt by the people of God on their return from exile. In the lectionary they are appropriated to express the joy we feel at the coming of Christ. This sort of re-use of material happens again and again in the scriptures; words which conveyed joy, or dismay, or grief on one occasion are taken over and used to express similar emotions evoked in quite different circumstances. There is nothing odd about this. In our own culture it happens perhaps more readily with music. Lovers enjoy love songs, regardless of the fact that they were composed for other lovers, perhaps of a quite different time. The most powerful experiences of life are felt as uniquely personal and individual. But they are also universal, which is why we can borrow language from each other. The Bible borrows its own language from itself, and the themes and words and images in which it speaks sew together the great acts of God, from creation to exodus to the ingathering of his people to the coming of the appointed, anointed Saviour, into one whole fabric, a single story of his will for the world.

Hebrews 1.1–4 (5–12)

No one is better at sewing things together than the writer to the Hebrews. The many and various ways in which God spoke of old are shown by him to come to a climax in the Word he is speaking now, in his Son. In Hebrews many of the great themes and images of the Old Testament are picked up, analysed, and shown to be pointers to the perfect revelation to come. That revelation is now ours. The writer also picks up texts, prophecies, allusions, from a whole variety of places in scripture and presses them into service as proofs that the incarnation was what God had in mind all along. To the exponent of historical criticism some of these 'proofs' may be less than compelling, but even the exponent of historical criticism can take the author's main point, that God's dealings with humanity are a seamless whole, and that in the incarnation we get a view of something like the total picture.

John 1.1–14

Our Epistle and Gospel are using different language, but they are saying some of the same things. Both St John and the writer to the Hebrews are setting out their understanding of the incarnation. Our Epistle and Gospel are, if you like, their Christmas sermons. They do not begin where most of us begin. Our Christmas sermons are inclined to dwell on babies in mangers, on songs of angels, on shepherds and wise men. St John and the writer to the Hebrews mention none of these things. Instead they dwell on Christ's part in creation. For them he is framed not by the crib, but by the cosmos. One of the things they are telling us is that the story of Christ and of Christmas did not begin in the reign of Herod the Great, or in an obscure little Judaean town. At the moment when the universe was created, its redemption had already begun.

St John here at the outset of his gospel piles up the titles and images of Christ to which he will return again and again. Christ is the Word of God, which is not just God's communication, but God's thought, reason and intelligence, closely allied to his wisdom. Through this Word the universe was brought into being. He is not only the life-giver, but Life itself. This foreshadows what St John is going to tell us later in his gospel about Christ's resurrection power. He is also the Light, with which God endowed his world on the first Sunday of creation. But all of this is summed up in the person of a man. This portentous being, who shared the essence of Godhead, somehow shrank to the dimensions of a local carpenter. Sometimes people use quite extravagant language in speaking of present day celebrities, or 'stars' as the media insist on calling them, but even the most extravagant comes nowhere near the immense significance that is claimed here for Jesus of Nazareth.

St John deviates, apparently, from his high theme, first to mention John the Baptist, who clearly had a great deal more significance for him and the other gospel writers than we usually allow. He is introduced as a witness, but he also functions to pin down the figure of the cosmic Christ, who is essentially beyond time and space, to the brief time of a few decades at the beginning of the first century AD, and to the little space of Roman-dominated Palestine. But secondly, St John pauses to mention those 'who received him'. He who was the eternal Word, and Life, and Light, came to an unresponsive world. Yet some did, and do, respond. And in speaking of them, of us, St John introduces yet another theme which he will expound later, that of birth: not the ordinary kind of birth, by which we all come into the world, but that other, special kind. Later he will call it the 'new' birth, but he does not do so here. So even amid all the breathtaking claims and the thought-provoking assertions about incarnation, we, the believers, find a place as those for whose sake all these things happened.

FIRST SUNDAY OF CHRISTMAS: 26 TO 31 DECEMBER INCLUSIVE

Isaiah 63.7–9; Hebrews 2.10–18; Matthew 2.13–23

Isaiah 63.7–9

This is an unusual prophetic reading. The prophets mostly speak of the exile as a punishment which God inflicted on his people because of their disobedience and unfaithfulness. Here, for once, a prophet speaks of the exile (retrospectively, for it is in the past at the time when he writes) as sufferings which, however well deserved they may have been, God *shared* with his people. 'In all their affliction he was afflicted.'

Hebrews 2.10–18

The Epistle has some striking things to say about the union of Christ with the humanity he came to serve. 'He who sanctifies and those who are sanctified have all one origin.' 'He is not ashamed to call them brethren', and 'He had to be made like his brethren in every respect'. He calls us his children, which implies that he and we 'partake of the same nature'. As our Old Testament lection says of God, Christ shares our sufferings; and not only our sufferings, but our temptations. Perhaps the most remarkable statement is in v. 10. He is made perfect through suffering. It is not only important *for us* that Christ suffers like us; it is important *for him*. The same author tells us elsewhere (5.8) that 'he learned obedience through what he suffered', and only when he was thus made perfect did he 'become the source of eternal salvation to all who obey him' (5.9). The idea that the eternal Son of God needed to learn, and to learn, so to speak, 'on the job', is one that some will find comforting.

Matthew 2.13–23

The Gospel reading is the story of the massacre of the innocents. However implausible the story may be, historically speaking, it is nevertheless an important one. If it did not happen in Bethlehem in the year AD 1 it has happened frequently enough since, and is still happening; and the reader may make his or her own catalogue of the places where the atrocity has recently taken place. Rachel still has cause to weep for her children. And our readings tell us that, wherever soldiers kill babies or rape their mothers, in all their affliction God is afflicted. St Matthew in this episode is telling us several important things. He is saying that here, right at the beginning of his earthly life, Christ shares the experience of his own people, Israel. As they were threatened and their children massacred at the time of the exodus from Egypt, so he is threatened. He shares the danger of persecution that his people have often been under. He shares the experience of dispossession and of exile to a strange land that they suffered at the time of exile in Babylon. He shares the experience of the homeless, the refugee. In Egypt he is the foreigner, the immigrant, the asylum seeker, the person without passport or papers, with no claim on the hospitality of his hosts but that of common humanity; the one without rights. It is through the sufferings of Christ that he brings about humanity's salvation, and here we see that he does not have to wait to begin. He does not have to wait for the cross: suffering starts while he is still in nappies.

SECOND SUNDAY OF CHRISTMAS: 1 TO 5 JANUARY INCLUSIVE

Jeremiah 31.7–14 *or* Sirach/Ecclesiasticus 24.1–12 *or* (*Canticle*)
Wisdom 10.15–21; Ephesians 1.3–14; John 1.(1–9) 10–18

Jeremiah 31.7–14

The subject is the ingathering of Israel, and the renewed prosperity of the restored nation. Curiously, it is the passage of Jeremiah which immediately precedes the oracle about Rachel weeping for her children, quoted by St Matthew in last week's Gospel. In another respect, too, it seems to relate better to last week's Gospel than to the Gospel and Epistle for the current week. It follows on from the story of the massacre of the innocents and the flight into Egypt by speaking of the return of the exiles and the bringing home of those who had been scattered.

There are two alternative readings, both of which are more helpful; both are from the Apocrypha, viz. Ecclus. (ben Sira) 24.1–12 and Wisdom 10.15–21.

Ecclesiasticus 24.1–12 is a declaration by the divine Wisdom. It pairs well with the appointed Gospel because it makes many of the same claims for Wisdom as John 1 makes for the Word. The two concepts, divine Word and divine Wisdom, run parallel in scripture, and Christ has been identified with both. Just as St John asserts that God created the world through his Word, so several passages of scripture (e.g. Proverbs 8) ascribe the same function to Wisdom. Ecclesiasticus 24 does not, in fact, quite do that. For ben Sira Wisdom remains, herself, part of the created order. She was there *from* the beginning, but not *before* the beginning. What ben Sira adds is the story of Wisdom seeking a home for herself and finding no place entirely appropriate for her, until God directed her to dwell with the people of Israel. Wisdom may be found everywhere (v. 6), but nevertheless she has a peculiar attachment to the people of God.

Wisdom 10.15–21 is prescribed as a *Canticle*, which means that it is intended as an alternative to the Psalm, rather than an alternative Old Testament lection. Nevertheless it is worth paying attention to. It makes a similar point to the reading from Ecclesiasticus but in a different way. It is concerned with the part played by Wisdom in the history of the chosen people, and in particular in the exodus from Egypt. The universalism of St John's doctrine of the Word is thus less in evidence in these two particular passages from the wisdom writings, though it is there by implication. Conversely, though John 1 emphasizes the universal, the apostle too is making the assumption that it is among the chosen people that the Word appears in flesh.

Ephesians 1.3–14

Both the Epistle and the Gospel focus on the cosmic dimensions of Christ's work of salvation. His work, and therefore our salvation, have their origin before the foundation of the world. God's plan was worked out through the ages and has come to fruition in our own time. The Ephesians passage focuses on atonement; 'In him we have redemption through his blood'. The Gospel concentrates on incarnation. In the Epistle we have a strong feeling of a grand design, pursued throughout the history of the universe 'according to the purpose of him who accomplishes all things according to the counsel of his will' (v. 11). The scope of this plan is cosmic and comprehensive. Its ultimate aim is 'to unite all things in him, things in heaven and things on earth' (v. 10). All this might seem designed to make the individual believer feel very marginal, but the intention is exactly the opposite. The apostle asserts that *we are part of the plan*, that our salvation is its primary purpose, and that our involvement in it has been in God's mind from the beginning.

John 1.1–9 (10–18)

The point that all was done for our sakes is not made in the Gospel reading, but the cosmic design is certainly emphasized. The lectionary gives us a choice. We can read either vv. 1–9 only, or go on to v. 18. This suggests that it is the first half of the reading that is considered most important for this Sunday. John the Baptist, who figured so largely in the pre-Christmas readings, is given prominence again, but the emphasis must be upon the Word, the light, and the life he brought and brings. The Epistle presents Christ as redeemer; the Gospel passage reminds us that the Christians of New Testament times also saw him as creator. The Bible does not draw a sharp distinction between creation and salvation. God's work is one: it is only from a human perspective that we see creation and salvation as separate activities. Creation itself is a saving act and the redemptive process begins from the first moment the world comes into being. The creation is not self-sustaining and only by a continuing act of grace can it endure.

Early Christians, and certainly those of Jewish background, would have read more into the expression 'the true light' than most modern readers are aware of. Jewish midrash notices that in Genesis 1, though God creates the light on the first day, the sun, moon and stars do not function until the fourth. The question arises, where did the light come from that illuminated the world from Sunday through to Wednesday? The answer is that Sunday's light was the original light, the true light, which God meant the world to have. But when he realized that the world was not worthy of it he withdrew it, and hid it away until the last times, replacing it with that of the sun, moon and stars, the workaday light of Wednesday. But when the last times are about to dawn and God makes a new heaven and a new earth, the true light will be restored. Christians live in a time when 'the darkness is passing away, and the true light is already shining' (I John 2.8).

THE EPIPHANY: 6 JANUARY

Isaiah 60.1–6; Ephesians 3.1–12; Matthew 2.1–12

The Epiphany lections are the same for all three years.

Most Christians are gentiles. We therefore have a vested interest in the festival of Epiphany and its message. That message, that gentiles, along with the Jews, are beneficiaries of the gospel, is prominent in the book of Acts, and St Paul's epistles are full of arguments showing that the inclusion of the gentiles was part of God's plan of salvation from the beginning. The Epiphany epistle is a fairly typical statement of Paul's conviction of the importance of the mission to gentiles, and the conviction, too, that he himself had a special commission to engage in it. But if the inclusion of gentiles figured so largely in the plan, why do the gospel writers keep so quiet about it? True, the gospels are not totally silent on the matter. Jesus is reported as having nice things to say about the Roman centurion whose servant was healed (Matt. 8.5–13; Luke 7.1–10). But apart from that there is only the very ambivalent story of his dealings with the Syro-Phoenician woman (Mark 7.24–30; Matt. 15.21–28). The general impression we derive from the gospels is that Jesus saw himself as concerned primarily, if not exclusively, 'with the lost sheep of the house of Israel'.

This is why the story of the coming of the Wise Men is important. We have only got as far as the second chapter of the New Testament, Jesus is still in his cradle, and here already he receives gentiles and is recognized by them. Matthew is trying to tell us that, appearances to the contrary notwithstanding, St Paul got it right, the gentiles *were* part of the plan from the outset.

The word 'gentiles' is not one we often find ourselves using. The tension between Jews and gentiles in the church disappeared centuries ago. But this is no archaic issue. What is at stake is the universality of the gospel. It really *is* for everybody, regardless of ethnic origin or any other accident of birth.

Isaiah 60.1–6

This is a prophecy about the restoration of Judah to prosperity and influence after the trauma of the exile, but if we read it in the context of Epiphany it is almost uncanny in the way it seems to foreshadow the themes, and even the details, of the story of the coming of the wise men. If we look carefully we have to admit that some of the uncanny parallels are in our minds, not in the text: 'and kings to the brightness of your rising' (v. 3). We all know that the wise men were kings. St Matthew, however, never says so. Christians have said so only because they were prompted by this very prophecy in the book of Isaiah. The 'multitude of camels' (v. 6) also recalls the gospel story. We all know that the wise men rode camels. Again, St Matthew never says so. He says only that they came from the East. Our collective imagination has contributed the camels. The prophet does speak of gold and frankincense, but is this the prophet foreshadowing the gospel story, or St Matthew echoing the words of the prophet? When we have, in honesty, recognized all this, the prophecy is still one which tells God's chosen people: 'The nations shall come to your light' (v. 3). The time will come, the prophet is saying to his people, when the nations will recognize that God has given you something that they envy, an illumination which they would like to share, and an excellence which they will be glad to acknowledge. He can hardly have known what form that illumination and that excellence would eventually take, but St Matthew and all we his fellow Christians think we know.

Ephesians 3.1–12

The apostle acknowledges here that the recognition of the gentiles' place in God's scheme of things is virtually a new discovery, 'which was not made known . . . in other generations as it has now been revealed' (v. 5). Nevertheless, theirs is no grudging inclusion; they are included on completely equal terms: 'fellow heirs, members of the same body, and partakers of the promise' (v. 6). That the church as a whole accepted this way of thinking is due in no small part to the work of Paul himself. If he had not won the argument in those early years, it is doubtful whether we would be here, celebrating Epiphany.

Matthew 2.1–12

St Matthew, as we all know, frequently quotes the Old Testament and spells out to the reader that the events he describes took place in fulfilment of prophecy. What is often overlooked is that even more frequently he does not make explicit quotations, but simply echoes the words of scripture and expects us to pick up the allusion. He does us the courtesy of assuming that we know our Bibles as well as he does. There can be little doubt that in his description of the homage of the wise men he not only has in mind our Old Testament lection but also the words of Ps. 72.10–11, neither of which he refers to explicitly. Here as elsewhere the prophecies are shaping the way the story is told.

My grandmother made wonderful patchwork quilts, but she never used new material in them. All the material came from cast-off dresses, shirts, old curtains or anything that came to hand. All the components had originally functioned as something quite different, and were mostly still readily identifiable as what they had been. But that didn't matter. Together they functioned excellently as a bed cover. St Matthew would have got on very well with my grandmother. He put together his gospel on much the same principles.

SUNDAY BETWEEN 7 AND 13 JANUARY INCLUSIVE

(Sunday after Epiphany and the First Sunday in Ordinary Time)

Isaiah 42.1–9; Acts 10.34–43; Matthew 3.13–17

Isaiah 42.1–9

Epiphany is about the manifestation of Christ to the gentiles, and this theme is continued in our Old Testament reading and Epistle for the following Sunday. Isa. 42.1–9 is about the servant of the Lord, whom Christians identify with Christ. The promises made here by God to the servant set out a programme which is strongly reminiscent of the activities of the earthly Jesus. He is 'to open the eyes of the blind, to bring out the prisoners from the dungeon, from the prison those who sit in darkness' (v. 7). But the theme of universality comes out clearly in the statements that he 'will bring forth justice to the nations' (v. 1), and that he is to be 'a covenant to the people, a light to the nations' (v. 6).

But perhaps the most important point for our present purpose is that the opening words of the lection, pointing to 'my servant, whom I uphold, my chosen, in whom my soul delights' are recalled in the words from heaven spoken at Jesus' baptism, recorded in today's Gospel reading. The parallelism is made all the closer by what follows: 'I have put my spirit upon him'. Isaiah 42 is talking about God's choosing of the servant, Matt. 3.13ff. is speaking of his choosing of the Son. (St. Matthew, thinking in Greek, would have been less conscious of the difference than we are; the Greek word *'pais'* covers both 'son' and 'servant'.) In both cases the bestowal of the Spirit is the mark of that divine choice.

Acts 10.34–43

The story of Peter and Cornelius is long (and, it must be admitted, somewhat repetitious). The lectionary offers us only the denouement of the story. The reading will surely require at least a brief introduction to explain what led up to it. It records Peter's conversion to the idea that gentiles are acceptable in the church. Peter is convinced not only by the vision which he had in Joppa, but by the facts of the case, that Cornelius and his associates have accepted the gospel. The lectionary reading curiously stops short at v. 43. We might have expected it to go on to v. 48 and include the account of how the gentiles received the Holy Spirit and were baptized. Just as in our Gospel reading Jesus himself begins by being baptized and having the Spirit alight on him, so in Acts do these hitherto rejected gentiles. The experience of Christ himself becomes their experience. Jesus was chosen by God. Cornelius and his friends have chosen to be chosen with him.

Matthew 3.13–17

This is one of the few overtly trinitarian passages in the New Testament, i.e. passages in which the Father, Son and Holy Spirit are explicitly mentioned together. Note also that the near-ubiquitous John the Baptist appears in it yet again. In the passage that precedes it, which was the appointed Gospel for Advent 2, John predicts of the coming Christ that 'He will baptize you with the Holy Spirit'. Here, in preparation for that work, the Christ is himself baptized with the Holy Spirit. Our Gospel reading says nothing about the scope of his saving work extending to all nations, but that is made clear enough in the accompanying Old Testament and Epistle.

SUNDAY BETWEEN 14 AND 20 JANUARY INCLUSIVE

(Second Sunday in Ordinary Time)

Isaiah 49.1–7; I Corinthians 1.1–9; John 1.29–42

Isaiah 49.1–7

Theme-watchers will have no trouble with today's readings. The word that links all our lections is 'call'. Isaiah 49 deals with the call and destiny of the servant of the Lord. We generally equate the servant with Christ himself, but the title 'servant of the Lord' is a very general and indeed open ended one. It could fittingly be applied to anyone who is committed to the service of God. It designates primarily a role and a relationship, rather than indicating a specific person. Jesus is the servant *par excellence* because he fulfils the role perfectly. Others of us fulfil it imperfectly, but are servants nonetheless. Christ's servanthood does not exclude the servanthood of others.

Isa. 49.1–7 begins with a statement that the servant was called 'from the womb'. His career was already chosen by God, and he was equipped by God for his task. He objects that nevertheless he has been a failure. In reply God promises that not only is he destined to succeed in his mission to his own people, 'the tribes of Jacob', but that he will also be 'a light to the nations' (v. 6). Though a failure hitherto (at least in his own eyes), the servant is thus being promised eventual success. Does a divine call always guarantee ultimate success? Our passage does not raise this question.

There is ambiguity in the passage, in that in v. 3 the servant appears to be identified as 'Israel', the nation, yet elsewhere he seems to be envisaged as an individual, and to have a mission *to* Israel (v. 6). It is best to recognize that this ambiguity cannot be readily resolved. What we can say with some certainty is that the experience of the nation, which suffered so grievously at the exile but is soon to be restored, has certainly coloured the description of the servant and his work.

I Corinthians 1.1–9

We all know how well the title 'servant of the Lord' fits Jesus. How well does it fit St Paul?

Paul knows himself to be called, 'called to be an apostle' (v. 1).

Those to whom he writes are also called, 'called to be saints' (v. 2), and 'called into the fellowship of . . . Jesus Christ' (v. 7). Two conclusions follow: first, each of us has a vocation. There are vocations such as those to holiness and fellowship, common to all, and more specialized vocations such as apostleship (and many others) which are only for particular people. Second, the initiative is not ours. A call by its nature comes from outside (though it may be felt inwardly). We do not determine it, we respond to it – or not. In these days when self-fulfilment is the order of the day, when the people most admired are those who know what they want and go for it, Christians are unusual in that they wait for God and try to take into account what are *his* purposes for them.

Verse 7 is a little startling. It implies that what the Corinthians are called to is a very short-term Christian career. They are simply waiting for a while. They are waiting 'for the revealing of our Lord Jesus Christ'.

In view of what follows in the rest of the letter, Paul in this opening passage says some surprisingly approving things about the Corinthian Christians. They 'are not lacking in any spiritual gift' (v. 7). (How many congregations could we say that about?)

John 1.29–42

Verses 29–34 contain the Johannine account of the baptism of Jesus. Since Matthew's account of the same event featured in last week's Gospel, most preachers will probably not wish to concentrate on it this week. It might be useful, however, to focus on the differences between the two, which are striking. The principal ones relate to the Baptist's double witness to Jesus, greeting him at the beginning of the passage as the Lamb of God (a phrase surely worth the attention of half a dozen sermons) and at the end of it as 'Son of God'.

But if the link with the other lections is important to us we shall wish to take up the 'call' theme. St John goes on immediately after his description of the baptism to speak of the call of the disciples. Again it is worth exploring the differences between John's version of the events and that of the other gospel writers. In the synoptics the call is very abrupt and appears to come 'out of the blue'. St John reveals that these men were already disciples of John the Baptist, and that Jesus had been pointed out to them by him.

By the time Paul wrote his letter to the Corinthians he was already an apostle. He knew what he had been called to. Though it was still early days, he knew, too, something of what his converts were called to, what Christian commitment would involve for them. The disciples at the beginning of John's gospel are being called to something which is as yet far less defined. They are intrigued by Jesus, and by John the Baptist's statements about him. They call him 'messiah'. But they still have little inkling of what discipleship of Jesus will mean. If they commit themselves, as they do, it is to a servanthood that has dimensions still unknown. A Christian may experience a call of either kind, i.e. either a call to something very specific, a defined task, or a broader conviction that God has work to be done, whose exact nature may only emerge with time.

SUNDAY BETWEEN 21 AND 27 JANUARY INCLUSIVE

(Third Sunday in Ordinary Time)

Isaiah 9.1–4; I Corinthians 1.10–18; Matthew 4.12–23

Isaiah 9.1–4

This reading appears more frequently in connection with Advent, but on this occasion we stop short of the key Advent verse (v. 6). The passage is selected because it is quoted in this week's Gospel. Zebulun and Naphtali had their tribal lands in the area of Galilee. Throughout most of biblical history the prestige of the Galilee region was not high, and the description of it quoted here, 'Galilee of the nations', is derogatory, implying that it is no better than gentile country. In Jesus' day Galilean rabbis (of whom, of course, Jesus was one) had a reputation for independence of mind, and in some quarters their orthodoxy was regarded as suspect. But Galilee had had its moments of glory, the 'day of Midian' referred to in v. 4 is the event described in Judges 6–8, the defeat of the invading Midianites by Gideon, whose chief supporters were the Galilean tribes of Asher, Zebulun and Naphtali. And it was to have glory again. For Christians, of course, Galilee is important as the location of Jesus' early ministry. But in purely Jewish terms it also came into prominence after the Jewish War of AD 66–70. By the end of that war the temple had been destroyed and worship there had ceased, and the rabbis who got together to begin the task of rebuilding Judaism did not see Jerusalem as an auspicious place to make the centre of their activities. Instead they gravitated to Galilee, which became for a while the rallying place for Jewish faith and piety.

I Corinthians 1.10–18

The Epistle offers only a little in the way of thematic connection with the other two readings. It does have something to say about apostleship, as Paul understands it, and what he says about baptism seems to imply that as far as his own work is concerned he sees the preaching of the gospel as more important than administering that sacrament. The call of the first disciples described in the Gospel reading also puts the emphasis firmly in the same place. It is a call to become 'fishers of men'. But the main thrust of the passage in I Corinthians is to express Paul's horror at the divisions within the Corinthian church. Apostles whose call is to the one work of preaching Christ are being treated, against their own will, as leaders of factions. It is implied in what is said here that Paul, Apollos and Cephas, the apostles mentioned, did have different approaches and different styles. We might reasonably take the Epistle as raising questions for us which Paul does not go on to tackle in the passage itself. There are bound to be in the church differences of approach, differences of emphasis, different ways not only of presenting the gospel but of understanding the gospel. How do we acknowledge these and allow dialogue between them without letting them become divisive? At Corinth they clearly *had* become divisive. Paul seems to suggest that part of the answer, at least, is to agree to put our emphasis on 'preaching Christ', and to regard as secondary any differences about *how* we 'preach Christ'.

Matthew 4.12–23

We mentioned last week the contrast between St John's account of the call of the first disciples and that found in the synoptics. It is relevant again here. According to Matthew Jesus' ministry does not begin in earnest until John the Baptist is effectively out of action. John may be only a forerunner, but Jesus seems to have left the field clear for him until his career was forcibly terminated. Matthew's summary of Jesus' message in v. 17 is not substantially different from John's own. The continuity between the two men is very clear at this point.

That Jesus' ministry begins in Galilee is seen by Matthew as a fulfilment of Isaiah's prophecy in 9.1. Jesus begins his ministry as a man on the edges. A Galilean teacher was outside the religious power structures which were centred in Jerusalem, and in the religious circles of Jerusalem such a teacher would not have been highly regarded. At the beginning Jesus' ministry is a ministry on the margins, and a ministry largely to the marginalized. This is not to say that Galilee was in other respects a backwater. Economically it certainly was not. Much of Galilee looks idyllically rural today, but in New Testament times it was well populated, with a considerable number of prosperous towns and villages, some of them, such as Magdala, and Sepphoris very large. So Jesus did not lack scope for his activities. Not until he has established a base in Galilee, where he belongs, does he move to the religious power centre, where he challenges and is challenged.

SUNDAY BETWEEN 28 JANUARY AND 3 FEBRUARY INCLUSIVE

(Fourth Sunday in Ordinary Time)

Micah 6.1–8; I Corinthians 1.18–31; Matthew 5.1–12

Micah 6.1–8

There are a number of cross threads tying together today's lections. Micah 6.1–8 is a famous passage which some see as a high-water mark of the Old Testament's thinking. What is not obvious in some translations is that the passage is couched in the language of the law court. The Lord has a case against his people Israel, and calls the mountains and the foundations of the earth to hear the evidence. He points to what he has done for them, rescuing them from Egypt and leading them to the promised land. After all this he could legitimately expect a response of love and gratitude. Verses 6–8 define that response. God is not much interested in a response expressed through sacrifice, even of the most lavish or precious kind. He looks for a response expressed in obedience. It is firstly a moral response. God wants his people to act justly and faithfully. It is secondly the response of piety, a religious response, in other words: to 'walk humbly with God'.

I Corinthians 1.18–31

In scripture 'wise' is normally a term of approbation, though there are exceptions, of which our Epistle offers one. Even wisdom, a God-given gift, may be perverted or misused. In today's Epistle 'wisdom' is treated as a very negative word. The reasons lie in the context in which Paul was operating. There were in his day teachers claiming special knowledge, knowledge not available except to the specially gifted or specially instructed. Such élitist ideas about knowledge and wisdom were even threatening to invade the church. Paul has no patience with them and sees them as potentially divisive and destructive.

Matthew 5.1–12

The beatitudes breathe the same air as the Old Testament and Epistle. Micah calls us to 'do justly'; Jesus blesses those who hunger and thirst for justice. Jesus blesses the merciful; the prophet says 'love mercy'. 'Walk humbly with God' advises Micah; 'Blessed are the meek', says Jesus. There is no place in the thinking either of Micah or of the Sermon on the Mount for the 'wisdom of the world' which Paul condemns. The Sermon on the Mount could almost be read as a commentary on St Paul's claim that 'God chose what is foolish . . . to shame the wise . . . chose what is weak to shame the strong . . . chose what is low and despised'. Both Jesus and Paul are standing the world's values on their heads, asserting that there is a poverty better than the world's wealth; a hunger preferable to the world's satiety; and a foolishness that makes better sense than worldly wisdom.

SUNDAY BETWEEN 4 AND 10 FEBRUARY INCLUSIVE

(Fifth Sunday in Ordinary Time)

Isaiah 58.1–9a (9b–12); I Corinthians 2.1–12 (13–16);
Matthew 5.13–20

The three readings appointed for this Sunday are not strongly linked, though they are not entirely unrelated. In such situations we need to be careful about picking out minor connections (or even manufacturing connections) which distort what the scriptures are saying. We need to ask first, of each passage: what is this passage saying, in its own right? What is its main thrust? If we can only make a real or fancied link with another lection by compromising that main thrust then we are not being true to the expository task. We have become sermon-cobblers. In such a situation it may be best to forget the possible links between lections and simply expound one of them.

Isaiah 58.1–9a (9b–12)

Here the prophet is criticizing formal religion which is divorced from righteous behaviour. The prophets do this frequently, of course, but Isaiah 58 is a particularly trenchant example of the genre. It is worth noting that this prophet is writing in the post-exilic period. The traumatic events of the exile were supposed to have taught the people of Israel a lesson. They were not going to repeat the mistakes of their pre-exilic forebears. But some lessons need to be learned afresh in every generation.

In all societies the responsibility of the rich and powerful towards the poor and powerless has always been an issue. In the days when there was no social security and the welfare state had not been invented (which is still the case in most parts of the world) there were plenty of calls on the charity of individuals. And even in our affluent West the need for such charity has not gone away. But in our own day we are more aware of this as an issue not *within* societies but *between* societies, between third world poverty and first world wealth. But this is simply a change of focus, a shift in the way the issue presents itself in our world. The basic question of the responsibility of rich towards poor is still there. The prophet is criticizing people who use religion and piety as a means either to salve their consciences or avoid the issue. Does this still happen?

I Corinthians 2.1–12 (13–16)

Paul is contrasting two wisdoms. The purveyors of what he sees as the dangerous and divisive wisdom of the world were offering a false intellectualism, a wisdom which, they thought, was not for everyone, but only for the privileged few. Paul says there is a better wisdom. He implies that his opponents are right about one thing; it is not for everybody. But in Paul's book real wisdom is available not as a privilege, but as a gift to the truly spiritual, whose 'knowledge' is not of intellectual mysteries, but only of 'Jesus Christ, and him crucified'. Paul here is pointing to an intellectualism which in his world was over-valued, to a 'wisdom' to which people were ready to grant an unwarranted prestige. Perhaps it is legitimate to raise the question: what, in our own world, are the kinds of expertise, the skills, the forms of achievement which we over-value? Should we be more ready to offer a Christian critique of society's values and priorities?

Matthew 5.13–20

Jesus often criticizes the scribes and Pharisees in similar terms to those used in our Old Testament lection, seeing them as people who are very careful about their piety and enthusiastic about the keeping of formal religious rules, sometimes to the neglect of more important ethical considerations. *But he does not do so in the present passage.* Here the scribes and Pharisees are seen as offering an example of the highest standards of exactitude in keeping the Law of God, an example which the Christian disciple is expected to surpass. The Christian is to outdo the scribes and Pharisees by beating them at their own game, being *more* scrupulous than they are. Just as the scribes and Pharisees are outstanding in their own kind of devotion, so (we are told in Matt. 5.13–16) Christian disciples must be shining examples of the way of Christ.

Thus, Isaiah 58 asserts that, though there is a false piety to be shunned, there *is* a true piety, which is acceptable to God. Paul says equally firmly that though there is false wisdom, which is dangerous and should be rejected, there *is* a true wisdom, worth pursuing; and Jesus in the Sermon on the Mount is pointing to a true righteousness, better and more exacting than some on offer elsewhere.

SUNDAY BETWEEN 11 AND 17 FEBRUARY INCLUSIVE

(Sixth Sunday in Ordinary Time)

Deuteronomy 30.15–20 *or* Sirach/Ecclesiasticus 15.15–20;
I Corinthians 3.1–9; Matthew 5.21–37

The Old Testament lections link closely with the Gospel.

Deuteronomy 30.15–20

Deut. 30.15–20 is a classic and clear statement of why the Law matters; the choice, whether to obey or disobey, is the choice between life and death. It is as stark as that. There is, of course, a multitude of circumstances in which it is by no means obvious what God would want us to do and how he would wish us to decide. There are thorny moral issues before which the conscience quails and falters. Our Old Testament reading does not deny that such situations exist. It simply does not address itself to them.

The rabbis said that when God sends a soul into the world everything about it is predetermined: whether it will be male or female, Jew or gentile, rich or poor; whether it will be healthy or unhealthy, happy or unhappy; whether it will live long or die young: everything is decided; *but not whether it will be righteous or unrighteous.* What they are saying is that, whatever our circumstances, whatever the constraints upon us (whether placed there by our upbringing, our social conditioning, or our genes), we always have a moral choice.

Sirach/Ecclesiasticus 15.15–20

This short reading from Jesus ben Sira offers clear reinforcement to the message of the Deuteronomy reading. In contrast to our Gospel it asserts that God does not face his people with impossible demands. The Law is there to be kept, and we are not incapable of keeping it. Paul's complaints in Romans 7 about the powerlessness of the human will to fulfil God's commands would have received no sympathy from ben Sira. This is a robust statement of traditional Jewish thinking.

I Corinthians 3.1–9

Paul is addressing the problem of divisions in the Corinthian church. He begins with his familiar contrast between the 'flesh' and the spirit. And here we learn that 'living in accordance with the flesh' is not just a matter of 'fornication, impurity, licentiousness . . . drunkenness, carousing, and the like', and the grosser sorts of immorality in general (which is how Paul characterizes it in Gal. 5.19–21), but that losing one's temper in the Church Council or plotting to get one's own cronies on to key committees is an equally 'fleshly' way to behave. It is interesting to see an apostle putting factionalism in church on the same moral level as adultery.

Equally interesting, a few verses further on, are Paul's assumptions about how the apostolate relates to the church. God, of course, does the real work; *he* is the one who gives the growth, Paul and Apollos are at best enablers. But they *are* dignified as 'God's fellow workers' (v. 9), a very prestigious title. But the Corinthian Christians themselves are not described in this way: they are the field, the building, mere objects on which God and his apostles work. No hint here of any partnership between ministers and those ministered to! No sense of mutuality. Paul had a lot to give the Corinthians. Had he nothing to receive? Are there things about the church that Paul has yet to learn?

Matthew 5.21–37

This is a longish reading, and virtually every verse would individually be worth making a sermon about. The preacher may of course do exactly that, and select one verse for special treatment, but if we look at the main thrust of the passage as a whole, it is about radicalizing the Law. If to take Deuteronomy 30 seriously is frightening, to take Matthew 5 seriously is terrifying. If we were to make a list of the Bible's most disturbing passages, today's Gospel would surely be near the top. Jesus' words are demanding because at some points they seem to be expecting a degree of self-control that is superhuman. Refraining from murder is not too difficult; but to refrain from hatred? Most of us manage to avoid adultery; but to avoid lust? To say that these sayings are mostly examples of hyperbole is certainly tempting, probably true, and extremely dangerous. The word of God is sharper than any two-edged sword. Cursed be he that blunteth the edge of it. Deuteronomy 30 gives us hope, because it presents the Law as something which we *could* keep, if we really decided to. It says this explicitly just a few verses earlier in the chapter (30.11–14). But our gospel reading drives us to despair. Jesus faces us with the tyranny of an impossible demand.

The answers to this dilemma do not lie within the passage itself. Our Gospel is part of the Sermon on the Mount, and the Sermon on the Mount begins with blessings, long before it gets to the demands. And if we turn to St Paul, there are pointers to an answer in passages like Gal. 5.16–25, which suggest that whoever is controlled by the Spirit need not fear too much the severe judgement of the demanding Christ.

SUNDAY BETWEEN 18 AND 24 FEBRUARY INCLUSIVE

(Seventh Sunday in Ordinary Time)

Leviticus 19.1–2, 9–18; I Corinthians 3.10–11, 16–23;
Matthew 5.38–48

Again the Old Testament reading closely supports the Gospel.

Leviticus 19.1–2, 9–18

Last week our Gospel passage was radicalizing the Law. This week
we see that the Old Testament Law can be pretty radical on its own
account. At the root of the Law is the demand for holiness; all the
detailed outworkings and individual commands are expressions of
this one basic demand, to be holy. And the reason why we are to be
holy is that God is holy. Our holiness is to be the mirror of his. The
closing words of this week's Gospel echo the opening ones of today's
Old Testament reading: 'You, therefore, must be perfect, as your
heavenly Father is perfect.' So this is the essence of what is required
of us, that we should be like God. Yet, we are assured elsewhere
(Deut. 30.11), 'This commandment which I command you this day is
not too hard for you'.

In the Old Testament Law, when it comes to spelling out what this
holiness actually means in practice, it does begin to look more
manageable. First, it involves the proper carrying out of religious
ritual. This is mentioned only in those verses which our lectionary
makers have carefully left out, but we would be untrue to the Old
Testament if we were not at least aware that for the people who wrote
it the proper ordering of sacrifices, etc., is all part of the sanctification
of the Name, of respect for the holiness of God. But for the rest,
vv. 9–18, holiness is spelled out in extremely practical terms. It
means becoming part of the social security system by deliberately
leaving some of one's harvest for the poor and the refugee. That
implies not screwing the last pennyworth of profit out of one's land
and business. It means being honest in word and action. It means not
making life more difficult than it has to be for other people. And all
this is summed up in the magnificent statement of principle which
Jesus apparently felt unable to improve on, 'You shall love your
neighbour as yourself'.

I Corinthians 3.10–11, 16–23

Today's Epistle contains echoes of the themes of disunity in the church, and of false wisdom, which most preachers will wish to leave aside, since they have already featured more prominently in readings for earlier weeks. Paul resorts to a favourite metaphor, that of the church as a building. (And note that for him it *is* a metaphor. The idea of the church as *primarily* a building, as it appears to many people today, he would have thought of as at least quaint, and probably dangerous.) The image of the temple, the temple which *grows*, is one that occurs again and again in the New Testament. Given that the building of the Temple of Herod went on throughout the lifetime of most of the New Testament writers, and that many of them had the opportunity to watch its progress, this is not surprising. The notes for the Fifth Sunday of Easter say a little more on this point. Paul here puts the emphasis on three things: (1) on getting the foundation right – the only foundation for the temple which is the Christian church, is Christ; (2) on the temple as the place where God's spirit dwells; and (3) on the fact that God's temple is holy, 'And that temple you are'. This last assertion offers at least a small link with the other lections for the day.

Matthew 5.38–48

Our Gospel reading quotes 'You shall love your neighbour...' at v. 43, but goes on to clarify what it means. It is not clear from the context in Leviticus 19 how comprehensively the word 'neighbour' is meant to be understood. It leaves open the possibility that it might be legitimate to love one's neighbour but hate one's enemy. (The words about hating one's enemy are not, of course, in scripture. They are popular interpretation of the injunction, not holy writ.) Jesus insists on an inclusive understanding of the word 'neighbour' that leaves no room for hatred. As in the parable of the Good Samaritan, the neighbour is universalized. The message of the Gospel reading is that our love must be *totally* undiscriminating, like the love of God, who does not reserve his rain and sunshine only for people he approves of. If we are to mirror God's holiness (Leviticus) or his perfection (St Matthew) then it must be through imitating his absolutely undiscriminating generosity.

SUNDAY BETWEEN 25 AND 29 FEBRUARY INCLUSIVE

(Eighth Sunday in Ordinary Time)

Isaiah 49.8–16a; I Corinthians 4.1–5; Matthew 6.24–34

Looking at today's three readings together, it would be perverse not to centre on the Gospel. Its content is so fundamental to the Christian view of life that the other two texts can only be regarded as adjuncts.

Isaiah 49.8–16a

The prophet is not, like Jesus in our Gospel passage, talking generally about God's dependability. He is talking about a particular situation, and expressing confidence that, in that situation, God's people can count on his care for them, and on the salvation that he has already prepared. He is speaking of the restoration of the people to their land after the exile. But the crucial verses are at the end of the lection (vv. 14–16a). Her experience of desolation had led Israel to lose faith. She had said, 'The Lord has forgotten me'. To Jesus, looking at the birds and the flowers, the evidence for God's care is staring us in the face, but to those who have passed through the waters the evidence often seems all the other way, and such was the experience of Israel at the time when the prophet wrote. The prophet asserts that what does not alter, what is constant in spite of all appearances, is the relationship which God has with us. We may be alienated from him: he is never alienated from us. His attachment to us and his feeling for us are stronger than the strongest of human ties. Even maternal affection, which may be stretched almost to infinity, has its limits. His divine affection has no end at all. In an unexpected, and for us, quaint metaphor, the prophet tells us that, as a lover might, God has our names tattooed on his hands.

I Corinthians 4.1–5

Paul here is trying to define his position and authority in relation to the church. He likens himself to a 'steward'. The 'steward' was a kind of housekeeper, the person who would be employed by a reasonably affluent family to oversee the day-to-day running of the household. A primary requirement for anyone holding such a post is that he should be trustworthy. This implies accountability. Paul acknowledges that he is accountable. But to whom? That is the main question he is addressing here. Paul is strongly denying that he is accountable to the church. He is accountable to God, and to God only.

The apostolate was a first-generation phenomenon. There was no second. Apart from the election of Matthias, no apostle was ever replaced. In this unique situation it may well be that Paul's assessment of his position is a proper one. But it would be hard to see him as providing a model, in this respect, for ministry in subsequent generations. Whatever position we may hold in the church we are, of course, primarily accountable to God, but that accountability is, in practice, largely expressed through our accountability to each other.

Matthew 6.24–34

Here some of Jesus' most characteristic teaching is uncompromisingly set out. At first sight it might be read as an invitation to improvidence, but there is nothing here to forbid the believer making sensible provision for the future. What it is doing, rather, is calling for a shift in our habitual attitudes. Having made what provision we can, we should leave the future where it belongs, in God's hands. This is not pious abandonment of responsibility. It is the purest realism. We insist on behaving as if we were in control, and we would do better to recognize that over much of our lives and nearly all of our future we have very little control at all. True confidence in God begins with the perception of our own vulnerability. So the underlying theme is trust. The answer to our anxieties is the assurance that God is in charge and won't let us down. And the message is a sound one, even if some of Jesus' examples may be less convincing to ourselves than they were to him. The mortality rates among wild birds are higher than Jesus probably knew.

The key verse of the Gospel reading is almost at the end (v. 33): 'Seek first his kingdom...'. At bottom, it is all about priorities, about putting first the things that matter most. To do so will result in placing in quite different perspective some of the things we often get worked up about. Many of us (most?) spend much of our time worrying about things which, in relation to the great issues of life, are trivia. Jesus here is calling for a re-ordering, a re-evaluation of the things to which we give attention, and on which we spend our time and money and our emotional energies.

SUNDAY BEFORE LENT

Exodus 24.12–18; II Peter 1.16–21; Matthew 17.1–9

Today's readings are focused tightly on the transfiguration.

The gospel accounts are connected by a whole web of allusions with the story in Exodus 24 of Moses' ascent of Mount Sinai and his encounter there with the divine presence. The Exodus account is complex and by no means consistent. The lectionary simplifies matters for us by selecting only one small part of it. But we should not expect to be able to sum up the significance of the transfiguration in any simple or straightforward way. The web of allusions mentioned above points us towards a multi-layered interpretation. What we are dealing with, both in Exodus 24 and in the gospel stories of the transfiguration, are accounts of what may broadly be called mystical experiences. Such experiences, by their nature, cannot be pinned down in words, and when the recipients of these experiences do try to describe them they often appear fanciful, contradictory, or simply bizarre. It is important to recognize at the outset that such are the descriptions that we are trying to elucidate here. Those who are unable to empathize with the mystical had better, perhaps, forget the lectionary for today and preach about something else. If we cannot take the transfiguration on its own terms we shall, in seeking to expound it, do more harm than good.

The Revised Common Lectionary does in fact offer alternative readings for Epiphany 9, which the *Methodist Service Book* omits. These are: Deut. 11.18–21, 26–28; Rom. 1.16–17; 3.22b–28 (29–31); Matt. 7.21–29.

Exodus 24.12–18

The closest parallels in the Old Testament to this story of Moses on Sinai are in the accounts of prophetic visions, such as we have in Isaiah 6 and the opening chapters of Ezekiel. Perhaps the oddest thing about the passage is that it stands here in the Law.

There are places in the Old Testament where we are told that no one can see God and live. Yet there are others where we are told plainly of people who did just that. The implication of Exodus 24 is that Moses on Sinai entered the very presence of the Holy One. It is also clear that though only he himself entered completely into that experience he did have company on the mountain. Here we have some of the inconsistencies. According to 24.9 (not included in the lection) he had three close companions, Aaron, Nadab and Abihu. This is one strand in the web of allusions. Jesus too had three companions. This invites us to see Jesus himself as a Moses figure. Or was Moses accompanied not only by the three but by seventy elders (24.9)? Nothing links these seventy with our gospel account, and in our actual Old Testament lection (24.13) only one companion, Joshua, gets a mention, and that a passing one. But though we are uncertain about how many companions were there, it *is* clear that in some respects they shared the vision. In Ex. 24.11 they have quite a party: 'They beheld God, and ate and drank'. Here we have, perhaps, the explanation for those very odd words of Peter on the mountain, about making three tabernacles. Peter has read Exodus 24 as well. He thinks he already knows the script. If there's going to be a party there ought to be somewhere to sit down.

But the companions do not share everything. In spite of what is said in Ex. 24.11, in 24.14 the elders are left firmly behind to mind the shop, just as in the Gospel, the bulk of the disciples are left behind and, as we learn in the subsequent passage (Matt. 17.14–20), the disciples' efforts at minding the shop are none too successful.

Both Exodus 24 and our Gospel reading are giving us essentially the onlookers' perspective. But the accounts do make it clear that the experience was not given primarily for the sake of the onlookers. It was important for the central figure himself, for Moses on the one hand, and for Jesus on the other. And this is the point at which every onlooker is ultimately left behind, and that includes ourselves, for Moses 'entered the cloud'. This is not the cloud that characteristically, routinely, gathers round mountain tops. This is the cloud, or smoke, of the divine presence, of which nearly all mystics speak. It is the cloud that surrounds the divine 'Glory' (Ex. 24.16), the *kabodh*, which is the real presence itself. Matthew does not mention the glory, though Luke does. But he does speak of the cloud (17.15).

II Peter 1.16–21

The Epistle does not contribute very much to our understanding, being a mere reference back to the incident of the transfiguration in this letter purporting to come from St Peter. It seems designed not so much to tell us anything about the transfiguration as to substantiate the author's claim to be the apostle himself.

Matthew 17.1–9

'And after six days...' Six days after what? Probably we are meant to understand that it was six days after the Caesarea Philippi confession (Matt. 16.13–20), but almost certainly Matthew also has in mind the six days' interval in Ex. 24.16 before Moses was called by God into the cloud. On the one hand Jesus is himself a Moses figure, repeating Moses' experience, but at the same time Moses is one of his companions on the mountain. Jesus does repeat Moses' experience, but also surpasses it. Moses, and Elijah, are prophets. But Jesus is more than a prophet. He is a son, indeed *the* Son. The voice from heaven (a standard device in rabbinic storytelling), reaffirms what was said at his baptism. This experience is not, after all, primarily given for the sake of the disciples. They manifestly don't really know what to make of it, though they may do later. Jesus presumably does, and presumably it was an experience that he needed.

ASH WEDNESDAY

Joel 2.1–2, 12–17 *or* Isaiah 58.1–12; II Corinthians 5.20b–6.10;
Matthew 6.1–6, 16–21

The readings are the same for all three years.

The lectionary today offers us a choice of Old Testament readings.
Isa. 58.1–12 has already been set in Year A for the Fifth Sunday in
Ordinary Time. See the notes at that point. In the context of Ash
Wednesday preachers may well wish to give prominence to the
theme of fasting, which is what holds this reading together. Its main
thrust is as described in the previous notes, but the prophet seizes on
fasting as one of the religious exercises which may be engaged in
without commitment to God's moral requirements, and therefore
vainly.

Joel 2.1–2, 12–17

The theme of the Joel passage is true repentance. The situation in
which Joel is prophesying is one of impending and serious national
disaster, an approaching locust plague. (The locusts are the 'black-
ness upon the mountains, the great and powerful people' of v. 2.) At
such times of threat it seems to have been customary to call a national
day of prayer, involving penitential exercises, which included fasting
(see v. 12). As in Isaiah 58, the prophet emphasizes that the penitence
must be sincere. 'Rend your hearts, and not your garments' (v. 13).
But with a national disaster looming, such insistence may have been
unnecessary. The people he addressed had plenty to concentrate their
minds. Our Ash Wednesday sermons will not normally be preached
in the shadow of such dire predicaments, but Christians should not
need a catastrophe to convince them of the necessity of repentance.
Rabbi Eliezer b. Hyrcanus used to say: 'Let the reputation of your
fellow be as dear to you as your own; be not easily moved to anger,
and repent, one day before your death.' For those who live their lives
before God every hour is the eleventh hour.

Repentance, as the Bible understands it, is not an emotion. It is a
matter of the will. It is not merely feeling sorry. It is a willingness to
change, or be changed. The Bible everywhere assumes that all of us
need to change, and that the society we live in needs to change. It also
assumes that change is possible. Repentance therefore presupposes
hope.

II Corinthians 5.20b–6.10

Paul, too, had plenty to concentrate his mind. His accounts of the dangers and harsh conditions he endured, one of which we have here (though it is not a very detailed one), even if they were only half true, would still justify his description of himself as being 'in jeopardy every hour' (I Cor. 15.30). Paul virtually lives permanently in a crisis. But he would probably say, 'So do we all, if only we recognized it.' We live, every day, under the judgement of God, and only survive it because we live, every day, under his grace. The Christian stands, all the time, before that throne, in that eternal 'Now' of God. For Paul, in our lectionary passage, it is for the time being the grace that is uppermost in mind, not the judgement. 'Now is the acceptable time; now is the day of salvation' (6.2). And the way from judgement to salvation is through repentance.

Matthew 6.1–6, 16–21

The Gospel picks up the same point as the Old Testament lection, that religious exercises, if they are to be worthwhile, must be sincere. But whereas the prophets criticize those who are enthusiastic for religion but lukewarm about morality, Jesus picks up quite a different point, criticizing those who, he thinks, engage in their religious practices primarily in order to impress other people. Fasting, of course, gets a mention as one of those practices (vv. 16–18), which provides a link with the Old Testament readings, but it is religious ostentation in general on which Jesus is focusing. He is not, of course, condemning public prayer, but private prayer practised in public places. It is probably fair to say that the sort of ostentation to which Jesus is referring is not much of a temptation in our own day. Today, praying on street corners would invite ridicule rather than respect. It *is* possible, however, to engage in religious practices in order to impress *ourselves*: to take pride, perhaps, in the extent of our charitable giving, or to congratulate ourselves on the assiduity of our devotions. But probably not many of us are tempted even at this level. Still, we must beware complacency or smugness, lest we find ourselves praying: 'We thank you, Lord, that we are not like this Pharisee'.

FIRST SUNDAY IN LENT

Genesis 2.15–17; 3.1–7; Romans 5.12–19; Matthew 4.1–11

The three readings together have a clear focus. They are concerned with temptation. Adam and Eve failed to resist it. The consequence was what Christian theology has traditionally seen as the Fall of the human race. Christ conquered temptation, and reversed the effects of the primordial sin, making salvation possible. This theme, of creation corrupted by the Fall, and its redemption by the work of Christ, the second Adam, undoing the first Adam's lapse, has for centuries been central to Christian understanding. Whatever hesitations we may have about it, and however we may wish to nuance it, we owe it to our congregations to explain to them what this traditional understanding is, because without a knowledge of it much of the New Testament will not make sense to them, half the hymns in the hymnbook will puzzle more than they illuminate, and much traditional Christian language will sound like gobbledegook. From the Christian point of view, this understanding, which can be set down in a couple of sentences, is what holds the Bible together.

Genesis 2.15–17; 3.1–7

'Of man's first disobedience.' In interpreting this enormously potent and influential story it is important to keep our minds on the essentials, on what the story is really trying to tell us, and not to be sidetracked into nit-picking. It is not about fruit; it is about obedience to God. In one sense, of course, God's prohibition is trivial. But that very triviality is significant. 'This commandment which I command you this day is not too hard for you' (Deut. 30.11). It is not beyond your capacities. Adam and Eve do not obey because they do not *trust*. They do not trust God. They do not trust what he has told them. Jesus in the wilderness rebuts every temptation by appealing to *what God has said*.

The serpent is not said to be evil; he is described simply as 'clever'. The serpent's 'cleverness' is the false wisdom which St Paul so frequently condemns. The pair who do not trust the simple command of God trust the specious reasoning of the clever serpent. Clever he certainly is. At no point in the story does he say anything that is not actually true. God has said: 'On the day that you eat of [the fruit] you shall die' (2.17). The serpent says, 'No you won't'. And they don't. The serpent promises them knowledge. And they get it. It wasn't, of course, quite the sort of knowledge they were looking for. 'Then the eyes of both were opened, and they *knew* – that they were naked.' It was the disconcerting knowledge of their own exposure. It does not at this point appear as if repentance is an option, perhaps because they are as yet incapable of appreciating the enormity of what they have done. Their own attempts to undo the results of their transgression are pathetic. 'They sewed fig leaves together and made themselves aprons' (3.7). One has to give them marks for trying. How were they to know what ages the true undoing would take, what waters would need to be crossed, and what the cost would be?

In some quarters there has in the past been a tendency to blame Eve more than Adam. The story as the Bible tells it gives no purchase to such an interpretation. It is only when both have eaten that 'the eyes of both were opened' (3.7). From the beginning we, i.e. man and woman, were in it together. And so we remain.

Romans 5.12–19

Paul does not refer explicitly to the story of Jesus' temptations in the wilderness. He may indeed not have known it. But he contrasts the obedience that Jesus showed throughout his earthly life with the disobedience of Adam. Paul's language is not perhaps as crystal clear as it might be, but the main thrust of his argument in this passage is nonetheless plain. The work of Adam and the work of Christ are mirror images of each other, and their consequences are equal and opposite. Adam's disobedience, according to Paul's interpretation of the Genesis story, involved the whole human race in guilt, condemnation and death. Christ's obedience bestows on us, by contrast, righteousness, forgiveness, and eternal life. Just how or why Adam's transgression should transmit guilt to all his descendants, and how or why Christ's righteousness should be passed on to those who believe in him, are questions which may give some of us difficulty. They are real questions, and serious, but they are not here addressed.

Matthew 4.1–11

The story of Jesus' temptations and the story of the transfiguration which was the Gospel for the previous Sunday are in some ways uncannily parallel. The transfiguration is essentially a private experience of Jesus, only partly shared by the witnesses. The temptations are a purely private experience, to which there are no witnesses at all. The transfiguration represents an encounter with the Divine. The temptations are an encounter with Evil. We may at first not recognize the story as an account of anything quite so momentous. It has none of the trappings of an apocalyptic confrontation. It presents us simply with an urbane conversation, not unlike the conversation between Eve and the snake. But as with Eve, so with Jesus, the restrained tone of the discussion belies the magnitude of the issues at stake, which in both cases are cosmic. Eve's interlocutor is a talking animal, and the writer of Genesis never suggests he is anything more sinister, but by Matthew's time the tempter had been firmly identified as the personification of all evil. Matthew refers to Jesus' opponent uncompromisingly as 'the Devil'. We, his readers, are left in no doubt as to what is going on: in spite of appearances this *is* a cosmic confrontation. The downward slide of humanity which began in Eden and has been continuing ever since, begins at this point to be put into reverse: the disobedience of the one man, Adam, is at last counteracted by the obedience of the one man, Christ, though we do not yet learn where that obedience will take him.

Like the serpent, the Devil is certainly clever. As with Adam and Eve, so with Jesus, what is at issue is trust in God. The Devil homes in on that very trust. If you really trust God, trust him to feed you. Turn stones into bread. If you really trust God, throw yourself from the pinnacle of the temple. Trust him to save you. (This 'pinnacle' was at the south-west corner of the temple mount, and from there to the valley bottom must have been a fearsome height.) 'Yes', says Jesus, 'I trust him but will not test him.' Only in what, for Matthew, is the last temptation does the Devil show himself in his true colours, for he admits that if Jesus accepts his advice it will mean worshipping him, the Devil. Now all is plain, for this contravenes the first commandment. Jesus for the first time calls him by his own name, Satan, and he concedes defeat, at least for the time being.

SECOND SUNDAY IN LENT

Genesis 12.1–4a; Romans 4.1–5, 13–17; John 3.1–17

Genesis 12.1–4a

The book of Genesis is very carefully structured. The first eleven chapters spell out the fall and decline of the created world. The disobedience of Adam and Eve, which was the subject of last Sunday's Old Testament reading, is followed by a rolling programme of catastrophes. The character weaknesses of Adam and Eve come out in their dysfunctional family, who end by murdering one another. Then we have the strange story in Gen. 6.1–4, pointing to a dysfunction which involved even the heavenly beings. The corruption becomes so widespread that God resolves to wipe out most of creation and make a fresh start. But after the flood the story of Noah's drunkenness (Gen. 9.10–27) shows ominously that the new humanity is no better at self control than the old. In chapter 11 we find that the new humanity has in fact learnt nothing. It makes a few technological discoveries, and the first thing it thinks of to do with them is to challenge God and take charge of its own destiny. God divides and scatters the human race.

Enter Abraham.

God has come to terms with the fact that the restoration of creation to the perfection he had in mind for it at the end of chapter 1 is going to be a long haul. Out of the scattered nations and families of the human race he has chosen one family and nation through whom blessing – even though by a long road – may come to the rest. The words quoted in today's Epistle, 'And Abraham believed God . . .' do not in fact occur in our Old Testament lection, but they are implicit in it. They are implicit in Abraham's action, his obedience: 'So Abraham went, as the Lord had told him' (12.4). The obedience of Abraham begins to answer the disobedience of Adam and foreshadows the obedience of Christ, through whom the process of salvation will eventually be completed. When we get to chapter 18 of Genesis we discover that Abraham is a great arguer. He is prepared to call even God to account, to demand that he explain himself and justify his actions. But this is when *other people's* futures are at stake. When his own future is on the line, here, and most remarkably in Genesis 22, he never says a word or raises a single objection. There is a time to question, and a time to obey without question.

Romans 4.1–5, 13–17

Abraham is an important figure for Paul, for on Abraham rests a large part of Paul's case for the inclusion of the gentiles. Here and elsewhere he puts great emphasis on Abraham's *faith*. He claims that Abraham is righteous in God's eyes because he *believed* God, trusted him; not because of what he achieved. In view of what we read in our Old Testament lection we may well feel that Paul is trying to force a distinction here which the text will scarcely bear. Abraham's faith is not something separate and distinct from his obedience. They are opposite sides of the same coin. But Paul is very concerned to establish that what made Abraham righteous in God's eyes was not any keeping of the Law (4.13). He makes no attempt to spell out the argument here, though he does so in Gal. 3.17, and a very easy argument it is. Abraham was not justified by keeping the Law of Moses because in Abraham's time Moses had not even been born and the Law was yet to be delivered. Abraham's standing before God must therefore rest on quite a different basis, namely, his trust in God. But there is another argument which Paul uses to buttress his conclusion, and which he does spell out in vv. 3–5. He puts a lot of weight on the word 'reckoned' in his quotation from Gen. 15.6. Abraham's faith 'was *reckoned* as righteousness', '*counted as* righteousness'. In Paul's mind this carries the implication that the righteousness wasn't real or deserved, it was simply credited to Abraham by God out of the goodness of his heart. This looks like verbal hair-splitting. We can be quite certain that whoever wrote the words of Gen. 15.6 did not mean them to be understood in this way. St Paul would have brushed such objections aside. This kind of emphasis on minute features of the sacred text, in defiance of the overall thrust of the passage, was standard rabbinical exegetical method in his day. But all of this is simply part of the huge battery of arguments which Paul uses to plead for the universality of the gospel. He has to show that there is an alternative way to God's favour, to salvation; alternative, that is, to the keeping of the Jewish Law. This alternative is the way of faith, and that way is already attested in scripture and in the career of Abraham, who antedates the Law by several centuries. Abraham is of course a Jew, the archetype and ancestor of all Jews. But he is also the archetype of gentiles, because his way to God is the way the gentiles have to take, the way of faith.

John 3.1–17

This is a passage whose very familiarity makes it almost impossible for us to appreciate its full impact. It is meant to baffle, and most readers no longer experience the bafflement. As we read it Nicodemus looks to us like a fool. But Nicodemus appreciates what we do not, the mind-blowing nature of the notion that one might be born for a second time. We do not experience the true force of the passage because the shatteringly radical idea of being 'born again' has for us become a cliché.

In his encounter with Nicodemus Jesus seems to set out deliberately to puzzle the man with teasing obscurities. And the reader is not helped by the fact that John's Greek contains two ambiguities which cannot be reproduced in English. To be 'born again' is also to be 'born from above'; and 'wind' and 'spirit' are exactly the same word, making possible the *double entendre* on which much of the meaning of the passage depends. One may be born painfully and messily by the normal obstetric processes, or one may be 'born from the wind'.

Yet this being 'born from the wind' is not something that happens totally 'out of the blue'. In 3.5 it is made plain that the new birth is 'of *water* and the spirit'; that is to say, it involves the mundane process and institution of baptism. Both the old birth and the new begin with the breaking of the waters.

The language of the new birth is closely parallel to the language of resurrection. Both images are conveying similar truths, and in not dissimilar ways. Both are ways of describing new life. Baptism, says St John, means a completely fresh start, where we begin again as God's babies. Baptism, says St Paul in numerous places, means 'dying with Christ', and coming through on the other side. To become a Christian, therefore, is a kind of birth, or a kind of death, which strangely turn out to be the same thing.

All of this may sound somewhat mystical. Perhaps it is, but it has very down-to-earth consequences. Abraham, too, was called to a new life, and that involved selling up and moving house; emigration; long distance travel; resettlement; getting used to a foreign people and foreign culture. It involved vulnerability, insecurity, uncertainty, 'not knowing' (Heb. 11.8). These are the practicalities of the life of faith.

THIRD SUNDAY IN LENT

Exodus 17.1–7; Romans 5.1–11; John 4.5–42

Exodus 17.1–7

At numerous places the gospel writers make it clear that they see Jesus as a Moses figure, repeating, and indeed surpassing, Moses' great deeds. St John in chapter 4 of his gospel does not specifically mention Moses, but he would expect all his readers to be familiar with the story in Exodus 17 and would assume he did not need to insult their intelligence by underlining the parallels. At the feeding of the five thousand Jesus, like Moses, gives people bread in the wilderness (John 6.31–34). 'This is the bread that comes down from heaven, that a man may eat of it and not die' (John 6.50). To the Samaritan woman he speaks of the water that will become in the believer 'a spring of water welling up to eternal life' (4.14). Like Moses, he assuages his people's thirst as well as their hunger. But Moses satisfied only their earthly appetites, and satisfied them temporarily: Christ gives the food and the drink of eternal life.

St John would also be familiar with the Jewish midrash quoted by St Paul in I Cor. 10.4, which said that the rock which Moses struck followed the Israelites around as they travelled through the wilderness, giving them water always 'on tap'. Jesus again goes one better, for the water he gives becomes a permanent spring within the believer's own being.

One further point emerges from our Old Testament lection. It is easy to assume that God's great gifts are made available only to people of faith, to the humbly receptive. The New Testament gives us some encouragement to think on such lines. But in the wilderness God's greatest benefits are bestowed on the contentious. It is the recalcitrant and doubting who are rewarded with water from the rock. It is the grumbling and faithless who are fed with manna. God does not always wait for his people to show penitence and trust, but offers his salvation 'while we were yet sinners'.

Romans 5.1–11

In our Epistle Paul is exploring precisely such divine initiatives. In any situation where people are estranged from one another deadlock can become permanent unless one or other party is prepared to make a move. And it is often necessary that the move should be made by the party that knows itself to have been most wronged. This, Paul is saying, is the case with God and humanity. *He* makes the first move towards reconciliation, though we are the ones who have failed him. He signals this through Christ's willingness to die for us. Nothing, surely, could more clearly indicate his readiness to repair the relationship between us. Paul seems to be thinking of a process of several stages, reconciliation, justification, salvation from God's wrath, though he does not explain this clearly and, if they *are* distinct stages in his mind, does not make plain how they relate to each other. But this uncertainty does not obscure his main point, which is that grace *precedes* repentance.

John 4.5–42

This rather lengthy but familiar story of Jesus' meeting with the woman of Samaria is notable for a number of reasons. John 4.26 is the one place in the whole of the gospels where Jesus himself claims to be the expected messiah. In Mark 14.62, if the received text is correct, he acknowledges his messiahship under interrogation at his trial, but in conversation with the Samaritan woman he volunteers the information. That he should be represented as doing so to someone who was socially so marginalized is very remarkable indeed. Samaritans are not mentioned very often in the gospels, but often enough to suggest that neither Jesus nor the gospel writers shared the common Jewish prejudice against them.

The setting, too, is interesting. The conversation takes place near the historic centre of the old Northern kingdom, close to the ancient city of Shechem where Joshua renewed Israel's covenant with God (Joshua 24), in the vicinity of the modern Arab town of Nablus, a site overshadowed by the two mountains of Gerizim and Ebal, the one for the blessing and the other for the curse (Deut. 27.11–14). Historically it is a place where momentous choices were made. In the person of this disdained woman the despised and rejected (and, in the eyes of the Jews, apostate) people of the ancient North, Jezebel's land, are being offered the opportunity to reclaim their heritage as members of the people of God.

There are in scripture at least two significant stories about meetings at wells. Abraham's servant, seeking a wife for Isaac, meets a girl at a well (Genesis 24) and by her good-mannered grace he knows he has found the right one. Moses, fleeing from Pharaoh (Ex. 2.15–22), meets seven sisters at a well. He defends them from harassment and, like Christ, he is the one who offers the water. Jesus is less fortunate. He doesn't meet good-mannered grace, but a woman who, faced with his simple request for a drink of water, only wants to start an argument. Poor old Jesus. Did he ever get his drink?

The well is still there, and the water from it is good water, cool and refreshing because the well is deep. But it is not 'living water', water that flows. It is Jacob's water, the water of the old covenant of promise. Jesus himself would be glad to drink it, but he also has something better, living and lasting.

When the conversation begins to get too personal the woman (we never do find out her name) tries to change the subject and talk about the ancient theological issues dividing her people from his. Jesus does have an opinion on these, an uncompromising and unapologetic one. If it is a choice between the two temples, Jerusalem and Gerizim, then the Jews are right and the Samaritans wrong, but there is a more fundamental issue. Where we worship is less important than what kind of God we serve; and less important (because Jesus does not allow her to avoid the personal questions) than what kind of people we are.

FOURTH SUNDAY IN LENT

I Samuel 16.1–13; Ephesians 5.8–14; John 9.1–41

On this Sunday we are offered a choice. There are lections suggested which are appropriate to Mothering Sunday, the same for all three years, and a separate set for Year A which ignore the Mothering Sunday theme. We shall first deal with the latter.

I Samuel 16.1–13

There are at least two possible approaches to this reading in the context of today's lectionary. We may see David as one of a line of Old Testament characters who prefigured Christ. In the previous two weeks we have been reminded of Abraham and his obedience, and of Moses, with his power, under God, to offer water out of the rock. Now we have David, the original messiah from Bethlehem, the good shepherd who risks his life for the sheep (I Sam. 17.34–36), and the fairest among ten thousand (I Sam. 16.12; S. of Sol. 5.10). This last estimate of David is echoed during the war against Absalom, when his generals dissuade him from risking his own person in battle, saying 'You are worth ten thousand of us' (II Sam. 18.3). It is totally at variance with David's valuation of himself in his grief over the rebellious and unrepentant son (II Sam. 18.33): 'Would that I had died for you'.

Or we may find a link, of sorts, with our New Testament readings by focusing on the text which in this passage is pivotal, I Sam. 16.7: 'The Lord sees not as man sees; man looks on the outward appearance, but the Lord looks on the heart.' In spite of what is said about David's attractive appearance, this is not what really matters. What matters is our true character, whether we are children of light rather than children of darkness. This is the test which at this point in the story David is claimed to pass.

Ephesians 5.8–14

In some editions of the New Testament this reading begins in the middle of a sentence.

The passage as a whole is spelling out some of the moral implications of the gospel, contrasting the deeds of 'the sons of disobedience' (5.6), which are the 'works of darkness' (5.11), with those of the 'children of light' (5.8). The writer has not, of course, invented this terminology, neither has St John. The writings of the Qumran community, the Dead Sea Scrolls, make it very clear that the contrast between 'the sons of light' and 'the sons of darkness' was a commonplace among Jews of the period. Both apostles are picking up words and phrases which were almost clichés in their day.

The Epistle is an important complement to the Gospel reading. St John's exposition of the work of Christ as light-bringer is very dramatic. That Christ offers us illumination comes out strongly, but a reader might be left with the impression that this illumination consists of spiritual understanding – something rather abstract, even intellectual. It *is*, of course, about spiritual understanding, but our reading from Ephesians puts us in no doubt that the Christian cannot leave it at that. If we have truly seen the light of Christ then this will have tangible effects on the way we live our lives. It will affect our behaviour from top to bottom, ruling out not only gross sins, such as fornication (5.3, 5), but also apparently trivial ones, such as 'silly talk' (5.4).

John 9.1–41

This is another long Johannine reading, an excitingly told story with a good deal of circumstantial detail. Like most of St John's narratives it is clearly intended to be read not merely as a record of events, but as a parable. That Christ is the bringer of light is a major theme in the Fourth Gospel. In John 9 this is demonstrated in a concrete way. John 1.4–5 identifies Christ as the giver of the primordial light which was God's first creation, bestowed on the universe on the first Sunday. In John 8.12 Jesus has reinforced this with his claim to be 'the light of the world'. In John 9 we see that light being bestowed on the individual believer. The cosmic becomes the personal. The healing of the blind man is set by John during the last period of Jesus' ministry, only a short time before the events of Holy Week, alongside the raising of Lazarus in chapter 11. Together the two make a statement at this approaching climax of our Lord's earthly career, that he is both Light and Life.

The man does not ask to be healed. Jesus does it as a demonstration, 'that the works of God might be made manifest' (9.3). There is an urgency in Jesus' words at this point (9.4–5). He knows he hasn't much time left. Jesus in the gospels generally works his miracles simply with a word, but he doesn't despise alternative medicine. Here he resorts to a folk remedy. The Pool of Siloam had long been Jerusalem's main source of water, though the Romans, in order to cope with the city's enormous expansion, had constructed aqueducts and improved supply by bringing water from outside the city area.

Imagine all this from the point of view of the blind man. At this point, when he is sent off to wash, he still can't see and doesn't know what Jesus looks like. He does not actually see Jesus until some time afterwards. On his way to Siloam does he even know what to expect? Jesus has not promised him anything, simply told him to go and wash in the pool. Neither has Jesus appealed to him for faith. The faith actually comes much later. He meets an unknown man, whom he cannot see and who promises him nothing. But he does what he is told to do. His salvation begins with an act of washing, which he undertakes, though the reason for it has not been explained to him (cf. II Kings 5.13).

St John spends a good deal of time on the authentication of the miracle. First, the identity of the man is established, as being the same one who had been a well-known blind beggar (vv. 8–12). Then there is a lengthy interrogation by the Pharisees, followed by questioning of the man's parents. This is followed by a second interrogation, in which the once-blind man stoutly defends his healer. The Pharisees, unable to deny that the healing has happened, try to explain it away as not being from God. The ex-blind man is not at all intimidated but replies with robust common sense. The incontrovertible crux of his answer is in v. 25: 'One thing I know, that though I was blind, now I see.' St John is no doubt reflecting the conditions of his own time when he makes it clear that those who thus affirm that they have been illuminated by the light of Christ do so at the cost of cutting themselves off from the synagogue. For St John and his contemporaries the choice was plain, one could not be both a Jew and a Christian.

There is still something missing from the ex-blind man's experience. He knows what has been done for him, and is prepared to affirm it uncompromisingly. He knows the name of the one to whom he owes his salvation, but he has not met Jesus face to face, and he has made no explicit affirmation of faith. The statement of faith comes surprisingly late in the story (v. 38). The initiative still belongs to Jesus. In the beginning he offered a healing for which the man never asked. And here at the end the man does not seek Jesus out; Jesus is still seeking him. The invitation to faith is strangely put, given that the title 'Son of Man' is not one that St John often uses. The man already knows that it is Jesus who has healed him, and has already firmly declared his conviction that Jesus comes from God. But what is new here is the acknowledgement of Jesus' lordship, his divine status. Now we have it all. Christ is the light-bringer, the giver of illumination, the saviour and healer. He is also Lord and Son of Man.

The story ends (vv. 39–41) with some important reflections on blindness, making it clear that physical blindness has never been the real issue. Jesus shows himself now to be not only saviour but judge, declaring that he is not just the bringer of sight but also of blindness. He comes 'that those who see may become blind'. This is a frighteningly uncompromising statement, but Jesus' exposition of it suggests that he is not so much the bringer of blindness as the revealer of blindness. What he exposes is the self-inflicted or self-chosen blindness of people like the Pharisees. In their interrogation of the blind man the Pharisees have already demonstrated this blindness, by their denial of the work of God which was staring them in the face.

MOTHERING SUNDAY

Exodus 2.1–10 *or* I Samuel 1.20–28; II Corinthians 1.3–7 *or*
Colossians 3.12–17; Luke 2.33–35 *or* John 19.25–27

Though the Mothering Sunday readings are the same for all years, we
are offered a choice of two Old Testament readings, two Epistles and
two Gospels.

Exodus 2.1–10

Things turn out all right in the end, of course, but we can hardly
ignore the fact that the baby was put at serious risk by his parents.
This could only be justified by the circumstance that the infant Moses
was already in very grave danger. This was an act of desperation. If
we refer to this story when there are children present we ought to be
aware of the possibility that some will perceive it as threatening.
Adults will be more receptive to the message that parents do sometimes find themselves in desperate situations and that, desperation
apart, parents may face hard choices about what best to do for their
children's future. And we need to recognize that in real life things do
not always turn out well. According to scripture, Moses was saved
because God had plans for him. Others were not so lucky. Mary and
Joseph fled to Egypt with their son. The other innocents were massacred. When mum and dad have done the best they know, the schizo-
phrenic son may yet end in jail, the anorexic daughter still die. For
some parents desperation has the last word.

I Samuel 1.20–28

Another abrupt beginning. Unless there is some sort of introduction
summarizing what has happened in the story so far, this lection will
not make a great deal of sense, except to listeners already very familiar
with it. It is also another reading which demands that we be sensitive
to the possible reactions of children. Most, doubtless, will take it in
their stride, but there may also be some who perceive it as a story
about a young child being abandoned by his mother to live with an
old man in a church, and who will feel strongly that he should have
stayed with his mummy. There may be adults who share this view.
The culture clash between the Bible's world and our own will probably cause us less trouble if we acknowledge it squarely and then
pass on to more positive features of the text. The biblical narrator

makes no adverse judgement on Hannah's treatment of Samuel and does not expect the reader to make any. Most of us will be very conscious that we could not treat our own child so.

But whatever our hesitations on such grounds, the principal feelings which the story is expressing are ones that most of us can fully share. The theme is Hannah's thankfulness. Children are a gift, and a gift which most couples earnestly desire. We desire them even more earnestly if, like Hannah, we have had difficulty producing them. Even in these modern days, our fertility is not entirely under our own control, so this (in the eyes of many of us) most precious gift of all is not something to be had on demand. Gift is what it remains.

An alternative approach to this lection would be to face head on the question of what rights parents have over their children. Hannah feels entitled to dedicate Samuel to religious service. Such dedications are scarcely in fashion in the third millennium Western world. But even in our world it is not rare for parents firmly to decide their children's future careers. There are those who will decide at a very early stage that their offspring is to become a concert pianist or an Olympic gymnast and give the child no options other than the decades of practice needed in order to fulfil the parental ambitions. What powers *should* parents exercise, or attempt to exercise? To what extent ought we to impose our wishes? Imposing our desires is perhaps always suspect. Inculcating our own standards and values needs more careful thought. Most of us would assume that Christian parents have the right to bring up their children in the Christian faith, while acknowledging that they may eventually reject it. The same may be said for other parental convictions. Perhaps the crux of the matter is that we may legitimately seek to persuade, but not to impose; that we may urge our point of view, but not in such a way as to attempt to deprive our children of choice; that we are entitled to make it clear where we stand, as long as we acknowledge their right to stand elsewhere.

II Corinthians 1.3–7

The first listed Epistle teams up fairly naturally with the reading from Exodus. Unexpectedly, it raises the question of suffering. Few parents find the experience of parenthood an unalloyed pleasure. The children do sometimes get us down. They are hard work. Most go through one or more rebellious phases, and many (most?) children at some point in their lives give their parents serious worry and heartache. But we love them and they love us, and unless we are extremely unlucky they are a source of profound joy and endless satisfaction. In our passage from II Corinthians St Paul is not talking about parenthood, he is talking about the Christian life in general, but he is drawing attention to that same balance between 'affliction' and 'comfort' which parents experience. And he is pointing out that this is not just universal *human* experience, it is rooted in the nature of God himself. (Perhaps we could say, though Paul does not, that it is rooted in the nature of personality as such, whether divine or human.) God shows us, in the person of Christ, that he knows suffering as none of us knows it. Yet God is also 'the God of comfort'.

Colossians 3.12–17

Again we have an epistolary reading which was not designed primarily to refer to family life, but which, without wrenching the meaning, may profitably be applied to family life. It is idealistic, but ideals are important: they show us what we are aiming at, even if we fall short. Central to it is the word 'love', which is a slippery, catch-all word that it is dangerous to use in discussion because we all think we understand it. Love does not in fact always produce the 'perfect harmony' of which the apostle speaks in v. 14. 'Love' needs a lot of unpacking. There are damaging and even pernicious forms of love, and perhaps no human love is ever entirely selfless. The Epistle does not raise these aspects of the matter but it does otherwise help a great deal with the unpacking. It is an interesting exercise to ask oneself how 'love' connects with the other words used in the passage. What, for instance, is the link between love and thankfulness? The apostle seems to be hinting that there is one. (Does the Old Testament reading give us a sidelight on that question?) But the words in vv. 12 and 13 have more obvious links. Living together successfully involves a degree of humility on the part of all concerned. It involves very ordinary and unassuming virtues like kindness and patience. It involves what the RSV translates as 'forbearing one another'. Would 'putting up with...' be a more modern rendering? The other virtues only get a mention, but forgiveness is spelled out a little more. Rightly, for in a family context it is the most practical daily expression of love.

Luke 2.33–35

The first listed Gospel reading briefly picks up the same theme. What we call the *Nunc Dimittis,* Simeon's hymn at the presentation of the infant Jesus in the temple, is of course well known and much sung, but we usually stop short of the blessing which immediately follows it. The lectionary here offers us only the blessing, with its ominous parenthesis: 'And a sword will pierce through your own soul also.' Protestants need no one to instruct them in the significance of the sufferings of the Son. It is the Catholic tradition which has been more conscious of the truth that the sufferings of a son are inevitably the sufferings of the mother. Part of the pain of being a parent is that one is tortured by the pain of one's child. Suffering that is occasioned by witnessing the suffering of another has a peculiarly horrid quality compounded of helplessness and frustration. Its essence is that we share, but cannot share.

John 19.25–27

It is easy when speaking of family life to assume the viewpoint of a parent. But in the context of the family we are all somebody's children. In the Old Testament the commandment, 'Honour your father and your mother' is fundamental. It was not addressed primarily to youngsters, but to mature adults for whom care of the older generation was to be a major duty. The gospel reading shifts our perspective in this direction. What does a man being tortured to death have on his mind? Pain, certainly. Desire for a quick end? Very probably. Hope for his own resurrection? One thing we do know Jesus had on his mind was regret; regret that he would not be able to fulfil his duty of care towards the woman who had brought him into the world. He does the next best thing.

Christ fully shares our human condition. Even for the incarnate God the next best thing is the best that he can do.

FIFTH SUNDAY IN LENT

(First Sunday of the Passion)

Ezekiel 37.1–14; Romans 8.6–11; John 11.1–45

Ezekiel 37.1–14

Ezekiel's vision of the valley of dry bones has often been seen as a prophecy about life after death. It is not, and was never intended to be, so understood. Ezekiel's meaning is made very clear in vv. 11–14. The prophet has his eyes firmly set on this world, not the next, and is addressing a severe problem facing his people. He is, like St John, using the language of the world to come in order to speak about the here and now.

Ezekiel is writing in exile to a people in exile. These people had lost everything. They had trekked hundreds of miles across deserts, taking with them no more than could be carried on their shoulders, on the way to a country they did not know and to which they had no wish to go. They had left behind homes, possessions and jobs. As always happens in such circumstances, many had been torn apart from their families and did not know what had happened to those they loved. They had left behind the one sanctuary in which their God could legitimately be worshipped, lost the God-anointed king who governed them and seen the destruction of the holy city from which he ruled. They had lost the land which God had promised they should hold in perpetuity, and witnessed the abrogation of the covenant between him and them which was supposed to bind them to their Lord for ever. To us, in our more comfortable circumstances, their sense of loss is unimaginable. What had they left? Not faith, certainly. That had gone with the rest.

The bones which Ezekiel sees in his vision are his people. Their condition is hopeless. Ezekiel, as only Ezekiel can, lays on and labours how very dead they are. They are deader even than Lazarus. Lazarus had only just begun to rot. They have rotted and been reduced to piles of bones; and even the bones are 'very dry', nothing juicy enough even for a dog to gnaw on. But to God, the life giver, nothing is too dead for revival. As for St Paul so for Ezekiel, the agent of renewal is the Spirit and also the word, the word of the prophet himself. Resurrection is not instantaneous. Ezekiel gives us the details of a multi-staged process. There is the coming together of the bones, each finding its proper place in the skeleton, rattling as they seek each other out; then the covering with flesh and skin, then, finally, their reanimation by the Spirit/wind (there is the same ambiguity in Ezekiel's Hebrew as in the Greek of John 3) enabling them to be born afresh.

This Old Testament lection probably gives us more opportunity even than either of the two New Testament ones to 'earth' the Bible's talk of resurrection and new life. Yes, there is an other-worldly dimension to it. It does relate to the world to come. But it also has to do with God's possibilities for us in this present world. It tells us that however great our traumas (and what earthly trauma could be much greater than that of the Jewish exiles?) whether as communities or as individuals, our lives can be put back together again, not instantaneously, and perhaps not without further pain. The new life may not, and almost certainly will not, restore all that was lost, but it can make possible a new beginning, so that even those already bound in the grave clothes may be loosed and let go.

Romans 8.6–11

Once more, Paul and John are in profound agreement, but express things in different ways and develop ideas in different ways. Paul in today's Epistle does not even raise the question of resurrection as an eschatological event, unless he is hinting at that in v. 11. In bodily terms, we are already dead, 'dead because of sin' (v. 10), but our 'spirits are alive'. And this is going on now. We are already at the post-resurrection stage, already living the risen life.

But in this passage Paul has two things to add to what St John says in chapter 11 of his gospel. First, he affirms what John is perhaps simply taking for granted, that the risen life is a *moral* life. Those who are still 'in the flesh', and do not therefore share the new life, are there because they are trapped there by sin. They do not 'submit to God's law' (v. 7). And secondly, what liberates us from that position and moves us from death to life is the Spirit. John elsewhere has plenty to say about the Spirit, but he does not refer to the Spirit in chapter 11. For Paul it is the Spirit who, in a sense, mediates the risen life of Christ to the believer. This is said very emphatically in 8.11.

John 11.1–45

The Gospel is clearly intended to be the key reading for this Sunday. In St John's narrative this raising of Lazarus happens just before the beginning of Holy Week. Like the account of the healing of the blind man in chapter 9, prescribed in the lectionary for last Sunday, the story of the raising of Lazarus is a miracle which is also a parable. It is the most striking of the Johannine 'signs', demonstrating that Christ is the life-giver. The lection stops at v. 45 (reasonably, since this is another very long reading) but if we take note of the verses immediately following, it becomes clear that in St John's mind this raising was the event which made Jesus' opponents finally decide that he had to be removed. It brings everything to a head, and in that sense seals Jesus' fate.

John's 'signs' are not chance events. They do not take place just because Jesus happened to meet someone he felt sorry for. They are presented as steps in a deeply laid divine plan. The blind man is there 'so that the works of God might be made manifest in him' (9.3). The death of Lazarus, which looked like a tragedy, 'is for the glory of God, so that the Son of God may be glorified by means of it' (11.4). This rather rigidly deterministic view of events is one that many of us will have difficulty fitting into our own theology, but if we wish to understand what St John is trying to say then we must agree, for the time being, to go along with his assumptions about the way God works. In John's account, Jesus, on hearing the news of his friend's sickness, does not rush to the bedside, but deliberately hangs around for a couple of days longer in order to make sure that Lazarus is good and dead (11.6). This raising is not designed as an act of mercy, but as a demonstration of power.

In Hebrew thinking death is not necessarily an event that takes place at a point in time. It is a process. A sick person is already partly dead – not necessarily irrecoverably so. Some are deader than others. To raise someone from the dead is therefore not in principle impossible; such a raising is merely an extreme example of a healing. But Lazarus is very dead indeed; a fact which St John emphasizes in words that most translators since those of the Authorized Version have been too mealy mouthed to render plainly. But Lazarus's name is a portent. It is a latinization of the Hebrew Eleazar. It means 'God helps'. And he does.

The crucial verses in the chapter are 23–27. They might even be described as some of the most crucial in the entire gospel. When Jesus promises Martha, 'Your brother will rise again', she interprets the words in the conventional eschatological sense. The resurrection is concerned with the far future. It is something that will usher in the world to come. This is *some* comfort to those mourning the loss of a loved one. Do not let us dismiss that. Jesus does not dismiss it. The resurrection at the last day is very much part of the belief system with which he has been brought up, and he does not abandon it now. But he adds something much more momentous. Resurrection is not *just* about the world to come. It is not *only* a matter of the distant future. The new life which Christ offers is something that may be had *now*, and the raising of Lazarus is a concrete demonstration of that fact. St John is not saying anything here which is at variance with what the other New Testament writers say. All the New Testament writers agree that the resurrection is not merely something that happens to Jesus; it is something which Christians share with him. Sharing Christ's resurrection is indeed what being a Christian is all about. And it is something we can share, and should be sharing, *now*, this minute. Eternal life is not something we have to wait for. Jesus sums all this up in perhaps the most potent of the 'I am…' sayings, in v. 25: '*I am* the resurrection, and the life.'

Scarcely less significant are the words of Martha's reply (v. 27): 'I believe that you are the Christ, the Son of God, he who is coming into the world.' Note that this is a statement of faith. Martha makes it *before* Jesus has raised her brother. Historically, much weight has been placed on Peter's confession in Matt. 16.16. Martha's confession has been paid much less attention, but it is just as striking, and in content virtually identical. In Jewish law and custom the testimony of women was not rated highly, but in the gospels women are some of the key witnesses. Two Sundays ago (Third in Lent) we noted that in the Fourth Gospel Jesus does what he never does elsewhere, he makes himself known, unsolicited, as messiah (John 4.26), and to a woman. Here in 11.27 he receives a woman's acknowledgement of that messiahship. We may usefully compare here St Luke's story about the same Bethany household (10.38–42), in which Mary refuses the woman's traditional role and asserts her claim to be a disciple on the same terms as the men, and receives Jesus' full support in doing so.

SIXTH SUNDAY IN LENT

(Second Sunday of the Passion or Palm Sunday)

Entry into Jerusalem: Matthew 21.1–11; Psalm 118.1–2, 19–29
The Passion: Isaiah 50.4–9a; Philippians 2.5–11;
Matthew 26.14–27.66 *or* Matthew 27.11–54.

Effectively, we have a choice here. We can treat Palm Sunday in the way that has become traditional and focus on the entry into Jerusalem, or we can give preference to the lectionary's alternative title for this Sunday, 'The Second Sunday of the Passion', and place the passion at the centre. It will probably not be easy to do both, at least if we are to do justice to the second gospel reading, Matt. 26.14 – 27.66 (or 27.11–54). The former is a *very* long reading consisting effectively of the whole of Matthew's passion narrative. The latter is more manageable but still very substantial.

There is a serious problem here. Many members of our congregations do not, or cannot, attend church during Holy Week. This is true of most of our children. They worship on Sundays. Such Sunday worshippers, if traditional practices are followed, celebrate Christ's entry into Jerusalem on Palm Sunday, and the next time they are in church we are celebrating Easter and Christ's resurrection. For them the story of the sufferings and death is skipped over. This cannot be satisfactory. An older solution was to designate the fifth Sunday in Lent as Passion Sunday and to take account of the passion theme at that point. This was never satisfactory either, because it played havoc with the chronological order of events and many of us were uncomfortable with the dislocation involved. This is presumably the problem the lectionary makers are addressing.

Palm Sunday Old Testament Reading: Psalm 118.1–2, 19–29

This reading contains the substance of what the Jews called the 'Hallel', a very important festal psalm. It is important not merely for what it says, but for its associations. It was characteristically recited during processions at the Feast of Tabernacles. Tabernacles is a festival rich in themes and motifs, but one of its most prominent features is that it is the festival of messianic hope. According to first-century Jewish expectations, when the king messiah came it would be at the time of the Feast of Tabernacles, and he would come down the Mount of Olives from the way of the wilderness and thus enter

Jerusalem. Tabernacles, of course, falls at the opposite end of the Jewish liturgical year from Passover/Unleavened Bread, which is the setting for the passion story, but according to Matthew the crowd borrowed the language of Tabernacles during the triumphal entry, unseasonable or not.

The Gospel for Palm Sunday: Matthew 21.1–11

The entry into Jerusalem is the grand opening of Holy Week. It is, in one sense, out of character with the rest of the passion story, and this is part of its significance. The rest of the week is filled with tension and foreboding and, at the end, dire suffering. The Palm Sunday events do, in fact, initiate the tension, but they are also omens that look beyond the suffering and foreboding to the recognition of the king of glory.

The entry is a carefully staged event. Jesus has obviously pre-arranged the borrowing of the donkey, and the demonstration deliberately recalls Zechariah's two-edged prophecy. By enacting this prophecy Jesus claims authority: he is a king. But he disclaims violence. This disclaimer was very important in the volatile political climate of Roman Jerusalem, and even more important in the light of what Jesus was about to do. According to Matthew's account Jesus immediately followed up the triumphal entry with the violent act that we call the cleansing of the temple, which the temple security forces would automatically have interpreted as the deliberate provocation of a riot. In doing this he was behaving in exactly the way any Jewish revolutionary would have behaved: he was taking control of the temple mount, militarily the strongest place in the city. But his activities after the cleansing are entirely peaceful (21.14–16). And he soon abandons the temple mount altogether and goes out to Bethany to his lodgings (21.17). The cleansing of the temple and what follows are outside the compass of the Palm Sunday lection, but we can hardly understand the significance of the Entry without some reference to these subsequent events.

What could not be prearranged, of course, were the reactions of the crowd. Their greetings, as Matthew records them, are unambiguously messianic. See the notes on Psalm 118.

It is common to contrast the reactions of the Palm Sunday crowd with those of the crowd on Good Friday who shouted 'Crucify!' St Matthew, in all likelihood, is conscious of the contrast and expects his readers to note it. Surprisingly, preachers often speak of the crowd's fickleness, as if we could take it for granted that the two crowds were composed of the same people. The gospel writers say nothing at all to encourage such an assumption and it is, of course, inherently extremely unlikely.

Old Testament Reading for the Second Sunday of the Passion: Isaiah 50.4–9a

There are some obscurities in this passage, but its main point is clear. It is about someone who experiences bitter suffering and contempt, but who does not respond with violence, even violent language. He sees his suffering as being a result of his obedience to God, a result which therefore he has to accept. This is made very clear in vv. 4–6. The details of cause and effect are not explained, but it is plainly stated that he listens to God and does not rebel or shy away from what God asks of him. He gives his 'back to the smiters' and his 'cheeks to those who pulled out the beard'. The suffering is therefore entailed by what God demands of him. We may take this, if we wish, simply as a prophecy of the passion of our Lord. It fits the experience of Christ uncannily. But it is of wider reference. The prophet is speaking of what is a common experience of the servants of God, that true obedience to what God demands of us involves suffering of one sort or another.

The passion of Christ was inevitable, not because God had already written the script and foreordained the part each character was to play and the lines that were to be spoken, but because human nature is what it is. We choose our own parts. We write our own lines. But because we are what we are, the drama that emerges, and that we enact, is the passion of God. That is the nature of tragedy. God does not predetermine it: we do.

The Epistle for the Second Sunday of the Passion: Philippians 2.5–11

This short passage, so packed with doctrine, is one we can hardly do justice to in the present circumstances. It needs to be expounded as the principal lesson, and even Phil 2.5–11 cannot be the principal lesson in the face of today's Gospel. For that we have to wait until the Twenty-sixth Sunday in Ordinary Time.

In one sense, however, we almost do the passage an injustice in giving it the sort of prominence I am looking for. True, it is one of the most powerful and important theological statements that even the New Testament has to offer us, but if we look at its context in the

Letter to the Philippians we find that Paul does not introduce it by saying: 'I am now going to make a powerful and important theological statement.' He introduces it, almost in passing, as backing for some advice he is giving about Christian behaviour. If, instead of starting at v. 5, we begin with v. 1 this becomes very clear. Paul's aim is not to expound the doctrine of the incarnation or of the atonement, but to encourage us to make the character of Christ a model for our own.

One effect of the passage is to set the passion firmly in the context of the incarnation. Jesus' sufferings and death on the cross are not some separate act of atonement, additional to his normal daily work of teaching and healing. They are all of a piece with his entire character and career. 'Obedience' sums up the whole. Paul in this passage never mentions Adam, but the doings of Adam are the presupposed contrast with everything he says about Christ, and we shall not make much of what Paul is saying unless we grasp this fact. The pre-existent Christ was 'in the form of God' (v. 6). Adam, too, was made 'in the image of God'. Adam grasped at what the serpent offered him, 'You will be like God, knowing good and evil' (Gen. 3.5). Christ had all that, already, but laid it aside and 'emptied himself' (v. 7). 'He became obedient' (v. 8), unlike the disobedient Adam. And death, which for Adam was a punishment to be endured, Christ embraced. Adam fell through pride, because he thought he knew better than God. Christ, having accepted humiliation, is now exalted above all things.

But for Paul the moral is clear. We now have the opportunity to reject the way of Adam and choose the way of Christ.

The Gospel for the Second Sunday of the Passion:
Matthew 26.14–27.66 *or* 27.11–54

Especially if we opt for the longer of the two Gospel lections, the reading itself will occupy a good deal of time and leave little room for lengthy exposition. Perhaps this does not matter. This is one of the points in the liturgical year at which scripture reminds us that it speaks for itself better than any of us can speak for it. To read the story and to stand out of the way and let it make its own impact is probably the best thing the preacher can do. 'God is in heaven, and you upon earth. Therefore let your words be few' (Eccles. 5.2). There are occasions when our words only get in the way of the Word.

Many worship leaders will feel the need to break up such a long reading. Assigning different sections to different voices is an obvious step. Perhaps different sections could be differently presented, some being offered as straight reading, others dramatized. Perhaps it would be helpful to intersperse appropriate hymns or other responses. The musical settings of the passion story by J. S. Bach, and several others less famous, are punctuated by opportunities for such responses, and this structure expresses an important insight into the nature of the narrative, for the passion story is not just about Jesus, it is about us. The story is so presented to us that it is hard not to find ourselves identifying with a whole series of characters in it. The gospel writers constantly thrust at us a question, and they do this all the more effectively by never actually articulating it. They force us to put the question to ourselves. Would I have done any better? *Do* I do any better? Maybe I am not Judas, but I am at least Peter. I would at least be among those who forsook and fled. Of the 137 verses in this reading, the first 71, just over half the lection, are concerned with betrayal. The story is not just an account of what happened to Jesus, it is an indictment of virtually every other character who appears in it, and it is hard for the attentive reader or hearer not to feel that it is an indictment also of ourselves.

There are actually a number of betrayers in this story, but only two are put centre stage. There is not in fact much to choose between Judas and Peter, except in their subsequent actions. The difference between them is the difference between repentance and remorse. Remorse is a response with no future. It leads to nothing but despair, destruction and death. The remorseful Judas cannot be forgiven, because he cannot accept forgiveness. But repentance leads to hope, and indeed springs from hope. The one who repents knows that forgiveness is possible. Repentance therefore brings life.

If chapter 26 is about two betrayers, chapter 27 is about two deaths. Both are, in different senses, self chosen. All the gospel writers are masters of irony. Judas goes to the priests, whose job it was to offer atoning sacrifices for the sins of their people. But when he confesses, 'I have sinned in betraying innocent blood' (27.4), they answer 'What is that to us?' There is no atonement to be had there. Matthew assumes we will see the contrast between Judas' despairing death and that other, which takes away the sin of the world.

Again and again the question arises, whose fault was it? Could anyone, by acting differently, have changed the outcome? Where does responsibility lie? Manifestly it lies with a whole range of people, but they differ in their willingness to accept it. Laughably, Pilate, the judge at the trial, in whose hands the verdict ultimately rested, tries to deny it has anything to do with him (27.24). 'I am innocent of this man's blood', he says as he signs the death warrant. Even Judas didn't have the cheek for that. Judas at least accepts responsibility. It is his one saving grace. And so does the crowd who shouted 'Crucify!' According to Matthew (though not any of the other gospel writers), 'All the people answered, "His blood be upon us and upon our children"' (27.25). Again, we ourselves can hardly avoid the challenge. We might not behave any better than the characters in the story, but do we accept responsibility for what we do?

MONDAY IN HOLY WEEK

Isaiah 42.1–9; Hebrews 9.11–15; John 12.1–11

The Holy Week readings broadly follow the Johannine account of the passion, but very selectively.

Isaiah 42.1–9

This reading has already been set for the First Sunday after Epiphany. There the context was Jesus' baptism and the beginning of his ministry. It is interesting to look at the passage again in the context of his anointing and the beginning of Holy Week. In this different setting different words seem to spring out of the text. It declares new things (v. 9). In the context of the baptism the accent seemed to be on promise, on God's choice of his servant/son, and his bestowal of the Spirit. The prophecy speaks of the great things he is to do, opening blind eyes, leading out prisoners from the dungeon, becoming a light to the nations. He has done all that. (See John 9, where he gave light to the blind man, and John 11, where he leads out the prisoner even from the grave.) Now we notice the hints about the cost of these achievements, the possibility of failure or discouragement, and patience under suffering, for 'he will not cry or lift up his voice'.

Hebrews 9.11–15

We tend to assume that anointing signifies kingship, but that is not all it may signify. Priests, too, were anointed when they assumed their offices. And we know from the Dead Sea Scrolls that some religious Jews, at least, expected two messiahs, the Messiah ben David and the Messiah ben Aaron, a kingly and a priestly messiah. Jesus is both, and the writer to the Hebrews is pointing us towards the latter. It is in his capacity as this other messiah that Christ makes atonement for the sin of the world. Looked at from this angle, the passion of Christ in the events of Holy Week represents not the sufferings of the messianic king but the self-offering of the messianic priest, who offers the blood, not of bulls and goats as on the Day of Atonement, but of himself. In v. 15 the writer abruptly changes the image with which he is working, and shifts the scene from Leviticus 16 and Yom Kippur to Exodus 24 and the events on Sinai. Here the archetypal priest is not Aaron, but Moses, and the sacrifices are not those of atonement but of covenant-making. In Ex. 24.8 Moses says to the people: 'This is the blood of the covenant which the Lord has made with you.' Later this week the anointed one will pick up those very words: 'This is *my* blood, of the *new* covenant.'

John 12.1–11

John dates the anointing at Bethany 'six days before the Passover' (12.1), which places it not on the Monday of Holy Week but on the previous Saturday, i.e. the day before Palm Sunday and Jesus' triumphal entry (John 12.12–19). In St Mark and St Matthew the anointing does not happen until the Wednesday. Either way, it was evidently seen by these three evangelists as a significant event in the run up to Jesus' arrest and trial. (Luke does not place it in the Holy Week context at all.) The story of Jesus' anointing is told in very different ways by different gospel writers, and placed in different settings. Only John claims that the woman concerned was Mary the sister of Lazarus. Whatever the woman's motivation, other people will have placed their own interpretations on the act. 'Messiah' means 'anointed'. In John's scheme, therefore, the messianic shouts of the Palm Sunday crowd follow, logically, Jesus' anointing on the previous day. All this (that is, anointing plus triumphal entry) concentrates the minds of those hostile to Jesus, but there is also a third factor (missing from the synoptic schemes), namely, the raising of Lazarus. John in 12.9–11 echoes the point he made in chapter 11, that in the minds of Jesus' opponents it was the raising of Lazarus that made it imperative to get rid of him. The events described in our lection, with Lazarus presiding, therefore, set the stage for what is to happen subsequently.

Though no ancient reader would miss the messianic significance of this anointing it is easy for the modern reader to miss it, because Jesus himself does not pick up the messianic meaning. He deliberately reinterprets the act. Disconcertingly, he interprets the ointment as a burial gift. It is not only kings and high priests who are anointed, but the dead. The act does prefigure what is to come, but in ways that the other characters in the story do not yet appreciate.

Mary's act is a gesture, an extravagant one, and one that might, from some points of view, be open to question. Judas certainly thinks so, and I can think of church treasurers who would react similarly. We should not dismiss the objection simply because it is Judas who makes it. (Incidentally, all the Gospel writers record the objection, but only John attributes it to Judas.) But when tragedy is imminent and we are overtaken by events which we cannot control, sometimes the gestures are the things that matter most.

TUESDAY IN HOLY WEEK

Isaiah 49.1–7; I Corinthians 1.18–31; John 12.20–36

Isaiah 49.1–7

This lection has already been set for the Second Sunday in Ordinary Time.

The oddity of our Gospel reading is that it introduces 'the Greeks' and hints at the appeal Christ has for the gentiles, but lacks any indication that Christ responds to their interest. Our Old Testament lection repairs this omission. The prophet clearly states that the mission to gentiles is a major purpose of the Servant's calling. The reading links neatly with other Holy Week themes, both those of suffering and contempt (the Servant is 'deeply despised, abhorred by the nations') and those of vindication (both mentioned in v. 7). The prophet seems to be thinking of the corporate Israel here, but the words are equally applicable to the Servant as an individual. The reading also unexpectedly introduces the theme of 'glorification' (v. 3) which echoes Jesus' words in John 12.28.

I Corinthians 1.18–31

This Epistle has already been set for the Fourth Sunday in Ordinary Time. It makes an interesting commentary on today's Gospel. In worldly terms the way of the cross does not make sense, whether one starts from a Jewish perspective or a Greek one. The Greeks were famous for their pursuit of wisdom. In our Gospel reading Jesus apparently does not expect his choice of the cross to make sense to his Greek visitors. To Paul it is God's foolish act, which actually confounds the expectations of the self-styled 'wise'. The Gospel's logic is a topsy-turvy one which stands the world's values on their heads. Paul in I Cor. 1.26–31 and Jesus in John 12.26 both point out that this has consequences not just for Christ but for those whose who follow him. In our Gospel reading vv. 29–34 reflect the puzzlement of Jesus' Jewish hearers. The things Jesus is doing and saying don't make sense to them either. Jesus himself is disturbed (John 12.27), but his choice is confirmed by a voice from heaven. But to the uncomprehending, even a voice from heaven can be dismissed as not significant (John 12.29).

John 12.20–36

St Mark, when it comes to Holy Week, has a tightly organized scheme and offers us a diary of events, so that we always know which day of the week we are up to. St John does not do this. After the account of the triumphal entry on the Sunday we have no precise notes of time until the Thursday evening. Whereas in the synoptic gospels the week is filled mainly with Jesus teaching in the temple and entering into public controversy, John tells us that Jesus withdrew and kept himself to himself (12.36b).

The event described in our reading, the approach to Jesus by 'some Greeks', is a mysterious one. We end up not knowing whether he received the Greeks or not. Their request to see him is significant only because it prompts the words about his coming fate. It has been suggested that perhaps the Greeks were offering him some kind of alternative future, possibly a career as a teacher elsewhere, that would avoid the challenge he was facing in Jerusalem. All this is no more than speculation, but unless something like this was in his mind, why does John mention the Greeks at all? Whatever else, they are certainly there as a portent. They function for St John rather as the wise men do in St Matthew's account of the nativity, as an earnest of the eventual success of the gospel among the gentiles. This is a point which is picked up in our Old Testament reading.

In vv. 23–26 Jesus embraces his passion. He sees it as the only road ahead. But it is described first as a *glorification* (v. 23). This is not a word we expect. Jesus' description of his passion in these terms signifies that in accepting the passion Jesus is already focusing beyond it. He describes it in vv. 32–34 in a highly ambivalent way as a 'lifting up'. He sees his death as a falling into the ground as the seed falls. The end of the seed is new life.

WEDNESDAY IN HOLY WEEK

Isaiah 50.4–9a; Hebrews 12.1–3; John 13.21–32

Isaiah 50.4–9a

This lection was set as recently as Palm Sunday. It chimes in with today's Gospel by emphasizing strongly that the Servant is a *willing* sufferer, who accepts the pain and the contempt as a necessary part of the task God has given him. The word 'glorification' is not used, but it is made clear that the Servant will ultimately be vindicated.

Hebrews 12.1–3

The Epistle shifts the perspective by looking at Christ's endurance of suffering as a model to be imitated by his followers. He is not the first or only 'servant' who has thus endured. The writer has just given us a long catalogue of other women and men of faith who have also displayed constancy in extreme circumstances. They are the 'cloud of witnesses' to which v. 1 refers. We are invited to join them. The writer leaves aside the imagery of temple and sacrifice for the imagery of the sports arena. The Christian is one who needs the dedication of the athlete, who has to be completely focused on his goal, and turns away from anything that might distract him or impede his efforts to win that coveted medal. We are encouraged by those 'witnesses' who have run the course before us, but now even more by Jesus, 'on whom faith depends from start to finish' (NEB).

John 13.21–32

The event described in our Gospel reading for Wednesday is actually placed by John in the setting of the Last Supper, on the Thursday. It concerns Judas's betrayal, and it makes clear that, at least as John sees it, that betrayal was part of the plan. Jesus knows about it and makes no attempt to forestall it. Jesus' sufferings and death are not a fate forced upon him, or that takes him unawares. His passion is something that he takes upon himself, as a means to an end. And the end, spelled out again in vv. 31–32, as it was in yesterday's reading, is 'glorification', the glorification of the Father by the Son, and the Son by the Father.

MAUNDY THURSDAY

Exodus 12.1–4 (5–10) 11–14; I Corinthians 11.23–26;
John 13.1–17, 31b–35

The three readings, as we would expect, relate to the Last Supper.

Exodus 12.1–4 (5–10) 11–14

The same reading is prescribed as the Old Testament continuous
reading for the Twenty-third Sunday in Ordinary Time.

These are the words of institution of the Passover. Whether the
Last Supper was itself a Passover meal is a thorny question, to which
St John on the one hand, and the Synoptic Gospels on the other, pre-
suppose different answers. This question need not detain us. The Last
Supper takes place at Passover time and much of its meaning derives
from its Passover context. Neither need we stop for the moment to
worry about what for us are negative aspects of the Passover story,
such as the vicious treatment of the Egyptians. The Passover stands
here as a celebration of one of God's great acts of salvation, his
rescue of his people from slavery. It is thus, from a Christian
perspective, an archetype of the work of Christ, who redeems those
who trust him from the slavery of sin. If we choose to examine these
parallel events closely, however, the exodus with its celebration in
the Passover, and the work of Christ with its celebration in the
eucharist, then there are more differences than similarities. The
exodus is an act of political liberation, which the work of Christ
emphatically is not. The exodus and Passover have nothing to do
with sin, a subject which in the entire story of deliverance never gets
a mention. And though an act of sacrifice appears to be central to
both the Old Testament and New Testament events, the Passover
sacrifice is not expiatory and no such significance is ever attributed to
it. It is noteworthy that when the writer to the Hebrews looks for an
Old Testament sacrifice which offers a model for the atoning sacrifice of Christ his instincts take him not to the Passover lamb but to the
goat of *yom kippur*. It is perhaps as well to be aware of these limitations of traditional Christian typology, lest we fool ourselves into
imagining that the typology proves more than it does, but the
typology is not to be ignored. It was clearly potent in the thinking of
the earliest Christians, including the apostles, and almost certainly in
the thinking of Jesus himself. Yet at the institution of the eucharist,
though the setting is undoubtedly that of Passover, Jesus' words do

not directly recall the Passover sacrifice but that of covenant renewal. What seems to be in his mind is not Exodus 12 but Exodus 24. So we have several strands woven together here, linking Old Testament and New Testament themes in a quite complex way.

I Corinthians 11.23–26

We need this Epistle since the Gospel reading follows St John's account of the Last Supper, which omits the institution of the eucharist. Again there is a large critical problem here, concerning the reasons for the omission, but it would not be appropriate to discuss them. We simply need to observe the fact and leave speculations about the reasons to other occasions. The words 'new covenant' recall Jer. 31.31, but this is a bare allusion; the primary reference of Jesus' words is to the covenant-making ceremony on Sinai (Ex. 24.7). The covenant in Exodus 24 is established through sacrifice, and the language of the eucharist is also undeniably sacrificial. By repeating Jesus' words and actions his followers 'proclaim the Lord's death until he comes' (11.26). But the 'flesh' and 'blood' to which Jesus refers are neither of them sacrifices in any literal sense. The 'blood', as we all know, was actually wine, and it was not sprinkled on the people, as in Exodus 24, but was to be drunk by them. It *represents* blood. This representational quality is more remarkable in the case of the 'body'. If the Last Supper was a Passover there was, on the table in front of Jesus, some *actual* flesh, indeed sacrificial flesh, the flesh of the Passover lamb itself. Yet when he says, 'This is my body' he does not say these words over the flesh of the lamb, he says them over the bread. He chooses something which *represents* flesh, even when the real thing is to hand. The language is certainly sacrificial, but the materials quite deliberately are not. It is the message that matters, not the medium.

John 13.1–17, 31b–35

The powerful story of the foot washing is a parable on several levels. It is an example to be emulated, as Jesus says specifically in v. 15. It is also a parable of the incarnation itself, in which the Son of God 'emptied himself, taking the form of a servant', 'and being found in human form humbled himself...' (Phil. 2.7–8). And it is a parable in that this humiliation is a prelude to his 'glorification', a theme to which our lection reverts in vv. 31–32, and to which St Paul immediately moves in Phil. 2.9–11: 'Therefore God has highly exalted him, and bestowed on him the name that is above every name.' Though the language is different, the parallels of thought between John 13 and Philippians 2 are so close that it is hard not to imagine that one apostle is familiar with the other's work.

It is interesting that the Gospel reading contains in v. 34 the reference to the 'new commandment', the *mandatum novum* which was anciently included in the Gospel for Maundy Thursday, and from which the name 'Maundy' is derived. It is properly *Mandatum* Thursday.

GOOD FRIDAY

Isaiah 52.13–53.12; Hebrews 10.16–25 *or* Hebrews 4.14–16; 5.7–9;
John 18.1–19.42

The readings are the same for all three years. The notes will not comment on the readings separately, but as a group. Though these notes
do not normally comment on the appointed psalm, it is worth observing that the psalm for Good Friday is Psalm 22. It is important for a
number of reasons, not least because it contains the words of the cry
of dereliction, which the Johannine account of the crucifixion does
not. It also contrasts strongly with the readings from Hebrews, which
make the offering of the blood sound like a rather stately and cere-
monial matter. The psalm does not let us forget the earthly reality of
that blood shedding.

The Gospel is once more a very lengthy reading, two long
chapters, which might be expected to form the substance of a Good
Friday service. It takes us from the end of the Last Supper to
Gethsemane, and from there through the two trials of Jesus and the
crucifixion to the burial. The readings from Hebrews constitute a
kind of commentary on these events. What an observer in Jerusalem
would have witnessed was messy legal arguments and mob justice
and the agony of a man being tortured to death. Nevertheless, what,
on the heavenly plane, was actually happening was that Jesus our
great high priest was entering the heavenly sanctuary, bearing the
blood of the one true and efficacious sacrifice, and making atonement, once, for all, for the sins of the world.

And if the Epistle is an interpretation after the event, the great
classic text of our Old Testament reading might be described as an
interpretation before the event. It provides us with the job specifica-
tion for the Servant of the Lord. This is the post to which Jesus has
been appointed. On this Friday he completes his work and sees that it
is good. It is the sixth day, on which he can say: 'It is finished.'

One possible way of relating these three readings might be round
the triple theme of prophet, priest and king. Isaiah 53 does not *explicitly* speak of the servant as a prophet, but this is one of the ways in
which interpreters often expound the passage, and the experience of
prophetic sufferers such as Jeremiah may well lie behind it. The readings from Hebrews certainly focus on Christ's high-priestly work,
and in our Gospel the primary issue is whether Jesus can be called a
king, and if so, what is the nature of that kingship.

HOLY SATURDAY

Job 14.1–14 *or* Lamentations 3.1–9, 19–24; I Peter 4.1–8;
Matthew 27.57–66 *or* John 19.38–42

Holy Saturday is not a blank in the Christian calendar, an arithmeti-
cally necessary hiatus between Good Friday and 'the third day'; a day
when we can get back to the shopping, ready for the bank holiday. It
is the Seventh Day, the Sabbath, on which 'he rested from all his
work'.

The readings are the same for all three years, but we have a choice
of two Old Testament readings and two Gospels.

Job 14.1–14 *or* Lamentations 3.1–9, 19–24

The Old Testament readings typify Israel's pre-Christian faith, or
lack of it, in any life beyond death. The passage from Job contains a
complex of ideas. The writer is wrestling with the question of death
and its apparent finality. Verses 1–12 contain a strong assertion of
human mortality, and of the view found almost throughout the Old
Testament that there is no life to come. But in v. 13 Job speaks of the
grave as a welcome refuge from his troubles, and then goes on to play
with the idea – and it *is* just playing. It isn't even a hope – of how the
grave might be not just a hiding place, but a respite, from which God
might draw him again after the storm has passed. Between them,
what these two readings offer us is the best the Old Testament can do.

The Lamentations reading sounds like a purely personal lament for
purely personal suffering. But it is worth remembering the context.
Behind the personal tragedy is a lament for a city, a community, a
society, destroyed and dismembered. The singer of the song (and it *is*
a song) has been in one of those processions of refugees which we
have seen on our television screens all too often, with all his worldly
possessions on a handcart. And here his cry of dereliction thrusts into
the foreground his own personal grief. The writer has no anticipation
of a life beyond death. He too knows about the Stone that seems to
terminate any such expectations (v. 9). He knows about the worm-
wood and the gall that he must drink on the way (v. 19), the cup that
will not pass from him. Nevertheless he can speak of hope (vv. 21
and 24). He does not articulate the hope that he will rise from the
dead, but he does assert his faith in God and seems to leave it to God
to determine how that hope is to be fulfilled. 'Great is thy faithfulness' (v. 23).

I Peter 4.1–8

The Epistle is without alternatives, and for good reason. It raises the subject of Christ's 'preaching to the dead', which is deemed to be an important one for Holy Saturday, and it is the only place in the New Testament where the topic is referred to. And it genuinely *is* important, for it deals with what some might see as a problem: are the pre-Christian saints, such as the faithful men and women of the Old Testament, to be excluded from salvation because, by the accident of time, they had no opportunity to hear the gospel? The apostle's suggestion that Christ preached to the dead amounts to an assertion that the accident of time excludes no one from salvation.

John 19.38–42 *or* Matthew 27.57–66

The Gospel readings shift the focus of attention back to Jesus himself and the burial of his body. Our choice is between John's account and the more elaborate one in Matthew. In John's description, though time is short because of the onset of the feast, everything proper to a Jewish burial is done, and even done lavishly. (The quantity of spices used is enormous. This is not the disposal of a felon's body, but the embalming of a king.) There is irony here. Those who carried out these careful obsequies had no idea that what they were doing was so very temporary. They bound Jesus in the grave clothes, as Lazarus had been bound. Lazarus was raised to life, but still as a bound man, who had to be released by others. Not so the Lord of life. His friends did their decent best. They responded to death as all civilized people do, by observing the proprieties. That is one of our coping mechanisms; one of our ways of recognizing and of coming to terms with realities and finalities. The details of the solemnities recorded in the Gospel do have a function. They are markers for us. Yes, it was all done properly, as it ought to have been. Yes, this death was real. They did for Jesus what they would have done for any other corpse. He was 'crucified, dead and buried', ending, as we all do, in the hands of the undertaker. And yet, somehow it was all irrelevant. The human decencies do matter; they matter for all concerned. Nevertheless the new life that is in Christ bursts through, questioning all our human responses. Our rituals acknowledge the reality of death. But Christian faith asserts the reality of something beyond it. Before the night is over the grave clothes will not be burst open, not unwound, but transcended and laid aside.

Current scholarship is fairly unanimous that Matthew's Gospel must be considerably earlier than John's, by several decades, yet it is John's account of the burial that feels closer to the event. Only he tells us that the garden in which Jesus' tomb stood was close by Golgotha, 'in the place where he was crucified', which seems to be confirmed by the fact that the Church of the Holy Sepulchre manages to cover both of them under the same roof. (In life or death Jesus didn't travel far. From Bethlehem to the Sepulchre is only a couple of shekels on the bus.) But Matthew seems less concerned to tell us what happened than to head off some attempts to explain the resurrection away. He tells us about the 'great stone' which would have deterred all but very determined intruders. He mentions, as the other synoptists do, that the women were close by, watching, when the burial took place. No chance, then, that in the poor morning light they went to the wrong tomb. He alone, of all the gospel writers, says that the tomb was not only sealed but guarded, precluding any possibility that the disciples stole the body and that the resurrection story was a deliberate hoax. With Christian hindsight all these precautions look almost amusing. If anyone really took such measures they clearly did not know what they were up against. They had killed Jesus and the 'great stone' with its seals seems designed to keep him dead. But great stones are no barrier to what St Paul calls the 'spiritual body', which is the resurrection body. When the great stone is rolled away at last, it will not be to let Jesus out but to let the witnesses in.

EASTER DAY

Acts 10.34–43 *or* Jeremiah 31.1–6; Colossians 3.1–4 *or*
Acts 10.34–43; John 20.1–18 *or* Matthew 28.1–10

The readings for the three years, A, B and C, again separate, but all
years include Acts 10.34–43 in place of either the Old Testament
reading or the Epistle. And in each year John 20.1–18 appears as the
Gospel, though with alternatives. In Year A the alternative is
Matthew 28.1–10. So the lectionary is giving us a very strong hint
that among the various options it offers, Acts 10.34–43 ought to be
read somewhere. This is Peter's speech to Cornelius and his party. It
is a summary of the Christian faith, the resurrection faith, as fine as
anything in scripture. It is a summary of the apostolic experience, a
witness, by one who was there, to us who were not. The lectionary
seems also to be suggesting that among the gospel accounts of the
resurrection St John's should have a certain primacy, though there is
clearly no wish to exclude the others.

Jeremiah 31.1–6

The choice on this important Sunday of Jer. 31.1–6 as the Old
Testament lection only demonstrates how hard it is to find an Old
Testament reading that genuinely relates to resurrection. We get a
much stronger set of lections if we take Acts 10 in place of the Old
Testament reading and let Col. 3.1–4 stand as the Epistle. Anyone
who feels an urgent need to include an Old Testament lesson might
be well satisfied by reading the appointed psalm.

Acts 10.34–43

This is a well chosen lection. Its importance is that it sets the resurrection in context. First, its context is universal. The resurrection of
Christ is central to a gospel which is for all. Second, the revelation
which was meant for all was made initially through Israel. It is
universal, but the key events of which the revelation is constituted
happened at a particular time and in a particular place. Third, the
resurrection is set in the context of a particular life and a particular
death. That someone should come back from the grave is no doubt
remarkable, but the significance of the resurrection we celebrate on
Easter Sunday depends on who it was who was thus restored to life.
The body which was raised was not just any old corpse, but that of

'Jesus Christ (he is Lord of all)', the one who 'preached good news of peace . . . throughout all Judaea', who already in life was anointed 'with the Holy Spirit and with power'. The resurrection we celebrate is that of the one 'who went about doing good and healing'. It is also the resurrection of the one who was 'put to death by hanging him on a tree'. We cannot know the significance of the resurrection unless we appreciate the significance of the life and death of the one who was thus raised. And we can know little or nothing of any of this without the witness of those who were there, and saw and heard these things, of whom the apostle speaking is one. True, as Christians we can experience the presence of the risen Lord in our own lives, but without the testimony of the apostles and first witnesses would we even know how to put a name to it? However much we may value the witness of the Spirit in our own hearts and minds, for access to those primary events on which faith rests we are entirely dependent on those who were present at the time. Fourth, the resurrection of Christ is placed in the context of mission. Those who know the significance of that resurrection know also that it commits them 'to preach . . . and to testify'. When the evidence for Christ's resurrection is set before us we may disbelieve, but to believe and be silent is not an option.

Colossians 3.1–4

On this day, of all days, the church's traditional practice of reading the Epistle before the Gospel is of vital significance. The witness of the New Testament Epistles, taken as a whole, is older than that of the Gospels. It is in the Epistles that our primary evidence for the resurrection is to be found. And outside the Gospels no apostle ever refers to the empty tomb. Clearly, for them that was not a major element of their resurrection faith. They did not, astonishing as it may seem to us, even find it worth mentioning. The primary evidence for the resurrection of Christ lies in where Christ *is,* not in where he isn't.

Our lection, Col. 3.1–4, is very brief, but it makes the essential point which all the New Testament writers everywhere assert or assume, that the resurrection of Christ is *something which we share.* The apostle says, '*You* are risen *with* Christ'. The story of the resurrection is not just about something that happened to Jesus; it is about something which happens, or can happen, to ourselves, The resurrection of Christ is a unique event, unique not because nobody else ever came back to life, but because it makes new life available to those who are willing to share his death. He is raised not for his benefit but for ours. There are other resurrections of which the New Testament speaks, but they do not possess this quality. Jairus's daughter was raised, which was no doubt nice for her and nice for her mum and dad, but no one is saved through faith in Jairus's daughter, or in the widow's son at Nain. Lazarus has two tombs, one in Bethany and one (allegedly) in Cyprus. He needed both, because he died twice. All these people had to die again. Christ does not die again, but as our Epistle tells us, is 'seated at the right hand of God'. *His* resurrection is a once for all event.

The apostle states most of this in a single verse and then goes on immediately to set out the consequences: the new life which is thus made available to us is a new *moral* life; the newborn, new-raised Christian is to 'seek the things that are above'. From v. 5 onwards, outside the compass of our lection, he spells this out in some detail.

John 20.1–18

No one saw Jesus rise from the dead. The first witnesses, in this account in the Fourth Gospel, though closer in time than we are to the event, are in essentially the same situation as ourselves. They are examining the evidence and drawing conclusions. Mary, the first person on the scene, initially assumes that the body has been taken away by persons unknown. When the men arrive they do not jump to immediate conclusions. John looks into the tomb without entering (understandably: actually getting into a rock-cut tomb of this period is usually a hands and knees job). Peter does go inside, and observes the disposition of the abandoned grave clothes. John follows him and at that point, we are told, 'believed'. It does not say that Peter did. We assume he was still reserving judgement. These people are behaving exactly as we would do in the circumstances. They are making deductions from evidence that was, and remains, ambiguous. By itself the empty tomb settles nothing, half a dozen possible explanations offer themselves. What settles the matter for these first witnesses is the actual appearance of the risen Lord to Mary. Her initial failure to recognize him is disconcerting, but is a feature of several of the accounts of resurrection appearances. The risen Jesus is the same Jesus; later he will show them his hands and his side, but he is a Jesus, it seems to be suggested, who is in some way transformed, or should we say transfigured?

Matthew 28.1–10

St Matthew's narrative of the events of the first Easter morning is easily the most spectacular. In his account the women (Matthew has two Marys where John has only one) actually witness the rolling away of the stone by a glorious angel who descends from heaven. The guards, who Matthew insists were there, drop unconscious. All this happens to the accompaniment of a 'great earthquake'. But not even St Matthew claims that the women saw Jesus actually emerge. The angel rolls away the stone to reveal to them that Jesus has already gone. There is here no ambiguity; no one needs to draw hesitating conclusions. Earthquakes and angels stun them into belief. When the risen Jesus meets the women on their way from the tomb there is no problem of recognition. No doubt St Matthew's presentation of the events of Easter morning is important, but in his story the witnesses do not stand where we stand. They affirm the reality of the resurrection, but they do not share with us the predicament of faith.

SECOND SUNDAY OF EASTER

Acts 2.14a, 22–32; I Peter 1.3–9; John 20.19–31

There is no Old Testament reading prescribed in the lectionary for the Principal Service from now until Pentecost. The Old Testament lections are replaced by readings from Acts. This accords with ancient practice. Preachers who feel a strong compulsion to include an Old Testament reading may note that the Anglican version of the lectionary does offer this option. The readings from Acts set for the post-Easter period relate in fact to events after Pentecost. A preacher aiming for continuity might consider focusing for the next five Sundays on the Acts readings. Alternatively, since the lections from the Epistle take us systematically through the First Letter of Peter, we might regard the Epistle as setting the agenda for this period of the liturgical year.

Acts 2.14a, 22–32

According to the New Testament record this is the very first time anyone ever set out the Christian gospel, the post-resurrection gospel. It is the first proclamation, the first act of mission. Of course we do not know what was really said on that occasion. What we have in Acts is what the author *imagined* would have been said, but there is every reason to believe that he was well acquainted with the nature of early Christian preaching, and that he was not likely to have got it badly wrong.

Peter's sermon, as here reconstructed, is surprisingly combative and confrontational. At its heart is an accusation: 'This Jesus . . . you crucified and killed by the hands of lawless men.' Not until his hearers have acknowledged their responsibility for the death of Jesus does Peter offer anything that might be called 'good news', and that is several verses later, beyond the confines of today's lection.

The sermon is typical of those in Acts in that it relies heavily on scripture to show that the death and resurrection of Jesus were all part of the divine plan. They were foreseen by the people who wrote what we call the Old Testament. Characteristically, the Psalms provide the main evidence, and David is treated as a prophet. (This is explicitly stated in v. 30.) The resurrection is presented as the clinching argument which establishes Jesus' status, and the climax of our lection (though not the climax of the sermon) is the claim that Peter himself, together with his fellow disciples, can confirm that Jesus really has been raised from the dead.

I Peter 1.3–9

Our Epistle picks up a similar point to our Gospel reading. Though addressed to Christians within the New Testament period they are Christians who have not known Jesus in the flesh. 'Without having seen him you love him; though you do not now see him you believe in him' (v. 8). We usually think of the language of new birth as being characteristically Johannine, but here it is in St Peter: 'We have been born anew to a living hope' (v. 3). And the language of the new birth is also the language of resurrection, for 'we have been born anew . . . through the resurrection of Jesus Christ from the dead'. And the salvation we have already received is itself only a foretaste, a step on the way to 'a salvation ready to be revealed in the last time' (v. 5).

John 20.19–31

This is a weighty passage of scripture. It contains first an account of the appearance, on the evening of the first Easter Day, of the risen Jesus to the main body of his disciples. Then in v. 21 we have the sending out of the disciples, a rather pale version of the great commission in Matt. 28.18–20. In v. 22 we have the Johannine parallel to the giving of the Holy Spirit, which in Acts does not happen until Pentecost. And in v. 23 we have an authorization of the disciples which seems to be St John's equivalent of the more famous one in Matt. 16.19. The one in Matthew 16 appears to be delivered to Peter alone; the Johannine version evidently has in mind all the disciples. St John is packing a lot in here, and even more if we let our eyes stray to verse 17, two verses before our lection begins, where he speaks of his ascension, not as something which will happen in forty days' time but as if it were imminent, something to be expected that very evening. St John's Gospel thus includes all the important elements which appear in the other Gospels, but without respecting their chronology. What they spread out over a considerable period he telescopes into a great earthquake of events, in which Christ's resurrection, his commissioning of his disciples, his ascension and the giving of the Holy Spirit all take place in the space of a single day. Together these constitute the 'lifting up' of the Lord and his 'glorification'. Perhaps the church has been wise to adopt the scheme offered us in the Synoptic Gospels and in Acts, which holds these elements more digestibly apart, and allows us to savour and to celebrate each one separately. But we ought to observe how different St John's scheme is, if only to convince ourselves that the Synoptic/ Acts scenario is not the only possible way of interpreting what happened.

As if all this were not enough, our Gospel lection goes on to include the appearance to Thomas, which may look like something of an afterthought, but is very far from being any such thing. Sometimes it is useful to think of the New Testament as a set of documents with a message for first-generation Christians, on which we, after twenty centuries, are still eavesdropping. But occasionally, and excitingly, its authors forget the readership in front of them and turn deliberately to address *us*. That is what happens here. The Easter Sunday lections emphasized the importance of the first witnesses, the people who were there and saw for themselves, and so does today's reading from Acts 2. But from Easter Sunday evening until more than a week later, Thomas, though belonging to that company, is in *our* position. He is *the one who wasn't there*. Like us, he is a disciple who didn't see for himself, and who was expected to take somebody else's word for it. He is still, of course, in a privileged position. He is still a first-generation disciple, and, come Monday week, will get the chance to check for himself. But in St John's mind he is here to represent all those later disciples who will never have that opportunity. When St John says 'Blessed are those who have not seen...' he is talking about you, and he is talking about me. This, I suppose, is still talking about us in the third person. But at the end of our reading the apostle stops doing even that. He turns directly to us, and says 'You'. He is getting near the end of his gospel. Very interesting, but what was it all for? Just in case we had any doubts, he tells us: 'I wrote it for you. I didn't do it for the other apostles, or for those many Christian brothers and sisters who weren't there at the time but can still ask somebody who was. I didn't write it for my housegroup in Ephesus. *You* are the people I was thinking of. These things are written that you may believe . . . and that you may have life in his name.'

THIRD SUNDAY OF EASTER

Acts 2.14a, 36–41; I Peter 1.17–23; Luke 24.13–35

Acts 2.14a, 36–41

Here we have the rest of Peter's first sermon, to which we were introduced last week, beginning with the verse that is really the climax of its first half: 'Let all the house of Israel therefore know assuredly that God has made him both Lord and Christ [i.e. messiah], this Jesus whom you crucified.' The combative tone is still there. Peter is not letting his hearers off the hook. But what follows is the remorseful response of at least some of those listening. In v. 38 we have a summary of the way forward for a Christian convert: repentance, baptism, forgiveness of sins and the receiving of the Holy Spirit. St Peter is here providing the blueprint which the rest of the New Testament follows. Note that those whom he addresses are assumed to be Jews. They are 'the house of Israel' (v. 36). This is no doubt true to the historic occasion being described, but by the time Acts was written the gentile mission was well established, and in v. 39 we are given a strong hint that eventually others might be included. The sermon includes what sounds like a quotation from scripture, though it is not an exact quotation of anything we recognize: 'The promise is to you and to your children *and to all that are far off, everyone whom the Lord our God calls to him.*'

I Peter 1.17–23

Again a New Testament writer manages to cover a lot of gospel in a mere seven verses. The passage opens firmly. If you are going to be Christians, then live like Christians. Once, the apostle says to his readers, you got up to all sorts of pagan tricks. But all that is behind you. Why? Because Christ has rescued you from such futility by his self-sacrifice on the cross (here the apostle gives us his atonement doctrine in one sentence). The resurrection of Christ is our ground of assurance that all this is true. 'Through him you have confidence in God, who raised him from the dead and gave him glory.' And the test of it, as he began by saying, is Christian behaviour, i.e. obedience, and love (v. 21). This is evidence of what has really happened to us, our being born anew. At this final point the apostle's thinking converges with that of our Gospel reading. We are born anew 'through the living and abiding word of God' (v. 23), just as the

Emmaus disciples became convinced of the reality of the living Christ as he opened to them the scriptures, making their hearts burn within them.

Luke 24.13–35

This is the well-known story of the Emmaus road, which Luke actually places on the first Easter evening. He begins with a compelling evocation of the mood of that first Sunday, before the news of resurrection has been taken in. The shock and horror of the previous three days are evident in what the disciples say, and the disappointment. These people have watched a close friend being publicly killed by slow torture. Not only that, he was a friend in whom they had placed high hopes, 'a prophet mighty in deed and word before God and all the people'. 'We had hoped he was the one to redeem Israel.' These are shattered people, living in a shattered world. Their report of the finding of the empty tomb, and of the talk of angels, is delivered without excitement. They profess puzzlement, but obviously don't believe a word of it. It is going to take more than a story about visiting angels to cheer them up.

But like St John in last week's Gospel, by the end of this account St Luke shifts the perspective dramatically. He may have skilfully evoked the feelings of that first Easter Day, but his message is for those of us who were not there and never met the risen Lord for ourselves. At the end of the story that risen Lord 'vanished out of their sight' (v. 31). He could afford to. From now his disciples no longer need to see him with their bodily eyes, because they have learnt to see him in the exposition of the scriptures and the breaking of the bread.

FOURTH SUNDAY OF EASTER

Acts 2.42–47; I Peter 2.19–25; John 10.1–10

Though there is no Old Testament reading, preachers may wish to note that the appointed psalm is Psalm 23.

Acts 2.42–47

Peter's first sermon, explored in the readings for the previous two Sundays, resulted in the making of the first converts. Our reading for today tells how these first converts initially behaved. They paid attention to the apostles' teaching, they broke bread together, and they prayed. These were the basic elements of their faith and worship, Christian piety at its simplest.

The rest of the reading fills out the picture, showing these converts experimenting with a pattern of living, some features of which did not survive. This is interesting, for it shows that the first Christians did not get everything right. Neither did the Holy Spirit give them infallible guidance straight away. They had to find out by trial and error what it meant to live the Christian life. They were in the process of finding out what things Christians could best do together, and what they had better do separately. They appear to have lived together and they lived on their capital. This may explain why St Paul later had to appeal so urgently for financial assistance for the poor saints in Jerusalem, though not all interpreters find this suggestion convincing. But clearly this was a precedent not to be followed. They broke bread in their homes. Does this mean they did in private what later Christians felt ought to be done in public worship? They still worshipped daily in the temple. This, too, was a practice that eventually lapsed. The church still had no rule book. These people were finding out the rules as they went along. But this did not matter. They were breaking new ground and it was all very exciting. And they did it 'with glad and generous hearts' (v. 46). And the people respected them (v. 47). And God honoured them by giving success to their mission, 'adding to their number day by day those who were being saved'.

I Peter 2.19–25

The principal theme of the reading is unjust suffering, and the Christian necessity to bear such suffering with patience. It is clear from the letter as a whole that those to whom it was written were not having an easy time. The apostle points them towards the example of Christ, which he describes in a brief but fine passage in vv. 22–23, and in summary offers us one of the New Testament's very rare quotations from Isaiah 53. 'By his wounds you have been healed'. His understanding of Christ's atoning work is, as in last week's lection, summarized in a verse (v. 24): 'He himself bore our sins in his body on the tree, that we might die to sin and live to righteousness.' We have noted how, in his speaking of the new birth, St Peter's language seems to echo closely that of St John. Here in v. 24 we have a sentence that could have come straight out of St Paul. But the final verse of our lection leads us into the theme of the Gospel reading: 'You have now returned to the Shepherd and Bishop of your souls.'

John 10.1–10

The theme of God as shepherd is as ancient as it is ubiquitous. It is not confined to scripture. Both gods and earthly rulers were in the Ancient Near East frequently described as shepherds of their people. Ezekiel, in a famous passage in Ezekiel 34, bitterly criticizes the leaders of his people, the 'shepherds of Israel', for their failure to care for those under their charge, and conducts his own public enquiry into their negligence and indifference. These are the bad shepherds. In Ezekiel's parable God gives them the sack and takes over the job himself. 'I myself will be the shepherd of my sheep,' he says (Ezek. 34.15). This is the prophecy which, St John is hinting, Jesus fulfils. Jesus does not explicitly say that his Pharisaic opponents are to be identified as the bad shepherds, but this seems to be clearly implied. He himself, by contrast, is 'the good shepherd'. (Our lection ends at v. 10. The phrase 'I am the good shepherd' does not appear until v. 11.) In this passage Jesus substantiates his claim first by affirming that he is the only *legitimate* shepherd (vv. 1–3), and second by asserting that he is the one whom the sheep recognize and to whom they respond (vv. 4–5).

Whether Jesus ever expressed himself in quite these terms or not (and he may well have said something like it) the present passage has surely been shaped in the light of the situation which had developed later, when St John was writing his gospel. By then, antagonism between Jews and Christians had become intense; they were competing with each other for converts, and membership of the synagogue and membership of the church had become incompatible. Christians were claiming to be the legitimate spiritual heirs of the prophets and saints of the Old Testament, and were trying to convince all who would listen that the Jews had got it all wrong. This is the situation clearly presupposed, for instance, in the story of the blind man in John 9. Appealing as the image of the Good Shepherd may be, St John gives it a polemical edge which modern Christians may regret.

FIFTH SUNDAY OF EASTER

Acts 7.55–60; I Peter 2.2–10; John 14.1–14

Acts 7.55–60

This is the stoning of Stephen, but only the very climax of the story. It would not be helpful to read this passage without some indication of what led up to it. St Stephen is usually designated the first martyr. There is a good deal of evidence in the New Testament that persecution and martyrdom began very early in the history of the church, and that it was one of the possibilities that all converts needed to be prepared for. There is a clear link between our reading from Acts and the Epistle, for the First Letter of Peter was demonstrably written to a Christian community that had some experience of persecution, and was anticipating more.

In one sense, of course, Stephen was not the first martyr. He was the second. The archetypal martyr is Christ himself. The martyrdom stories from the early centuries of the church, which were a very popular form of Christian literature, invariably point up the parallels between the sufferings of the martyr and the passion of Christ, and it is interesting to find this already happening in the description in Acts of the death of Stephen. Stephen's words in v. 56, 'I see the heavens opened...', strongly recall those of Jesus to the high priest at his trial (Matt. 26.64 and parallels). 'Lord Jesus, receive my spirit' (v. 59) is an interesting variant of the Lord's own words, 'Father, into your hands...' (Luke 23.46). And Stephen's final prayer, 'Lord, do not hold this sin against them' (v. 60) echoes Jesus' 'Father, forgive them...' (Luke 23.34). Like the many martyrs who were to follow him, Stephen is treading a path already marked out by 'the pioneer' (Heb. 12.2).

I Peter 2.2–10

Only when one tries to analyse this passage does it become evident what a diversity of images it contains. To try to expound them all is to risk making a sermon that looks like a mishmash. The biblical author manages to hold them together and make smooth transitions from one to another but preachers without comparable skills might be well advised to select one image and focus sharply on that.

Readings in previous weeks have alerted us to Peter's fondness for the theme of the new birth. In vv. 2–3 he reminds us that being born is not an end, it is a beginning. Those who are born again need to grow up again. This can be the difficult bit.

At the end of our lection (v. 9) the apostle introduces a theme drawn straight from Ex. 19.5–6 (though he has skilfully given us a pre-echo of it in v. 5). Language which in the old scriptures described the destiny of God's ancient people is now applied to his new people, the community of Christians. They, he seems to be suggesting, have taken over Israel's role. By the time this epistle was written there can be no doubt that the church contained substantial numbers of gentiles. The words of v. 10, 'Once you were no people...', are surely addressed directly to gentile Christians. This letter purports to be by St Peter. Is this the same Peter who in Acts 10 needed so much persuasion to accept gentiles into the church; the Peter who, even after that, was criticized by St Paul for still being in two minds about the issue (see Gal. 2.11–13)? If so, then the author himself has done some growing in the faith. The whole passage is a tissue of scriptural quotations and allusions. The final verse, 'Once you were no people but now you are God's people; once you had not received mercy but now you have received mercy,' is deliberately reminding us of Lo ammi and Lo ruhamah, the rejected children of Hosea (Hos. 1.6–8), who in Hos. 2.1 are eventually accepted and acknowledged. Our author sees this as a foreshadowing of the homecoming of the gentiles.

But the central part of our lection is exploring the image of the stone. In ancient scripture this image has both positive and negative aspects. It is sometimes an image of judgement. The stone may be 'a stone of stumbling and a rock of offence' (Isa. 8.14–15). See also Daniel 2.34–35, 44–45. Our author recognizes this in 2.8, but he is chiefly concerned with the positive.

If the letter really is by St Peter we may readily see why the image of the stone should have resonances for him. Herod the Great began the rebuilding of the temple in Jerusalem in 20 BC and it was not completed until more than eighty years later. All through the lifetime of Peter, the other apostles, and Jesus himself, that temple was in process of being built, and as good Jews going up to Jerusalem three times a year, they would doubtless have been interested to observe its progress. Since no noise was allowed in the temple precincts, all the stones were cut to shape off-site, labelled, transported to the temple mount and fitted into place. If the quarrymen knew their job, any stone which the builders were inclined to reject would have its proper place somewhere in the scheme. Jesus and his apostles would have spent the better part of a lifetime watching that temple grow, and the building metaphors which abound in the New Testament are doubtless informed by that experience.

The other element in Peter's experience is more personal. 'Peter', of course, was not really his name. He was Simon. It was Jesus who had rechristened him 'the Stone man' and said he would build a church with him. So the idea of 'living stones', which we might think a contradiction in terms, is an idea that would come readily to Peter. He was one. Christ himself is the original 'living stone', the one destined to be the cornerstone. But one stone does not make a temple, which is why he tells us: 'Like living stones yourselves be built into a spiritual house' (v. 5). Fitted each in place, and living and growing up together, the people of God become an edifice more glorious even than the temple of Herod.

John 14.1–14

The words of v. 12, 'He who believes in me will also do the works that I do', make an interesting comment on the death of Stephen. But there is much else in this reading, enough to keep a preacher busy for weeks on end. 'No one comes to the Father but by me' (v. 6) is seen by some as ruling out non-Christian faiths as possible ways to God. But how is this modified by Jesus' assurance that 'In my Father's house are many rooms' (v. 2)? It is a passage of puzzled questions and demands. 'We do not know where you are going' (v. 5). And, surely the most naïve query in scripture: 'Show us the Father, and we shall be satisfied' (v. 8). Here, only a day before his death, the disciples are still asking questions to which Jesus thought he had already given them the answers. Yet above all it is a comforting passage. It begins with profound reassurances and ends with the most tremendous promises This is not an age of certainties. Thinking Christians do not have an easy time of it. Thomas is our patron saint. He asks our questions for us: 'How can we know the way?' Jesus' answer is, 'You know *me*. Let that be sufficient.' The martyrs, too, may have had their uncertainties. They may have been more ambivalent people than we know, but when push came to shove, they were clear about what was worth dying for. Can we at least be clear, in the middle of our ambivalences, about what is worth living for?

SIXTH SUNDAY OF EASTER

Acts 17.22–31; I Peter 3.13–22; John 14.15–21

Acts 17.22–31

There are a number of apostolic sermons or speeches recorded in Acts, of which Peter's speech on the day of Pentecost, set in the lectionary for the First and Second Sundays of Easter, is typical. They have several characteristic features in common. But lest we should imagine that there is only one proper way of preaching the gospel, our reading for today offers us an example of apostolic preaching that is very untypical indeed. This is St Paul's speech on the Areopagus at Athens. The speech is remarkable for what it does not do and what it does not say. It does not quote or allude to scripture, or contain any arguments from Old Testament prophecy. The only quotations it contains are from two pagan authors. It does not begin with Jesus, or give any information about his life and teaching. It does not refer to his death. Jesus, indeed, does not get a mention until almost the end. Even then Paul does not use the name of Jesus or of Christ, but refers to him with astonishing indirectness as 'a man whom [God] has appointed' (v. 31). We are told only two things about him; first, that he is the one through whom God will judge the world; and, second, that God has raised him from the dead. Few of us, if challenged to reduce the gospel to its most basic elements, would come up with anything quite so minimalist as this.

But Paul is beginning where he thinks his gentile audience stand, and with the beliefs and attitudes he hopes he and they already share. He begins with deity, with creation and with universal humanity. And he begins with reason. These are not bad starting points. We preachers ought to try them occasionally.

I Peter 3.13–22

There are themes here which we have already encountered in our progress through I Peter: the possibility of being 'called to account for the hope that is in' us, and the possibility of having to suffer for our faith. If such circumstances arise, the Christian's response must be one of 'gentleness and reverence', like that of Christ himself. But a theme which we have not so far mentioned is that of baptism. The subject of baptism is a prominent one in this epistle, and nowhere more prominent than in our present lection. The baptism of the believer and the resurrection of Christ are strongly associated in the apostle's mind. Baptism is the entry to new life, and that new life is something of which Christ assured us when he was raised from the dead. The author draws both on Christian mythology and Jewish midrash in expounding this. The Christian mythology is that of Christ's preaching 'to the spirits in prison' (v. 19), a subject alluded to in the Epistle for Holy Saturday. The apostle here relates this, not to the pre-Christian saints, the faithful and virtuous of Old Testament times, but to the unfaithful and ungodly, and specifically to the generation of the Flood, whose wickedness was a byword. Jewish tradition has it that during the long period while Noah was building the ark he preached to his neighbours, explaining to them what he was doing, and why. But they were headstrong and only mocked him. Their fate was judgement by the waters. Noah and his family, by contrast, were saved by the waters. This for the apostle is the archetype of baptism. But in Christ, even the generation of the Flood are given a second chance to make the right choice. In the midrash there is a curious tie-up between this passage and Genesis 18. In Genesis 18 Abraham conducts a Dutch auction in his attempt to avert the judgement of Sodom. He drives the Lord down until he admits that the presence of even ten righteous persons would be enough to save the city. Every Christian reader of the story must cry out: 'Why does he stop at ten? Why not push the argument to five, or three, or One?' The rabbis had an answer. They knew the story of the Flood and they were sure that Abraham was familiar with it too. So they reckoned that if in Noah's day the presence of eight righteous persons had not been enough to save the world, it was clearly no good trying to drive the Lord much lower than ten. Ten righteous might be enough to save the world from judgement; but eight were enough only to save themselves. Christians are those who have opted for faith and for baptism, and for them therefore the waters are not waters of judgement, but of salvation.

John 14.15–21

We are not far now from Pentecost and the lectionary is beginning to prepare us for the coming of the Holy Spirit. Our present lection, indeed, is not just about the Holy Spirit, it is one of the most clearly trinitarian passages in the New Testament. Its context is that of the Last Supper and Jesus' farewell words to his disciples. Before he leaves them he tries to address that sense of profound loss which they are going to feel. But he will not leave them bereft. He will give them another *paraclete*. What is the best translation of this word? Counsellor? Advocate? In the context I do not think we can improve on 'Comforter'. This Comforter is also called 'the Spirit', and Jesus tells the disciples they know him already. Then he says to them: '*I will come to you.*' The clear implication seems to be that the Comforter/Spirit is the presence of Jesus himself. After he is no longer with them in the flesh he will still be real to them. The Spirit is the one through whom Christ becomes real to us after his death and resurrection and ascension. And if Christ is real to us then *ipso facto* his Father is real to us. But all this is set in a framework. The first verse of our lection and the last mention a condition. All this, says Jesus, is for those who love him. And those who love him are defined as those who obey him. Love and obedience are the doorway to the presence.

ASCENSION DAY

Acts 1.1–11; Ephesians 1.15–23; Luke 24.44–53

Acts 1.1–11

For the author of Acts the ascension is a kind of marker. It seals off the forty-day period during which Jesus made sporadic appearances to his disciples and it initiates a new phase in his relationship with them. In this new phase, the implication is, they could no longer expect to see him in the same way. The occasional presence of the risen Jesus in the flesh is to be replaced by the continual presence of the Holy Spirit. What changes at this point, therefore, is the mode of the divine presence. The ascension is telling us that the incarnate phase of our Lord's life is over. What is going on here may be regarded as a kind of progressive liberation of the Spirit of Christ. The risen Lord is not limited in the way he was before his resurrection. Neither sealed tombs nor locked doors are barriers to him. He appears and disappears at will. Nothing in the gospels suggests that the pre-resurrection Jesus ever behaved in this way. He shared our normal human limitations. The risen Jesus in some respects evidently does not, but it seems to be assumed that, even so, the risen Jesus could still only be in one place at once. After the ascension he is liberated even from this constraint. In the person of the Holy Spirit the presence of God can be with anybody, anywhere, and all at the same time. The ascended Christ is also free of particularity. The incarnate Christ must perforce be either a Jew or a gentile, male or female, black or white, blond or brunette. The ascended Son is none of these things, but is, to borrow a Pauline phrase, 'all in all'.

Ephesians 1.15–23

The risen and ascended Christ transcends the limits of the incarnate life. Incarnation means that he shared human limitations, but now no longer. To understand what the apostle is saying here we need to take account of the world view with which he and most of his contemporaries operated. To them it was not a simple matter of an earth peopled by human beings, above which was heaven, the habitation of God and his angels. They took for granted the existence of a great hierarchy of superhuman beings and forces, principalities, thrones, dominions and powers. The pagans attributed to each of these forces a degree of independence. They had wills and influence of their own.

They could be beneficent or malign. In the thinking of Jews and Christians all such forces were in the last resort subject to the one God, but nonetheless their existence was taken seriously. Together they made up a great pyramid of being, with the more refined and spiritual at the top, nearest to God, and becoming less spiritual and more earthy as one descended through the levels. In the minds of some people it was only indirectly, through these various strata of being, that God had any contact with the created world. The totality of these intermediaries was referred to as the *pleroma*, which is translated literally, but rather unhelpfully, as the 'fullness' of the divine. All this, of course, is remote from our own way of thinking about the world, but we need to know about it if we are to understand the New Testament's language. The apostle, in our lection from Ephesians, is claiming that Christ, at his resurrection and ascension, was established at the very top of this pyramid of being, 'far above all rule and authority and power and dominion [all of these are technical labels for the various 'powers'] and above every name that is named' (v. 21). And when he says that 'he [God] has put all things under his feet', (v. 22), the 'all things' does not mean merely what we ourselves would think of as the entire creation, but also that vast array of beings in the superhuman world. This is the apostle's picture of the cosmic Christ, the one who, in his own person, *is* the *pleroma*, who absorbs into himself the totality of heavenly existences, 'the fullness of him who fills all in all'. This is what the ascension means to the mind of the apostle: this is the magnitude of what he is claiming for a Galilean carpenter. How we express all this in terms of our own twenty-first-century world view is, of course, another matter altogether.

Luke 24.44–53

The ascension of Jesus is described both at the end of St Luke's Gospel and the beginning of Acts. The significant difference between them is that in the Gospel the ascension takes place on the evening of the first Easter Day. In Acts it happens forty days later. It is the chronology of Acts which has determined our church calendar. During what for Luke is his final meeting with the disciples Jesus first expounds the scriptures, explaining that all that has happened to him is in accordance with ancient prophecy and the divine will (vv. 45–46). Second, he summons them to mission. His passion and resurrection took place so that 'repentance and forgiveness of sins should be preached . . . to all nations' (v. 47). Third, he makes it clear that this is their job and they ought soon to get on with it, because they are the witnesses to what has taken place (v. 48). But, fourth, in the interim they are to wait until they are 'clothed with power from on high'. (This last phrase is curiously reminiscent of the ancient 'judges'. See, e.g., Judg. 6.34, where the Hebrew actually says that 'The spirit of the Lord clothed itself with Gideon'.) The actual ascension is spoken of very briefly. Jesus took the disciples for a walk 'as far as Bethany' (just on the far side of the Mount of Olives), blessed them and left them, being 'carried up into heaven'. The emphasis throughout is not on what was happening to Jesus, but on what he was expecting of the disciples.

SEVENTH SUNDAY OF EASTER

(Sunday in Ascensiontide)

Acts 1.6–14; 1 Peter 4.12–14; 5.6–11; John 17.1–11

Acts 1.6–14

The reading from Acts is almost, but not quite, co-terminous with the one appointed for Ascension Day. The description of the ascension itself is more detailed than in St Luke's account in the Gospel reading for Ascension Day but, even so, there is a good deal of emphasis on the disciples themselves and on their mission. The disciples begin by raising the eschatological question. After all that has happened, are they now to expect the kingdom of God to dawn? The answer is a firm one; they are not to bother their heads about that. It isn't their business. They are to prepare themselves for what *is* their business, being Christ's witnesses. And they will be equipped to do this by receiving the power of the Holy Spirit. This emphasis is confirmed by the final words of 'the people in white robes': 'Men of Galilee, why do you stand looking into heaven?' (v. 11). Jesus has departed, but that doesn't mean attention has to be focused up there where he has gone. The disciples' business is down here. The message of the ascension is: Get on with it.

But before Pentecost there is to be a brief hiatus. In the final verses of our lection the disciples gather themselves. The names of the men are listed. But in addition there are 'the women', unlisted except for Mary the Lord's mother. There are also his brothers. The addition of these family members is interesting. Our impression is that during our Lord's earthly life they were less than supportive, but here they are at the end – or the beginning.

I Peter 4.12–14; 5.6–11

We have commented already on the frequency with which this letter of Peter mentions persecution and suffering. This is also a feature of our present reading. For the Christian, says our apostle, suffering is to be expected (4.12). It is 'required of the brotherhood throughout the world' (5.9). And it is a sharing in the sufferings of Christ himself (4.13). But if we are to share Christ's sufferings we shall also share his glory (4.14; 5.10). We might get the impression from our other readings that at the ascension Christ goes off to be in glory with the

Father, leaving us behind. That is not the case, says the apostle. Glory is our destination too. Mission is our business for the moment, and that may involve pain as well as joy, but Christ's will for us is that eventually we shall be with him. At the incarnation the Lord became as we are, so that at last we should become as he is. This perspective has always, at least since the time of St Athanasius, been a feature of the thinking of the Eastern church. It has been less fashionable in the West, but it is a valuable aspect of the meaning of the ascension. The disciple shares not only the risen life but also the ascended life of Christ.

John 17.1–11

Our Gospel reading is again part of the farewell discourse delivered by our Lord on Maundy Thursday. It does not specifically speak of ascension, though v. 5 is as clear a reference to the ascension as we could expect to have. Its theme is 'glorification', and in St John's mind 'glorification' is an inclusive concept which comprehends the lifting up of Christ on the cross, his resurrection and his 'going to the Father'. Jesus' work is to glorify the Father, and the Father's response is to glorify the Son.

In this prayer Jesus' words about his relation to the Father are followed by others about how he relates to his disciples. His 'glorification' in some way includes them too (v. 10). This is made more explicit in v. 22, beyond the confines of our lection. Eventually they will be with him (v. 24), but for now, he says, 'I am no more in the world, but they are in the world' (v. 11). As in our Epistle, and in Acts, the separation of Jesus from those who trust him is only apparent or temporary. It is apparent in that his presence will shortly take the form of the Holy Spirit. It is temporary in that at the last they will share his glory.

PENTECOST

Acts 2.1–21 *or* Numbers 11.24–30; I Corinthians 12.3b–13 *or*
Acts 2.1–21; John 20.19–23 *or* John 7.37–39

The lectionary offers us a number of options here. Clearly the intention is that Acts 2.1–21 should be read, either in the Old Testament slot or in place of the Epistle.

Acts 2.1–21

Examples of ecstatic experiences may be found in many religions, both in ancient times and today. A number of such experiences are described in scripture, and they are still a feature of Christian life (at least for some Christians) in our own time. But because we may be minded to put this single label on them, 'ecstatic experience' does not mean that they are all the same. Such experiences are indeed very varied, both in the manner of their happening and in content. As it is described in Acts, the coming of the Holy Spirit at the first Christian Pentecost, though manifestly an example of ecstasy, has some very striking features, some of them unique.

The event is unique in that it is such a momentous happening in the life of the church. It is an initial moment of empowerment, like the lighting of a fuse, following which the church exploded into mission. It is another face to the resurrection of Christ. At his resurrection Christ shares his life with his disciples: Pentecost shows us how. Those who have themselves encountered the Holy Spirit will recognize at least part of the Acts experience as their own. There is the feeling of being 'taken over', of being swept along; the finding ourselves doing things we did not know we could, and discovering abilities we did not know we had.

The speaking in tongues is not, in itself, a unique feature. In some Christian communities this is commonplace. The author of Acts, however, gives the impression that what was manifested was not merely ecstatic speech but the speaking of actual foreign languages. This is less usual, to say the least. But as St Paul attests (e.g. in I Cor. 14.27–28, and 12.2, in today's Epistle), when a Christian speaks in tongues, even if what is said is not immediately intelligible to all, a fellow worshipper may be given 'the gift of interpretation' and be able to translate. Perhaps something of the sort happened at the first Christian Pentecost. The Old Testament makes it clear that the prophets were sometimes carried away and spoke in ecstasy, occasionally in what seemed an uncontrolled manner. The Bible's descriptions of these occurrences lack detail, but what we can say for certain is that what eventually emerged was intelligible speech. And in Acts 2, whatever was said in tongues, when Peter gets up to address the crowd he uses not glossolalia but the Greek that would be understood by all his hearers.

One of the features of the Pentecost experience which some of us find a challenge to our imaginations is its corporate nature. Spiritual experience is something most Christians would claim to know about, but our instinct is to think of such experiences as essentially individual. They go on inside our heads. At Pentecost we have a spiritual experience which is unambiguously corporate (as well as being very public – and extremely noisy). In the twenty-first-century West this is not, for the most part, how we like to do things. Especially for the restrained English, Pentecost is a rather foreign-looking event, and perhaps just a little distasteful. No doubt this is our own shortcoming.

Numbers 11.24–30

This lection will require a little introduction. The context is the wanderings in the wilderness. Moses has complained that he is stressed and overworked. The Lord suggests that he appoint seventy elders to share the burden. These elders are taken to the tabernacle outside the Israelite encampment. There the spirit comes upon them and they prophesy (which is likely to have been rather like speaking in tongues). Nothing is said of the content of the prophesying. That is not important. The important thing is that they did it. The prophesying is evidence that the elders genuinely do now share the gifts needed for the job in hand. It is, in effect, their authorization. We are told in v. 25 that though they prophesied on this occasion, 'They did so no more'. They did not need to. Prophesying was not their primary job. Once the gift of prophecy had shown that the Lord approved their appointment they were not required to exercise it on a regular basis.

Now comes the interesting part: Eldad and Medad, who were not among the appointed seventy and who had remained within the camp, also prophesy. Joshua suggests they should be stopped. They have not been officially chosen or appointed and therefore, in Joshua's view, have no business to prophesy at all. Moses rebuts the suggestion, with his reply, 'Would that all the Lord's people were prophets, and that the Lord would put his spirit upon them' (v. 29).

What the seventy elders on the one hand, and Eldad and Medad on the other, represent are respectively institutional and non-institutional prophecy. Israel was familiar with both. Most prophets, no doubt, were professionals. They may have inherited the job from their fathers, and undoubtedly served some sort of apprenticeship, possibly with a prophetic guild, a company of 'the sons of the prophets'. This story in Numbers 11 is asserting that not all prophecy is institutional. There is always room for the unauthorized inspired person, the prophet after the order of Eldad and Medad, who can say: 'No prophet I, nor prophet's son; but the Lord took me . . . and said, "Go, prophesy"' (Amos 7.14–15). Priesthood in the Old Testament is a hereditary and closed order (and there are dire penalties for usurping priestly functions, as is demonstrated in Numbers 16) but Numbers 11 is telling us that the order of prophets is not and must not be like this. There are no penalties for usurping prophetic functions. At Pentecost Moses' wish in v. 29 is fulfilled.

I Corinthians 12.3b–13

The opening half verse is important. Some of us would hardly claim to be Spirit possessed. We have not spoken in tongues and are not given to ecstasy. But the apostle assures us that if we can say, 'Jesus is Lord', and acknowledge him as our Master, then whether we realize it or not, we have the Holy Spirit within us. The 'gifts' of which St Paul goes on to speak seem to be envisaged as ones which are exercised in the church context, especially in worship. If we, in our day, were making such a list of gifts to be used within the church it would not include many of those mentioned here by St Paul. His is a first-century list. Can we learn anything from it? Why would it not occur to most of us to include in our list the gift of prophecy, or of miracle-working? Are our reasons for missing them out good reasons? What gifts would we want to include that Paul does not? And if we are listing gifts of the Spirit, do we not wish to include gifts that a Christian would find valuable in the wider world, outside the immediate confines of the church and its worship? Whatever gifts we might think useful, Paul's main conclusions (which he expands as the chapter proceeds, beyond today's lection) are that no Christian has them all; no Christian needs them all. And above all, *gifts* is what they are, and gifts is what they remain. We can take no personal credit for them whatever.

John 20.19–23

This reading has already appeared in the lectionary as part of the Gospel for the Second Sunday of Easter. It is St John's account of the bestowal of the Holy Spirit. It differs from the Acts description in that it happens not at Pentecost but on the evening of Easter Day. It does not take place in Jesus' absence, after the ascension, but in his actual risen presence. 'He breathed on them' (v. 22). It is his personal gift. It is much less spectacular, and does not lead there and then to any ecstatic behaviour. And it is bound up with Christ's authorization of the apostles, his giving them the power to grant or withhold the forgiveness of sins (v. 23), and his sending of them out into the world (v. 21b). This is rather like the institutional bestowal of the Holy Spirit that takes place through the laying on of hands at an ordination. There is nothing here of the wind and fire.

John 7.37–39

This reading picks up the theme of John 4, which was the prescribed reading for the Third Sunday in Lent. The setting, however, is completely different. In John 4 the setting is the centre of the estranged North, in the shadow of Mount Gerizim. Here it is the centre of Judah and Jerusalem, the temple mount itself. On both mountains the living water is being made available to those who worship in spirit and in truth. 'On the last day of the feast, the great day...' (v. 37). The feast referred to was the Feast of Tabernacles. On the last day of the eight-day festival there was a procession from the spring of Gihon in the Kidron valley, with much waving of branches of palm, myrtle and willow, and singing of psalms. The procession escorted a priest carrying a jar of water, which was ceremonially poured out at the foot of the great altar in the temple court. After the vast numbers of sacrifices offered at the Feast of Tabernacles, sacrifices of slaughtered animals, and offerings of the produce of the land, here is the simplest and most basic sacrifice of all, the libation of water, the water of life which makes all growth and all production possible. And on this very occasion, says St John, Jesus stood in the temple court and proclaimed, 'If anyone thirst, let him come to *me* and drink.' Faith in Christ is not an optional extra, something to be indulged in by those who haven't anything more exciting to do on Sunday mornings. What he offers is something that satisfies our most fundamental needs. St John sees this as a prophecy of the coming of the Holy Spirit, which is contingent upon Christ's 'glorification', but this interpretation does not exhaust the meaning of the saying.

TRINITY SUNDAY

Genesis 1.1–2.4a; II Corinthians 13.11–13; Matthew 28.16–20

Genesis 1.1–2.4a

This lection consists of the whole of the first account of creation, i.e. stopping short of the story of the Garden of Eden. On the occasion of Trinity Sunday it is clearly sensible to focus on its relevance to the subject of the Trinity. The Trinity is patent in the New Testament, but at least latent in the Old. In this reading the work of the Father/Creator of course constitutes the substance, but the presence of the Spirit is explicitly acknowledged in 1.2, and Christians at least from the time of St John have identified the creative Word which the Father speaks with the Son who became incarnate as Jesus Christ. Creation is therefore not exclusively the province of the Father. All three persons of the Trinity have a part in the creative work. And later in scripture it becomes apparent that all three are concerned in the work of salvation. St John further suggests that Christ is to be identified not only with the Word but also with the primal Light (John 1.9–10). A further hint of the triune nature of God has also traditionally been found by Christians in Gen. 1.26, where God says: 'Let us make man...' Though the text says nothing explicit of trinity it does clearly imply plurality. The writers of the Old Testament, though they powerfully affirm the unity of God, perceive that there is a sense in which it is proper to speak of God as a social entity. It is such perceptions that the doctrine of the Trinity crystallizes under the Christian dispensation.

II Corinthians 13.11–13

Warning! Different editions of the New Testament have different ways of numbering the verses at the end of II Corinthians. If your Bible has a v. 14, do not stop at v. 13 or you will miss out the words that matter most. Whatever the numbers say, read to the end of the chapter.

We believe II Corinthians to have been written relatively early in St Paul's career. It is interesting therefore to find the trinitarian formula apparently already established. Our Gospel reading, though St Matthew is probably writing a little later, confirms the general picture. The Trinity, therefore, is not an idea dreamt up by fourth-century church councils. Here it is, embedded in quite early layers of the New Testament.

The doctrine of the Trinity is a mystery, but it is not complicated. The first Christians were Jews. They knew about God the Father, who created the world and who was the saviour of his people. They then encountered Jesus. His effect on them was such that they felt compelled to say: 'In meeting Jesus we meet God'. Then they encountered the Holy Spirit. When he took over their lives they had no doubt that it was God taking over. So then: the Father was God; Jesus Christ was God; the Holy Spirit was God. Those were convictions that came straight out of their common experience as Christians. Yet they knew there could only be one God. That, for them, was a statement of how things are. And that is the doctrine of the Trinity. Complications and disagreements arose when Christians tried to put it all into philosophical terms and explain how these apparently contradictory statements could hang together, but for St Paul writing his letters or St Matthew writing his gospel these complications are still for the most part over the horizon. The formula they were already familiar with still stands as a statement of how Christians find things. They know God as Father, and observe his work in creation and providence. They meet God in Christ the Son, and believe his words, and trust him as their saviour. And they are guided and empowered by the Holy Spirit, who is able to do for them more than they can ask or think. And they assert the mystery, that these three are One God, blessed for ever.

Matthew 28.16–20

The doctrine of the Trinity is not an intellectual construction put together by theologians who wanted to make things complicated. Neither is it a difficult bit of dogma which ordinary Christians can afford to ignore. It is rooted in the experience of Christians and in the life of the church. The setting in which it is introduced here by St Matthew shows it to be the basis of mission. To preach the gospel of the Father, the Son and the Holy Spirit is our whole business. Quite properly our celebration of the Trinity stands, liturgically, at the end and climax of the Christian year, the sum and essence of all that has gone before.

In St Matthew's telling of the post-resurrection story there is no account of the ascension as such, but our present lection describes what Matthew evidently understands as our Lord's final appearance to his disciples, and Jesus' words in v. 18, 'All authority in heaven and on earth has been given to me', convey the *meaning* of the ascension, though we are given no description of the event. Matthew also differs from Luke and Acts in that they set the parting scene near Jerusalem, whereas he puts it in Galilee. In this Matthew has some support from Mark (see Mark 16.7). These discrepancies do not affect the main issue.

SUNDAY BETWEEN 24 AND 28 MAY INCLUSIVE (if after Trinity Sunday)

(Eighth Sunday in Ordinary Time)

Isaiah 49.8–16a; I Corinthians 4.1–5; Matthew 6.24–34

The Eighth Sunday in Ordinary Time also occurs two Sundays before Lent and the appropriate readings are commented on at that point.

SUNDAY BETWEEN 29 MAY AND 4 JUNE INCLUSIVE (if after Trinity Sunday)

(Ninth Sunday in Ordinary Time)

Genesis 6.9–22; 7.24; 8.14–19; Deuteronomy 11.18–21, 26–28; Romans 1.16–17; 3.22b–28 (29–31); Matthew 7.21–29

For the rest of the liturgical year we work our way steadily through what remains of St Matthew's Gospel, i.e. from chapter 7 onwards, and for the next sixteen weeks we similarly work through Romans.

Genesis 6.9–22; 7.24; 8.14–19

The story of the Flood is a long one and the lectionary makers have done their best to edit it down to manageable proportions, but the reading might still benefit from a sentence or two to help hearers bridge the gaps. This is not offered as a 'related' lection, but it might be taken as such. It makes a good commentary on Rom. 3.23. It is about the universality of sin. After Adam and Eve's disobedience, the writer of Genesis is telling us, the world slid downhill into corruption, and by the time of Noah that corruption had become total (6.11–12). This was the human race doing what comes naturally to it. Noah and his family appear to be an exception to the general rule, but are they? Jewish tradition regards the words of 6.9, 'Noah was a righteous man, blameless in his generation', as ambiguous. He was blameless *in his generation.* This could be taken to mean that he was righteous by the standards of his time, which, not to put too fine a point on it, were abysmal. In other words, he was the best of a bad bunch. On this understanding the most important statement about Noah is not the one in 6.9, that he was righteous, but the one in 6.8, that 'Noah found grace in the eyes of the Lord'. All this plays straight into St Paul's hands. It also fits in with the story in Gen. 9.20–27, about how Noah's first act after the Flood was to plant a vineyard, make wine from the grapes and get drunk. Righteous he may have been, but he had his little weaknesses.

It is true that the text also says (6.9) that 'Noah walked with God'. And he does have faith. When God tells him to build the ark he immediately orders the wood and starts going to carpentry classes. He 'did all that God commanded him' (6.22). The Deuteronomist

113

would have approved of his obedience, and Jesus of his wisdom. But St Paul still gets it right. Whatever Noah's merits, or lack of them, it is by grace that he is saved.

Deuteronomy 11.18–21, 26–28

To bind God's words on the hands and forehead and on one's door-posts and gates is an instruction that orthodox Jews take literally. Christians do not. But we can take it seriously. We can take scripture seriously without necessarily taking it literally. Deuteronomy uses less picturesque language than Jesus in our Gospel, but the message is much the same. Obedience to God is what matters most. And both Jesus and the Deuteronomist are telling us that in any case this obedience is in our own best interests. This week's parable is about wisdom and foolishness. The man who builds his house on sand isn't necessarily immoral. He is simply stupid. The person who fails to keep God's commandments has made a choice. And in choosing disobedience he has chosen curse rather than blessing. Judgement is not something that God inflicts: it is something we bring upon ourselves.

Romans 1.16–17; 3.22b–28 (29–31)

Romans 1 does offer us a link with the Gospel reading, though it is in verses which the lectionary omits (vv. 18–29). These are strictures aimed at idol worshippers. 'Claiming to be wise, they became fools' (v. 22). The apostle is condemning the self-chosen foolishness of those who 'exchange the glory of the immortal God for images resembling mortal man' (v. 23).

In the lection itself there are too many possible directions in which the interpreter might go for us to pursue them all here, but the crucial verses are 3.23–24, beginning with the statement that 'All have sinned and fall short of the glory of God'. This might be regarded as a summary of the argument of the entire passage, Romans 1–3. Both Jesus and the Deuteronomist in our readings for today assume that the choice between obedience and disobedience is an open one. It is up to us which way we go. This is a typically Jewish perspective. Paul is questioning it. Yes, we do have a choice, but in practice, he says, we all get it wrong. Jews and gentiles get it wrong in different ways, but both fall under the judgement of God. This seems a much more sombre view of human nature than that of Jesus and the Deuteronomist. So is our situation hopeless? Far from it, says Paul. The bad news is: all have sinned; all need to be saved. The good news is: all *can* be saved, through faith in Christ (3.24). In this matter, Jews and gentiles are in the same situation. Their roads to condemnation may be different, but there is only one road to salvation. In the final paragraph of our lection (and this is true whether we opt for its shorter or for its longer form) Paul points out one of the consequences. We all have the opportunity to be redeemed from our errors and end up on the right side, but if we do, none of us can take any credit for it.

Matthew 7.21–29

This lection, together with the related Old Testament reading, could be suitably entitled 'Taking God seriously'. The opening verse of the Gospel declares that lip service is not enough. For Jesus' first hearers the parable would have made the point admirably. We can still get the point, even though our houses are stouter than theirs. Most Palestinian houses, throughout the biblical period, were made mainly of mud brick. Only public buildings and the houses of the very rich commonly had much stone in them. An ordinary house might have three rows of stones at the base of the walls, but after that the mud brick took over. Mud brick is an excellent building material, as long as it doesn't rain. When it gets wet it has a powerful tendency to return, like Adam, to the earth whence it was taken. To keep the rain out it needs constant repair and replastering. If it is neglected even for one winter the consequences can be dire. So when the rain descended and the wind blew and beat upon ancient Palestinian houses they not infrequently fell. And of course such houses needed proper foundations. In most parts of Palestine bedrock is not far below the surface and the sensible builder starts on the bedrock. It looks as if the foolish man in the parable built his house in the bottom of a wadi, where the sand accumulates, and where the building would in any case be very vulnerable to winter floods. A dry wadi can turn into a raging torrent in minutes. All this Jesus' hearers would not need to have explained to them. They knew about wadis, and about houses that fell down.

SUNDAY BETWEEN 5 AND 11 JUNE INCLUSIVE (if after Trinity Sunday)

(Tenth Sunday in Ordinary Time)

Genesis 12.1–9; Hosea 5.15–6.6; Romans 4.13–25; Matthew 9.9–13, 18–26

Genesis 12.1–9

This lection also appeared in part (12.1–4a) on the second Sunday in Lent. The notes at that point are very relevant to the reading's present function as a continuous reading. In its position on the Tenth Sunday in Ordinary Time it actually connects very well with the Epistle, for it is one of the principal places where the promises to Abraham, to which St Paul is referring in Romans 4, are set out.

Hosea 5.15–6.6

This lection is presumably chosen because it includes the words quoted in the Gospel reading, Matt. 9.13. Its content only relates to that of the Gospel in the most general way. It consists of two oracles of Hosea (5.15–6.3 and 6.4–6). The theme of the first is the return to God of penitent sinners. The words of penitence in 6.1–3 are not in fact uttered by the sinners. They are what God is *hoping* they will say. Perhaps we could see the response of sinners to Jesus as the eventual fulfilment of this hope. The second oracle is a complaint by God about his erring nation (or rather, his two nations, Ephraim and Judah), but it is a despairing complaint: 'What shall I do with you?' It says nothing of any response by the two nations, and apparently none is seriously expected.

Romans 4.13–25

Part of this lection, 4.13–17, has already been set as the Epistle for the second Sunday in Lent. See the notes offered at that point. Verses 18–25, which did not appear in the lenten reading, mainly expand the argument we examined earlier. The expansion relates to the sacrifice of Isaac, into which Paul introduces the theme of resurrection. For St Paul and any Jewish readers of his letter this coupling would seem very natural. His willingness to sacrifice his son is the outstanding example of Abraham's faith. Even though God had promised that he would have descendants through Isaac, he was prepared to put him to death. How could this be? It is because, says Paul, he believed in God 'who gives life to the dead' (v. 17). Paul is drawing on a well-known Jewish tradition at this point. The rabbis reasoned that Abraham was willing to sacrifice Isaac because he believed that God would raise him from death. In v. 24 Paul is implying that this is one of the points of contact between Abraham's faith and ours.

Matthew 9.9–13, 18–26

The call of Matthew (v. 9) appears to be as abrupt as the earlier call of Peter and Andrew, James and John, and is even more briefly described than theirs. Apart from the appearance of his name in lists of the twelve apostles, and of course in the title to this gospel, Matthew is never mentioned again in the New Testament. All that we know of him is that he was called, and that he answered.

In any case, what for Matthew was doubtless a momentous and life-changing experience is referred to here merely in order to explain how on this occasion Jesus came to be entertaining, or to be entertained by, tax collectors and 'sinners'. Do not take too seriously the designation 'sinner'. In Pharisaic parlance anybody was a 'sinner' who was less fussy about observing the details of Jewish law than they were. These people were not thieves and murderers; they probably just didn't bother to tithe the salt and pepper. If we know anything at all for certain about Jesus of Nazareth it was that he was not choosy about the company he kept. This was very unrabbinic behaviour and he was bitterly criticized for it. In many ways Jesus was a typical rabbi of his period (he certainly argues like one) but in some ways he was not, which accounts for the slight air of scandal that seems more or less permanently to have surrounded him. Galilean rabbis in general appear to have had a reputation for unorthodoxy, especially in the way they related to women, but Jesus was more suspect than most. No Pharisee would have sat down at table with 'sinners'; for them it was a question of religious purity. Jesus' reply, 'Healthy people aren't the ones that need the doctor,' is indicating that for him purity is not the issue, but human need. In v. 13 he quotes Hosea: 'I desire faithfulness and not sacrifice.' Neither Mark nor Luke at this point include the Hosea citation, perhaps because it is not really clear what Jesus means by it, unless he is using it as a dismissal of ritual law in general.

Our lection moves on to the healing of the woman with the haemorrhage and the raising of Jairus's daughter (though Matthew never tells us he is called Jairus). Indeed, Matthew's account of these two miracles is much shorter than that found in the other Synoptics and lacks all detail. All three Synoptic Gospels tell the two stories together like this, the one inside the other. When Jairus asks for help Jesus goes willingly. But on the way he is presented by other needs, and another, acute, purity question. This woman has no business to be there. She is ritually unclean. She should not be in the crowd at all, silently polluting all the unsuspecting people around her. She has even, and quite deliberately, touched and polluted the great man himself. She has done the unthinkable. No wonder St Mark tells us that when Jesus confronted her she was extremely worried. Matthew probably assumes we know this without being told. But she is driven by need and isolation. The most extraordinary thing about this event to Jesus' contemporaries would have been his silence. About the purity question he does not say one word. For him, it wasn't worth a mention.

And then he goes on, to the house of the 'ruler of the synagogue'. Jairus is part of the religious establishment. But on this occasion he too needs a healer. He does not have to be a 'sinner' or a down-and-out to receive the Lord's attention. He only has to have a need and acknowledge it.

SUNDAY BETWEEN 12 AND 18 JUNE INCLUSIVE (if after Trinity Sunday)

(Eleventh Sunday in Ordinary Time)

Genesis 18.1–15; (21.1–7); Exodus 19.2–8a; Romans 5.1–8; Matthew 9.35–10.8 (9–23)

Genesis 18.1–15; (21.1–7)

In last week's lection Abraham was called by God to leave his home-land, and God promised to make of him a great nation. But, as we subsequently learn, he is childless and both he and his wife are very elderly. The episode in our present reading concerns the visit to Abraham and Sarah of three 'men'. We are of course meant to under-stand that they were angels. There is, however, some ambiguity in the text. Did Abraham really have three visitors, or only one? Genesis 18.1 says that '*The Lord* appeared to Abraham', but by v. 2 the Lord has become three 'men'. Abraham, however, has apparently not noticed this, because in v. 3 he still addresses the Lord in the singular (a fact more obvious in the Hebrew than in translation). Throughout most of the rest of the episode he treats his guests in the plural, but after v. 13 he seems again to be speaking to the Lord alone. Modern interpreters are inclined for the most part to treat these oddities as oddities, but older generations of Christians were convinced that the oscillation between oneness and threeness was clear evidence that even in the Old Testament the triune nature of God was acknow-ledged.

The writer assumes that Abraham is unaware of the divine nature of the three 'men', and entertains them lavishly because he is a generous man and because the lavish entertainment of guests is a mark of virtue. Lavish the provision certainly was. The three have a whole calf to themselves (Abraham does not eat with his guests) and the quantity of bread works out at roughly half a hundredweight (about 25 kilos). Still, the preparation of the meal must have taken some time and they had opportunity to work up an appetite. But the purpose of the visit is to announce that Sarah is to give birth to a son. There are a number of occasions in scripture when an angel announces an imminent birth. Usually the announcement is made direct to the mother (though the birth of John the Baptist is an exception). Here the news is given to Abraham, and Sarah overhears. Sarah's incredulous laughter, and the conversation to which it gives rise, are important only because they relate to the child's name. Isaac (*yitshaq* in Hebrew) is a verbal form meaning 'he shall laugh'. The longer form of the lection records an alternative explanation of Sarah's laughter, which reflects rather better on Sarah.

But the main point of the story is to record another stage on the road to redemption. Abraham has been called and has obeyed. He has received God's promises. The birth of Isaac is the first step towards their fulfilment.

Exodus 19.2–8a

This is the beginning of the account of the revelation on Sinai. The Israelites have come to the foot of the mountain. Over the next few days impressive things will happen, and Moses will go up on to the mountain to meet God himself and to receive his Law, which will from now on form the basis of their relationship. In v. 5 God summons the people to 'obey my voice and keep my covenant'. In v. 8 they answer, 'Everything that the Lord has spoken we will do.' But the answer turns out to be rather too glib. They do not in fact know at this stage what they are letting themselves in for. In the event, the ink is barely dry on the tablets of stone before they find the covenant to which they have committed themselves too onerous to keep. They disobey both the first and the second commandments and worship the golden calf. The Old Testament makes it very plain throughout its pages that the people of God found themselves incapable of keeping the Law on which their salvation rested, and that this was so from the very beginning. This is the basis of Paul's case, which underlies today's lection from Romans, that a better way than the Law had to be found. That way was the way of faith in Christ; and the human nature which the Law could not tame was reconciled to God through his death.

Matthew 9.35–10.8 (9–23)

The sending out of the disciples is presented as an extension of Jesus' own ministry. According to 9.35 that ministry is twofold: Jesus proclaims the good news of the kingdom, and he heals the sick. In 10.7–8 the ministry of the disciples has exactly the same double focus. Jesus himself seems overwhelmed by his feelings of compassion for those coming to him and by the scale of their needs. Alone, he cannot do all that clamours to be done. The disciples are the extra labourers he is sending into the harvest fields. The episode is a kind of practice for the mission they will all be swept up into after the first Christian Pentecost. But there are two significant differences between the post-Pentecost mission and the present one. First, the present mission is a temporary and short-term project. It is assumed that it ends and the disciples return, though this is not explicitly reported. Second, as St Matthew describes it, the mission is a restricted one. It is to Jews only. It does not include gentiles, or even Samaritans. The terms of the briefing leave no room for misunderstanding about this (10.5).

If we use the longer version of the lection we find the briefing extended into a description of the sort of treatment disciples of Jesus may expect (10.16–23). Most of this does not seem readily applicable to the situation of that first small-scale mission. The evangelist has got carried away. He is clearly thinking of the conditions of his own time and has in mind the sort of problems that arose for the church later.

Two other aspects of the mission are emphasized in these additional verses (10.9–15). The disciples are to travel light – *very* light. They do not even take food with them, but are to depend on what their hearers give them. Neither are they to take a change of clothes. This is more surprising. It seems to confirm the supposition that the present mission is to be brief (we hope!).

The other, perhaps unexpected, aspect of the mission is the spirit in which it is to be carried out. Good news is to be announced, healing offered, but the basis on which it is all done is 'take it or leave it'. The disciples are not there to persuade, but to proclaim. If people do not listen, they have no time to waste and must pass on. There are others who will. The implications are actually quite harsh: those who choose to reject what is offered have chosen judgement for themselves (10.14–15).

A final salutary thought: is this first mission of the disciples meant to offer a pattern for the ministry of the church throughout the ages? Its restriction to Jews, and perhaps some of its other peculiarities, raise the possibility that it is not. But if it is, then it prompts the thought that the ministry of healing, which has a very high profile in the New Testament, and which is presented here as a major part of the disciples' activities, has been seriously neglected by most of the church since.

SUNDAY BETWEEN 19 AND 25 JUNE INCLUSIVE (if after Trinity Sunday)

(Twelfth Sunday in Ordinary Time)

Genesis 21.8–21; Jeremiah 20.7–13; Romans 6.1b–11; Matthew 10.24–39

Genesis 21.8–21

This is one of the most shocking stories in the Old Testament. It reflects no credit either on Abraham or on Sarah his wife. Their behaviour is reprehensible not only by the standards of our time, but by the standards of theirs. Our continuous lectionary readings have leapt from the call of Abraham in Genesis 12 to the promise of the birth of Isaac in Genesis 18. In between, ignored by the lectionary, is the account of the birth of Ishmael. In the society of the biblical patriarchs polygamy was common; nevertheless, in marriage contracts of the period, at least where wealthy families were concerned, the bridegroom was sometimes prohibited from taking any additional wives. This caused problems if the first wife proved childless, so an additional clause was often added, obliging the bride in such circumstances to provide a slave-wife to replace her as a childbearer. Such a slave woman might be included as part of the bride's dowry. She acted as a kind of spare wheel on the marriage, in case the worst came to the worst. Reading between the lines, it looks as if the marriage contract of Abraham and Sarah was of just this type, and Hagar was the spare wheel. Eventually Sarah does have to hand Hagar over and she gives birth to Ishmael. Ancient Near Eastern law in general takes steps to protect the rights of slave-wives. Ex. 21.7–11 (a law which is of course later than Abraham's time) lays down that a woman sold for purposes of cohabitation is entitled to have her status protected and must not later be sold on as a common slave. And non-Israelite law codes prohibit the repudiation of a slave-wife once she has borne her master's children.

Abraham and Sarah therefore violate moral standards which were clearly defined throughout the Ancient Near East. The initiative comes from Sarah. We are told that Abraham was reluctant, and that he only agreed to expel Hagar after God gave him permission (vv. 11–12). This will not do. Only three chapters earlier, in Genesis 18,

Abraham has put God himself on the spot by demanding, 'Shall not the judge of all the earth do right?' (18.25). God himself, Abraham is asserting, is bound by the moral law. Now all that is forgotten and Hagar is driven out into the desert with her baby, a bottle of water and a loaf, and the pious hope that God will look after her. He does, of course. But that excuses nothing.

Jeremiah 20.7–13

This is part of one of Jeremiah's so-called 'confessions'. They are not in the usual sense of the word 'confessions' at all, but a species of complaint. Jeremiah 20.7–18 is perhaps the most powerful and out-spoken of them. The prophet begins by accusing God of having made a fool of him. God has called him to be a prophet, and given him the words to say, but the prophecies never come true. This has made him a laughing-stock. God has overpowered him and *made* him prophesy (v. 7), but then has let him down. The obvious answer is to stop proph-esying. Jeremiah has tried that, but the word became 'like a burning fire shut up in [his] bones' (v. 9) and he could not hold it back. This might not be so bad, but the word God has given him to speak is deeply unpopular and has made the prophet many enemies, and their opposition is both strong and violent. The hardest of these enemies to cope with are Jeremiah's own family and friends. To find enmity where we look for support is especially difficult to take. And the hatred Jeremiah faced really was virulent. Elsewhere in the book it is made plain that his very life was in danger. This, of course, is where the Old Testament lection converges with our Gospel reading. What Jesus prophesied for his disciples had already been found true by this man of God in the Old Testament. Precisely why Jeremiah's closest associates took such strong exception to his prophesying is a matter of debate. The book of Jeremiah never makes it clear. But we do know that Jeremiah's family belonged to a local provincial priesthood. Many such priests lost their livelihoods at the time of King Josiah's reform, which closed down all the provincial sanctuaries. If Jeremiah had been a supporter of the reform, and had spoken in favour of it (and we cannot be really sure whether he did) this would be enough to account for the opposition. But there may be other explanations. In vv. 11–12 the prophet returns to protestations of faith, to assertions that the Lord will support him, and to prayers that God will take vengeance on his persecutors. In v. 13 he ends this section of his com-plaint in the way the psalmists do, by thanking God for a deliverance which he has not yet experienced, but which he takes on trust.

Romans 6.1b–11

Paul begins by countering a naïve objection. He has been arguing, earlier in this letter, that all human beings stand convicted of sin in the sight of God. The only hope any of us has, therefore, of acceptance by God is by putting our faith in Christ, and through him God will forgive our sins by his grace. The naïve objection is: If God is prepared to forgive us all anyway, why not carry on sinning, and give his grace plenty to do? The more sin, the more grace, and the more grace, the more of a good thing. Put in this way the idea seems ridiculous, and of course it is, but there were people in the early church who espoused it, and there have been people since who have fallen into a similar error of taking the grace of God for granted. 'Dieu me pardonnera, c'est son métier': 'God will forgive: that's his job.' Paul does not really argue against this idea, he dismisses it. He expounds his basic teaching about where Christians stand. Anyone who really shares the new life in Christ knows that to get there we must share his death, something which we express by baptism. If we have died then we are now 'dead to sin'. It is a sufficient answer to the naïve objection to say, as he does in v. 2, 'How can those who have died to sin still live in it?' No one whose faith is serious, no one who truly understands the gospel and what the cost of grace can be, will take the forgiveness of God for granted. To think thus would be to trivialize the whole work of salvation.

Matthew 10.24–39

On the evidence of the gospels Jesus is the great enemy of the family; a fact worth remembering if we belong to the sort of church that periodically plans cosy 'family services'.

The reading begins exactly where last week's Gospel left off, and continues to explore the subject of persecution. If Jesus himself has been vilified, his disciples can expect no kinder treatment (vv. 24–25). The central part of the reading (vv. 26–33) emphasizes that whatever unpleasant things may happen to the disciples, they are in God's careful hands, and they will ultimately be vindicated.

The final paragraph, vv. 34–39, introduces the subject of the family. It is very disturbing, and would have been found even more disturbing by first-century listeners or readers than it is by us. Family solidarity and family duty are no doubt important to most of us, but they were infinitely more important to Jews of the biblical period. For Jesus to say that he was in the business of dividing families and setting close relatives at odds with each other would have been profoundly shocking. Most shocking of all is v. 37: 'Whoever loves father or mother more than me is not worthy of me; and whoever loves son or daughter more than me is not worthy of me.' When we think of our own attachment to our fathers and mothers, and to our children, can we face Christ's demand that we should put them second? Everyone in Jesus' day was thoroughly familiar with the totalitarian state, the Empire which demanded the first claim on the loyalty of all its subjects, beyond all national and lesser loyalties. Jesus proclaims an alternative empire, the empire of God. But the totalitarianism of God's empire is at least as unforgiving as that of its rival, and 'the King of the kings of kings' makes claims more far-reaching and uncompromising than those of Caesar. Jesus did not invent this totalitarianism; it is there already in Deuteronomy (Deut. 13.6–11), but the absolute demand, which in the Old Testament only God is entitled to make, Jesus appropriates to himself.

There is nothing theoretical about all this. Christian faith still divides families. There are places in the world where someone who converts to Christianity can face ostracism by those who have been closest. In our own country a Christian in a non-Christian family is unlikely to meet any opposition so dramatic, but there can certainly be tensions, if only over minor-seeming things like family outings on Sunday mornings. A Christian may in many ways find relations with the family problematic, and within the church the issue receives much less attention than it deserves. Our people do need help in this matter. Passages of scripture like today's Gospel raise the questions in very sharp form. They do not make them easier to discuss.

SUNDAY BETWEEN 26 JUNE AND 2 JULY INCLUSIVE

(Thirteenth Sunday in Ordinary Time)

Genesis 22.1–14; Jeremiah 28.5–9; Romans 6.12–23;
Matthew 10.40–42

Genesis 22.1–14

We now come to the powerful and disturbing story of the binding of Isaac. It is perhaps the Bible's most outstanding example of faith. Abraham believes that God has promised him descendants through Isaac. He also becomes convinced that God wants him to put Isaac to death as a sacrifice. He is ready to obey. It is all, of course, a big mistake on Abraham's part. God could not have demanded human sacrifice, but maybe a Middle-Bronze-Age man could be excused for not knowing that, and the mistake does not diminish the faith.

The story is remarkable for its reticence. It leaves out so much, and leaves so much unexplained. Did Abraham make no objections? None are recorded. What did Sarah think about it? Was she consulted? And what about Isaac himself? Isaac's question in v. 7 suggests that at that point Abraham had not told him what he had in mind. But Jewish interpreters assert that the repeated words, 'And they went on, both of them together' signify the assent of Isaac to the enterprise, that Isaac was a willing victim. They also claim that the binding of Isaac (v. 9) was done at Isaac's own request, lest he struggle involuntarily and mar the sacrifice. And Jewish tradition identifies the unnamed mountain in the land of Moriah as the hill that later became the temple mount, the one place where sacrifice could legitimately be offered according to the yet undelivered Law. Some even say that every sacrifice that was ever to be offered there in the future was a mere memorial and drew its efficacy from the sacrifice of that only son who offered himself willingly on the altar. Be that as it may, Christian tradition has long seen Isaac as a type of Christ, treading his own *via dolorosa*, bearing the wood. But perhaps to focus on Isaac is to do violence to the story itself. As it stands, it is not about Isaac, who remains a passive figure (though that very passivity is itself important). It is the story of a lonely father who in hope is prepared to sacrifice even hope itself, and who is justified by faith.

Jeremiah 28.5–9

This lection ought not to be read without some attempt being made to set it in context. It links neatly with the Gospel reading since it is a story about the rejection of a prophet; curiously enough, the rejection of a prophet by a prophet. At the point in history at which these events take place Jerusalem has already fallen once to the Babylonians, the king has been deported, the temple has been looted and the holy vessels taken off to Babylon. But some prophets are prophesying that Babylon's days are numbered, that Judah will soon be free and that the holy vessels will be restored. Jeremiah is convinced that all this is delusion. At the beginning of chapter 27 he engages in a piece of enacted prophecy. He appears in public wearing a yoke, the sort worn by draught cattle. In biblical imagery the 'yoke' usually signifies servitude, and so it is here. The message conveyed by the enactment is that Babylon will continue to dominate the region, that this is God's will and that Judah would be well advised to accept it. Jeremiah explains that if she does not accept it, the Babylonians will come back and the second destruction will be far worse than the first.

At the beginning of chapter 28 the prophet Hananiah contradicts Jeremiah. He repeats the prediction that the holy vessels will be returned, and that so will Judah's exiled king. The yoke of Babylon will be broken. Our lection reports Jeremiah's answer, which is remarkably mild. He hopes Hananiah's prophecies are correct. Nevertheless he goes on to observe that generally speaking it is the prophets who prophesy disaster who turn out to be right. After our lection closes Hananiah engages in some enacted prophecy of his own. He dramatically breaks Jeremiah's yoke. But before the chapter ends Jeremiah has reappeared, this time wearing a yoke of iron.

It is easy to talk about respecting the prophetic word, but what if prophets disagree? A question raised again and again in the book of Jeremiah is: How do we know which are the true prophets? In retrospect of course it is obvious. But who are the true prophets of our own time? If, as our Gospel suggests, to recognize a righteous person is to be one, then perhaps to recognize a true prophet is to share at least a little of the prophetic spirit oneself.

Romans 6.12–23

St Paul is still exploring the idea that Christians have somehow passed through death. One consequence is that they are 'dead to sin';

sin no longer has power over them. He then moves on to the imagery of slavery. To be 'set free from sin' means that we becomes 'slaves of righteousness' (v. 18). The interesting thing is that he does not here speak of Christ giving us freedom. He assumes that what we have is a choice of servitude.

Matthew 10.40–42

In these days of telephones, e-mails and other instantaneous methods of communication it is easy to forget that until very recent times all messages had to be conveyed in person. Every messenger was a kind of ambassador, representing the person who sent him. The words of the messenger were the words of the one from whom he came, and demanded the respect due to the one from whom he came. In this scheme, Jesus is the representative of God (one might say, though this passage does not, that he is both the messenger and the message). Whoever receives Jesus receives God himself. Whoever listens to a prophet and respects the word he speaks listens to God. The prophet and the listener share the same virtue, for if the message is to get through, the speaker and the hearer are of equal importance. In this respect those of us who pay attention to scripture are as important as the people who wrote it. Without us their words fade on the air. The two final sayings in this reading are expressed a little obscurely, but what Jesus seems to be saying is that to welcome a righteous person is a righteous act, and therefore to be righteous oneself. To welcome one is to be one. In v. 42, the phrase 'little ones' seems to mean the disciples themselves. (Whether Jesus meant this by it or not, it is probably what Matthew thinks he meant.) In this case the saying is telling us is that anyone who does a disciple even the smallest service will be counted as being on God's side.

SUNDAY BETWEEN 3 AND 9 JULY INCLUSIVE

(Fourteenth Sunday in Ordinary Time)

Genesis 24.34–38, 42–49, 58–67; Zechariah 9.9–12;
Romans 7.15–25a; Matthew 11.16–19, 25–30

Genesis 24.34–38, 42–49, 58–67

The story of the finding of a wife for Isaac is a very long one, and for use in public worship it doubtless needs to be abbreviated, but the lectionary makers have given us a regrettably abrupt beginning. The story is an important one. All those grandiose promises to Abraham would have fallen rather flat if Isaac had stayed a bachelor. The marriage is arranged by proxy, through the agency of Abraham's servant. Isaac has nothing to do with it until the bride arrives on her camel. In the Old Testament all the virtuous characters marry within the family: only the suspect ones look elsewhere for their wives. Abraham makes two stipulations: first, a wife for Isaac must be sought among his own kin, in the land from which he came; second, Isaac must not be required to return to that land, the bride must agree to come to him. These people were pastoralists, travelling over large areas. Abraham had travelled further than most. Families could become widely separated, and Abraham is hundreds of miles from his closest relatives. A bride who agreed to join her husband's family might never see her own people again. A lot is being asked of Rebekah but she willingly agrees. She may not know how momentous her decision is, but she has chosen to belong to the covenant people, and Abraham's second stipulation is an assertion that the covenant people do not go back.

We customarily call these stories about Abraham, Isaac and Jacob 'the patriarchal stories', but they are just as much about the matriarchs. The founding fathers of the nation set the tone for much that is to come, but the choice of the founding mothers is no less significant. What comes through in this account is Rebekah's character. The servant's chosen test, which would tell him whether he had found the right girl, may seem an arbitrary one to us, but it was not. The point is that camels, after a journey over several hundred miles of desert, have a powerful thirst. To water them, jarful by jarful, is a job not undertaken by any but generous hearts. Even after Abraham's servant has made his speech, Rebekah still knows very little. Was it really wise to commit herself to joining a family known only by distant repute, and to marrying a bridegroom of whom she had not even seen a photograph? She does not use Mary's words, 'Behold the handmaid of the Lord. Be it unto me according to your word', but Rebecca demonstrates a kind of faith, and she is a decisive girl; and on this delicate rock the people of God is built.

Zechariah 9.9–12

This passage, more commonly associated with Palm Sunday, is chosen because it emphasizes the meekness of Christ. When at his entry into Jerusalem he fulfils this prophecy of Zechariah he is deliberately disclaiming political ambitions and military methods. But this does not mean that he cannot be fierce when the occasion for it arises. He is fierce with the money changers in the temple, and fierce with his Pharisaic opponents; and he can pronounce judgement as well as forgiveness. Neither does his meekness mean that he is undemanding.

Romans 7.15–25a

There is a lot of perceptive psychology here. This passage is a crucial link in Paul's argument about the human need for salvation. Paul is describing his own personal experience. He confuses the discussion by using the word 'law' in several different senses, but if we can ignore that we can see him to be speaking of a situation in which people not uncommonly find themselves. Perhaps the clearest example is that of the alcoholic or the drug addict who knows what effects his behaviour is having and regrets it, but feels unable to do otherwise. Such a person feels himself to be in the grip of a power, within him, but not himself, and which he cannot control. He wishes to be different, but does not know how. Presumably the alcoholic or the addict did once make an act of choice; chose to drink, or chose to take drugs. But the choice no longer seems open. Sometimes no choice appears at any stage to be involved. A person suffering from clinical depression never chose that state of mind. Such a person wants nothing more than to be able to cheer up, but continues to look on the black side of everything; then, in a lucid moment, says, 'That's not me. It's the depression talking.' That is exactly the feeling St Paul is trying to express; the feeling that one has been taken over, manipulated by an alternative self. But we do not need to be addicts, or alcoholics or depressed people to be familiar with situations where our best intentions are constantly frustrated, and apparently by ourselves. Where a relationship, perhaps within the family, has become fraught, we may make all kinds of resolutions that we will handle things better. 'This time, I will not lose my temper.' 'This time, I will not shout.' 'This time I will listen patiently to what my partner has to say.' And even before we start, we know really that it isn't going to work. Five minutes into the conversation we shall be shouting, losing our temper and not listening. Why does this happen? Paul says it is sin, which he seems to visualize as a nasty, other self which has a will of its own and won't do what we tell it; an other self which lives inside our skin and makes us do things we don't really want to do and say things we didn't really mean to say, and gives us feelings that we do not recognize as properly our feelings, and messes up our lives.

There are two matters for serious debate here. Most interpreters agree that Paul is describing his own experience, but is it his experience in the past, before his conversion? Is he talking about a dilemma from which now, in Christ, he has been released? Or does he mean that even the faithful Christian still constantly faces this problem? Interpreters continue to differ about the answer to this question.

The second matter for debate is if anything more fundamental. Many of us recognize the intractable situation Paul is describing, and feel bound to agree that, though the words and ideas which he uses are not ones we ourselves might choose, he gets the description devastatingly right. He is talking about somewhere we have been. But is he right in the way he generalizes from this, and assumes it to be a description of the universal human condition? Is he right to conclude that all human beings, by their very nature, are powerless in the face of sin and incapable of choosing what is good? There is a strong strand of Christian tradition that says Yes to this question and erects on St Paul's words the doctrine of original sin. And yet there is also abundant evidence within scripture that this is not the only possible way to understand human nature.

Today's lection sets up the problem, as Paul sees it. It contains at the end only a hint of what the solution might be. The lectionary is sometimes rather like the television serials: we have to wait until next week for the answers.

Matthew 11.16–19, 25–30

The immediately preceding verses have been about John the Baptist, about Jesus' relations with him and Jesus' testimony to him. Verses 16–19 of our lection take up the theme. Jesus complains that there is no satisfying his hearers. They are like peevish children, who reject every suggestion of their companions about what game they should play. John was an ascetic: they could not approve of such a killjoy. Jesus himself was anything but ascetic. That did not suit them either. They accused him of being too fond of his food and drink, and said, 'Look at the company he keeps'. The rather obscure sentence in v. 19, 'Yet wisdom is justified…', seems to mean that though they are critical of both John's lifestyle and his own, Jesus wants to affirm both.

Verses 25–27 are remarkable. When we read St John's Gospel the style of Jesus' teaching there is quite different from what we normally encounter in the synoptics. Did Jesus really teach in the manner St John shows us? This little passage, in typical Johannine style but embedded here in St Matthew, suggests that sometimes he did. The vocabulary and turns of phrase are not only very Johannine but very typically Jewish.

The comfortable words of vv. 28–30 are also very Jewish-sounding. In rabbinic vocabulary the 'yoke' was the yoke of the Law. The rabbis, to be fair to them, did not see obedience to the Law as a burden, but Jesus suggests elsewhere, in some rather outspoken comments (Matt. 23.4), that the Pharisaic teachers' version of the Law *was* experienced by some as burdensome. He himself, he claims here, is far gentler in his approach. It is difficult to reconcile this perception with some of the extraordinarily radical demands he makes on his disciples in the Sermon on the Mount. But both radical demands and reassuring promises have their place. Religion needs to offer both comfort and challenge if it is to be complete.

SUNDAY BETWEEN 10 AND 16 JULY INCLUSIVE

(Fifteenth Sunday in Ordinary Time)

Genesis 25.19–34; Isaiah 55.10–13; Romans 8.1–11;
Matthew 13.1–9, 18–23

Genesis 25.19–34

One has to feel sorry for Esau. The rabbis tried hard to invent reasons why God did not favour him. But there are none. Sometimes the God of the Old Testament is very arbitrary. Esau's only real offence was that he was a hairy man, whereas Jacob was smooth – too smooth by half.

Rebekah has a problem conceiving. According to the dates given it took her twenty years. Then she has a difficult pregnancy. No wonder: carrying twins is never any joke. But the struggles in her womb are only a portent of the struggles to come. The boys didn't get on. Chalk and cheese, evidently. Jacob is favoured by Rebekah, and by God, but he's a nasty piece of work. Esau comes in from an unsuccessful hunt, literally starving. 'For God's sake, Jacob,' he says, 'give me some of that stew you've got there. I'm at my last gasp.' 'No,' says Jacob, 'I won't. I'll *sell* you some.' God works out his purposes and he gets there in the end. But he doesn't always do it through the nice people. I wish he did, though.

Isaiah 55.10–13

The imagery of sowing and growing, reaping and winnowing, runs all through scripture, unsurprisingly, given that Israel, like virtually all ancient societies, lived off its land. The point our Old Testament reading is making is similar to the one made by Jesus in the parable of the sower: there is a reliability about the agricultural process. The prophet, indeed, is talking about certainties. When it rains, there is growth. Anyone who has seen the brown summer landscape of much of Israel burst into green in response to the rain will need no convincing of that. It is a question of simple cause and effect. The prophet is saying, the word of God is like that. When God speaks, things happen. In particular contexts, we are all familiar with the idea of the powerful word. If you are the person in the dock, and the foreman of the jury utters the word, 'Guilty!', you know there will be consequences. If it is your examination paper and the external examiner says, 'This one fails, I think, decisively', there will be consequences. If you are on the parade ground and the drill sergeant shouts 'Atten-shun!', there had better be consequences. If a man says to a woman, 'Will you marry me?' and she says, 'Yes', a good many things are going to change in consequence. Mere words? In their appropriate places, all of these are words of power. They change things; they make things happen. Indeed, the utterance of such words may in itself constitute a happening. When a prime minister said, 'We are at war with Germany', that word was an event. All God's words are like that, all of them words of power. They create. They save. They destroy. The prophet in our lection is, as it happens, speaking of salvation, of the bringing back of his people from captivity, and in that context of the return from exile he is making a very specific point. If God's word is always powerful, always effective, then we can trust his promises.

Romans 8.1–11

This is the climax of Paul's argument in chapters 6, 7 and 8 of this letter. Again he obscures his reasoning by using the word 'law' in a multiplicity of senses, but his main point is clear enough. He has given us a picture in chapter 7 of humanity enslaved by sin and therefore worthy of condemnation. Now he tells us that for us it does not need to be like that. There is no condemnation for those who are 'in Christ Jesus'. We have moved out of the realm of sin and death and into the realm of life. This realm of life is the realm of the Spirit. The Spirit is described in this passage as 'the Spirit of God', 'the Spirit of him who raised Jesus from the dead', 'the Spirit of Christ', and (twice) as 'the Spirit of life'. He is also 'the Spirit who dwells in you'. And St Paul contrasts the 'things of the Spirit' with the 'things of the flesh'. 'The flesh' he makes no attempt in this passage to define, except by saying that it is 'hostile to God'. But perhaps we do not need to define it, because as Christians we have left it behind and have become Spirit-controlled. The really good news in this passage is that these things are not promises. They are not possibilities which, if we persevere, we may attain to some day. What Paul thinks he is describing is where we are *now*, already. We have already passed from death to life. All we need to do is to get on and live up to it, to be what we are.

Matthew 13.1–9, 18–23

Much of the hilly ground regularly cultivated by Palestinian peasants is of the steep, rocky sort that in Britain we would consider has only two possible uses: grazing sheep or planting trees. But they cultivate it, painstakingly building little terraces to hold back the soil, terraces often no more than a couple of square metres in extent. When it comes to sowing, one might expect they would be careful with the seed, making sure it was only sown where there was enough soil to give it a reasonable chance of survival. But that is not the peasant's method. In an apparently wasteful way he scatters the seed broadcast. He knows what he is doing. Appearances can be deceptive. Where the soil looks sparse there may in fact be deep cracks between the stones where the seed can put down good roots. Where it looks deep, it may in reality be only a thin covering over the underlying rock. The method that works is to scatter the seed everywhere and let it take its chance. Yes, the sower knows that much will not survive. Some will wither, some be eaten by birds, some choked by weeds. It is always so. But the sower also trusts that enough will survive to provide a harvest. This is the wasteful, prodigal way of faith, and it is justified by its results. No one can teach a Palestinian peasant anything about faith. Faith is his livelihood. Perhaps God is a peasant at heart. The losses he knows are inevitable, but he is confident about his harvest.

SUNDAY BETWEEN 17 AND 23 JULY INCLUSIVE

(Sixteenth Sunday in Ordinary Time)

Genesis 28.10–19a; Wisdom of Solomon 12.13, 16–19 *or*
Isaiah 44.6–8; Romans 8.12–25; Matthew 13.24–30, 36–43

Genesis 28.10–19a

In last week's reading Jacob coerced his brother into giving up his birthright (Genesis 25). In Genesis 27, which does not appear in the lectionary, he takes advantage of his blind father in order to steal his brother's blessing. Now even the smooth Jacob has made life too difficult for himself at home. He sets off for Syria, ostensibly to find a wife. He heads in the direction of his mother's brother, Laban. He may be a rotter, but he knows that marrying within the family is one way to social approval. So Jacob is leaving home to seek his fortune and everything before him is uncertainty. And he lies down in a desolate place with only a rock for a pillow. And he dreams. And in his dream the place where he lies is at the foot of a staircase, with its top in heaven, and angelic beings are going up and down, presumably minding their angelic business. And God himself addresses Jacob. And to the undeserving Jacob God repeats the promises he made to Abraham and promises him success in his journeying, and promises, too, that he will eventually return. And Jacob is impressed and in the morning marks the place as sacred and names it 'Bethel', 'God's-house'. The lectionary reading unaccountably stops at this point, yet the last three verses of the chapter, which it leaves out, are vital to understanding the significance of the story. However impressed Jacob may have been in the night, in the cold light of day he reverts to type. Wheeling and dealing is Jacob's nature and he cannot help trying it on, even with God. He tries to strike a bargain. If God will look after him, and see that his business prospers, Jacob will sign over to him ten per cent of the profits. Jacob still has a lot to learn. God doesn't meet him again for twenty years. But his journey does prosper, because, in the next chapter, Jacob too will meet a girl at a well.

Wisdom of Solomon 12.13, 16–19

These verses from the book of Wisdom, taken by themselves, are far from transparent in their meaning, but if we look at their context they are much more comprehensible. The writer is speaking about divine omnipotence and divine justice. God's power, he says, is absolute. He is accountable to no one (vv. 13–14). But in God's case absolute power expresses itself in absolute righteousness (v. 16a). His righteousness, however, is not hard-edged. His justice is a benign justice. 'Although you are sovereign in strength, you judge with mildness, and with great forbearance you govern us' (v. 18). And just as his power is universal, his concern for his creation is universal (11.24–26, outside the compass of the lection). This concern extends even to the sinners and the ungodly. Even with them he is unfailingly fair, and indeed compassionate, for when they manifestly deserve judgement he does not execute it immediately and catastrophically, but little by little, giving them time for amendment of life. This last point is made very fully in the verses that precede the lection, 12.1–11, and is worth mentioning because it is here that the sentiments of the writer of Wisdom impinge most directly on today's Gospel reading. The parable declares that God will 'let both grow together until the harvest', but gives the impression that this is only because it is administratively easier that way. Wisdom suggests that there might be a more positive reason for God to hold his fire.

Isaiah 44.6–8

What this reading has in common with the other Old Testament lection is a powerful emphasis on God's omnipotence and sole deity. Presumably the lectionary makers thought this theme connected with the content of the parable. Perhaps we could say that this omnipotence carries with it an implication of the eventual triumph of righteousness, which is also implicit in the parable, but the connection is scarcely to be described as a totally convincing one. The second half of the book of Isaiah abounds in these fine statements of God's complete authority and oneness. The writer is in Babylon, and the magnificence of Babylonian religion, with its multiplicity of gods and temples and the spectacle of their worship and festivities, is daily evident around him. What is also evident is Babylon's 'great power' status and its domination of the known world. In the face of all this the prophet, a man from an obscure backwater on the fringes of the empire, asserts that his national God is the One really in charge. He is the one whose prophets have accurately predicted the course of events, ands even the rise of Babylon herself. And he is the Redeemer, the one who will restore his people.

One way of beginning a new life is by being born again. An alternative is to be adopted. Adoption was very common throughout most of the ancient world, from Old Testament times and earlier, through to the period of the Roman empire when St Paul was writing. Not all of those adopted were babies or young children; many were adult. For an adult to adopt an adult was quite usual. The person adopted was not infrequently a slave. We are, of course, well acquainted with the institution of adoption, and many of its implications are clear to us, but in the ancient world the social reasons behind it were to some extent different from what they are among ourselves. Ancient reasons for adoption were often economic. In our sense of the word, there was no social security. The only social security available was one's children. It was they who would provide support and care in one's old age. And if one had no children? Adoption offered a remedy. The adoptee, of course, also benefited. He could expect, eventually, to become heir to the estate. It was by no means impossible to begin as a slave and end up as the heir. So a person would begin as a member of one family and become the child of another. Familiarity with this institution is assumed by Paul and by other writers of the New Testament. This is why they can speak so readily of the possibility that we might *become* children of God.

When he writes our present passage Paul assumes that we, his readers, know all this. We began as slaves; slaves to sin and death and fear, but the Spirit enables us to escape from this slavery. He is 'the Spirit of sonship', through whom we become children of God, members of his family, 'and if children, then heirs, heirs of God and fellow heirs with Christ' (v. 17). For a slave, the prospect is dizzying. The second half of the reading, vv. 18–25, is harder to follow, but it expresses Paul's conviction, which he explains more fully elsewhere in his letters, that what happens to redeemed Christians does not affect them alone, but is of universal significance. Somehow, when we are set free 'the creation itself will be set free from its bondage to decay' (v. 21). Liberty for us means liberty for the cosmos. Paul has moved on from the mundane and comprehensible business of adoption to something apparently more abstruse, that makes sense in terms of his world view but is more difficult to express in terms of our own. This need not worry us too much. What his words should warn us against, however, is any assumption that salvation is just a matter of individual people making individual decisions to be Christians, and saving their own souls. As Paul sees it, there is very much more to the work of Christ and his Spirit than that.

Matthew 13.24–30, 36–43

Another parable about seeds and sowing, this time unique to St Matthew. Whereas the parable of the sower, which appeared in last week's Gospel, accurately reflects the agricultural practices of the region, the parable of the wheat and the tares not only does not do so, but appears inherently implausible. A farmer (he is not a mere peasant, he employs labourers) sows a field with wheat. When the seed germinates, weeds are found among the crop. In the days before selective weedkillers this was a fairly normal scenario, yet the landowner immediately concludes, 'An enemy has done this.' It sounds an unlikely kind of sabotage. Did such things really happen? The labourers ask if they should go and weed the field; surely an impractical suggestion, as their boss quickly decides. His verdict is: 'Let both grow together until the harvest.' But then once more implausibility takes over. Would it really be possible to reap the weeds first, and make a bonfire of them before starting on the wheat? Any such attempt would surely only have resulted in trampling the wheat into the ground. Whoever invented this story did not know much about the practicalities of agriculture.

Whoever he was, he was not thinking realistically about farming, he was thinking allegorically. But he was raising a genuine issue. He was thinking of his own time, later than the ministry of Jesus, when the church had attracted into itself a wide range of people with mixed motivations and varying degrees of seriousness. We have not much information about what was going on in the evangelist's time, but we do know that in the early centuries of the church's life there was often heated debate about church discipline. There were the rigorists, who thought the church should aim at being a small, hard core of the ultra dedicated whose total commitment was not in doubt, and should vigorously purge any whose devotion was in any way suspect. And there were their opponents who felt that the church of the God of grace ought to be more tolerant of human frailty. We know where the author of our parable stood on the issue. Too much haste to weed out the unsatisfactory, he thinks, could only lead to errors. The more excellent way is to reserve human judgement, and leave it all to the judgement of God, who will sort everything out on the last day. If he can put up with the weeds until then, so should we.

SUNDAY BETWEEN 24 AND 30 JULY INCLUSIVE

(Seventeenth Sunday in Ordinary Time)

Genesis 29.15–28; I Kings 3.5–12; Romans 8.26–39;
Matthew 13.31–33, 44–52

Genesis 29.15–28

Jacob and Laban are two of a kind. Jacob is in a weak position. He wants a wife, but has no capital. Laban exploits this weakness (as Jacob earlier had exploited the weakness of Esau) to get as much work out of Jacob as possible. Jacob puts in seven years work in lieu of a bridewealth payment for Rachel. We are to assume that the marriage is consummated in the dark. Laban has made a substitution and in the morning Jacob finds not Rachel in the bed, but Leah, whom he did not fancy at all. It makes a good story and ancient Israelites will have relished it. Jacob has his contract extended by another seven years but has two wives to show for it instead of one. The custom of the times allows this, but it spells trouble ahead. The importance of this episode, as far as the story of salvation is concerned, is that the promises are on course for being fulfilled. The people of God are still not numerous, but the potential is clearly there. Its importance in the history of Jacob himself is that it shows us a Jacob who has still not changed much (though he is evidently hardworking enough to impress his uncle), and who for once seems to have met his match.

I Kings 3.5–12

This is rather like one of those fairy stories in which the hero is offered three wishes. Such offers are always an invitation to think very carefully indeed. But to put the matter in religious terms, God is raising with Solomon the question that Jesus raises in two of the parables in our Gospel reading: What do you really want most? Solomon might have asked for health, wealth and happiness, but asks for wisdom. This is a moral choice, for health, wealth and happiness would have benefited himself, whereas wisdom benefits his kingdom and his people. The wisdom literature says many of the same things about Wisdom as Jesus says about the kingdom of God. For example, it says that Wisdom is not only God's gift, but that she is freely available. Anyone can have her, for she is an accommodating lady. But those who choose her have to make her their first priority. Where Wisdom differs from the kingdom is that those who choose her are promised health, wealth and happiness as well, for these are in her gift. I suspect Solomon knew this all along (see 3.13–14, outside the lection). Perhaps it is only those who are wise already who choose Wisdom.

Solomon of course has this reputation for wisdom, but any study of Old Testament history is bound to prompt the question: Was he really as wise as he is made out to be? Perhaps the narrator of Kings had his own suspicions about this too, and perhaps we should let him have the last word, for he says in v. 15: 'And Solomon awoke, and behold, it was a dream.'

Romans 8.26–39

This passage follows on immediately from the previous week's Epistle. The word 'likewise' indicates that Paul is still exploring the work of the Spirit in the life of the Christian. That life, as the apostle goes on to describe it here, is one that has been entirely taken over by God. The Christian does nothing for himself or herself. Even our prayers and appeals to God are effective only in so far as they are not our prayers at all, but the Spirit praying in us and for us. The translation of v. 28 has been hotly disputed. But one way of understanding it is that only in so far as God works in us and through us do we effect anything or achieve anything worthwhile. Verses 29 and 30 go on to speak of God's foreknowledge and foreordination of us believers. Such words raise thorny and difficult issues, but we can at least understand that they are the apostle's attempt to express his feeling that nothing of what he has been given is of his deserving. All we have to do to find salvation is to say Yes to God and open our hands to receive, but the apostle seems determined to deny himself the merit of doing even so little. If he has received, it is only what God has, of his volition, thrust upon him. The rest of our reading is a kind of great hymn of confidence, a thanksgiving for the glorious place in which Christians stand. God is on our side (v. 31) as he has already proved (v. 32). What have we to worry about? Even the superhuman cosmic powers hold no terrors for us (vv. 38–39). This is the culmination of the argument which Paul has been pursuing throughout the epistle so far.

Matthew 13.31–33, 44–52

This reading is part of a collection by St Matthew of 'parables of the kingdom'. Verses 31–33 are about the apparent insignificance of the kingdom. Throughout New Testament times the public face of the kingdom was never more than a few handfuls of people, who would have been dismissed by most of those who encountered them as a 'fringe sect'. But they believed that behind them was the cosmic power who was about to save and judge the world. These are very encouraging parables to those of us who belong to small Christian congregations. We have no membership statistics for the New Testament church, but we do know that the numbers of people involved were by our standards tiny.

In the second pair of parables the point is quite different. They might be regarded as an expansion of Matt. 6.33, 'Seek first his kingdom…'. To gain the kingdom we have to see it as the most important thing in life. It must have first priority, or none. The parables are about people who knew a good thing when they saw it. To the man who found the treasure in the field *of course* it was worth taking out a second mortgage and pawning everything he possessed in order to buy the field. He was on to a winner, and knew it. With the kingdom of God we are on to a winner, if only we could see it. Jesus is raising the question for us all the time: What really matters most to you?

The last parable is different again. It is about the comprehensiveness of the kingdom. In one sense, of course, we have a choice, whether to join the kingdom or not. But in the long term we have no choice at all. We pray: 'Your kingdom come', but as Luther observes in his catechism: 'God's kingdom comes, whether we pray for it or not.' Eventually God asserts his imperial rule, and then we are all in the kingdom. But for those who have chosen the kingdom willingly, that will be one thing. For those who have not chosen it, it will be another. The sort of judgement imagery which St Matthew favours, and which he seems to enjoy using (and which is not especially common elsewhere in the New Testament), the imagery of fiery furnaces and gnashing teeth, is not very congenial to the modern mind. But I suppose if we voiced such objections to St Matthew he would only reply, 'It wasn't meant to be congenial.'

SUNDAY BETWEEN 31 JULY AND 6 AUGUST INCLUSIVE

(Eighteenth Sunday in Ordinary Time)

Genesis 32.22–31; Isaiah 55.1–5; Romans 9.1–5; Matthew 14.13–21

Genesis 32.22–31

The stories about Jacob in the book of Genesis are not a collection of separate, disjointed tales. They add up to a coherent story of a character who is all too believable. To understand any one of the stories we need to see where it fits into the pattern of the Jacob saga as a whole. The lectionary, dipping into the saga week by week, does not make it easy for us.

In Genesis 28, appointed for the Sixteenth Sunday in Ordinary Time, we saw Jacob leaving home and venturing into the wider world. On the way out he met God at Bethel, and though he was impressed by the experience, his response to it can hardly be considered satisfactory. He appears to have been unmarked by that meeting, for, as he goes his way, neither his behaviour nor his character seem to change at all. Twenty years on, he is returning as God said he would. He is returning because he has outstayed his welcome among the Syrian branch of the family. He is returning a wealthy man. But he is returning to face a brother he had wronged and who (he has just heard before our reading opens) is approaching with a small army of four hundred men. As a precaution he puts his cattle, his wives and children and all he possesses across the ford of the river Jabbok, 'and Jacob was left alone, and a man wrestled with him until the breaking of the day'. Who was this 'man'? Our natural expectation is that the narrator, perhaps at the denouement of the story, will reveal all. He drops a few hints, but we are never plainly told. What we discover is that in this story the real issue is not the identity of the 'man' at all, but the identity of Jacob. Jacob is a tough one. As dawn approaches the 'man' dislocates Jacob's thigh (it was probably a foul) but Jacob hangs on. His opponent tries to break free, but Jacob demands from him a blessing.

Jacob had asked for a blessing before. He had come in before his father. And the blind Isaac had faced him with a question: 'Who are you?' And Jacob had replied, 'I am Esau your firstborn.' Now when he asks for the blessing of this spectral 'man' he is asked again. The words are different; the question is the same. 'What is your name?'

Jacob won't get this one by false pretences. God will deal only with our authentic selves. It is only when we acknowledge who we are, and what we have let ourselves become, that he can work with us and make us different. For as soon as Jacob does acknowledge his name, God changes it. Jacob gets his blessing, this time a legitimate one. And we have a new Jacob. There he is, the morning after, battered, not unmarked by the experience. He too has his suspicions about the 'man'. Where he dreamed of the ladder he called the place 'God's-house'. This place at the ford he now calls 'God's-face'. And the sun rises as he crosses over.

Isaiah 55.1–5

Moses not only gave bread in the wilderness, he gave water from the rock. The prophet who wrote the words of our lection is living in exile, in Babylon, along with many of his fellow countrymen. He believes that salvation is imminent and that God is about to lead his people home. As in the time of Moses, there is a promised land at the end of the journey but, as before, the journey lies through a desert. But this time, the prophet promises, there will be no hardship. This time God will make highways through the wilderness and the desert itself will spring into blossom as his people pass. Some of this is not in our lection but in the surrounding chapters. What is in the lection is the promise that God will liberally supply not only food (though food will be on offer) but what the desert traveller needs even more, drink. And he will provide it freely. The food will not just be bread, but richer fare (v. 2b). And the drink will not just be water, but milk, and wine, which is not a desert drink at all. And just as the prophet sees the expected events of his own time surpassing those of the time of Moses, the gospel writers pick up the imagery of both of them and see Jesus as outdoing them all, and offering a salvation which surpasses anything that God has yet done.

Romans 9.1–5

The first half of St Paul's letter to the Romans came to a climax with last week's reading. Now he turns to quite a different subject. Paul has a problem. He has spent half his letter demonstrating that all have sinned, Jews and gentiles alike, and that all, therefore, are offered salvation by God on the same terms, namely, faith in Christ. So what becomes of the Jews? Paul's own mission to the gentiles had confirmed that many of them were waiting and ready to accept the gospel. The Jews, for the most part, were not. So has all that was given to Israel, 'the glory, the covenants, the giving of the law, the worship and the promises', and everything else God has done for them and revealed through them – has all that gone for nothing? Paul is reluctant to think so. He himself is a Jew, and his pain at seeing his own people rejected, or opting for their own rejection, as it were, is palpable. In v. 3 he makes the striking statement, 'I could wish that I myself were accursed and cut off from Christ for the sake of my brethren.' This is a statement not quite without precedent, for it echoes that of Moses in Ex. 32.32. But in today's reading the apostle only raises the subject; he will continue wrestling with it throughout chapters 9, 10 and 11, though with what success we shall have to wait and see.

Matthew 14.13–21

This is St Matthew's first account of the feeding of the multitude. The story, in one form or another, is told by all four evangelists, and St Mark and St Matthew both tell it twice. We may reasonably deduce from this that for the gospel writers the event had considerable significance. At least part of its significance for them was that in it they saw Jesus repeating, or even outdoing, the work of Moses, who fed Israel in the wilderness with manna. Five out of the six accounts of the feeding drop us a strong hint by describing the place where it happened as 'desert'. But the evangelists also see the event as a fore-shadowing of the eucharist, and they make this clear in the way they describe it. All six accounts say that Jesus took the bread, gave thanks, broke it, and gave it to his disciples. No Christian could possibly miss the eucharistic allusion. And in case we do miss it, three of the accounts, when they speak of giving thanks, actually use the Greek verb *eucharistein*. On Maundy Thursday Jesus broke bread with his disciples. We call this the Last Supper, but we usually insist on talking about it as if it was the First Supper, as if Jesus had never done this before. The various stories about the feeding of the multitude suggest that for Jesus to take bread, give thanks, break it and give it to his disciples was something which he did habitually, even though on the occasion of the Last Supper he may have added a fresh interpretation to what he was doing.

And Jesus was trying to get away from it all! Our lection begins: 'Now when Jesus heard this…'. The 'this' was the news of John the Baptist's horrific death. Jesus immediately does what most of us do when suddenly receiving tragic news. He goes off on his own – or tries to. The crowd won't leave him alone. (At least he didn't have the media reporters as well, pestering him for his reactions.) His turning back to the crowd, first to heal them and then to feed them, is an act of compassion (v. 14). He has needs of his own, but he puts theirs first. Already, though we have not yet reached that final Thursday evening, when Jesus takes, and blesses, and breaks and gives, it is something more than bread that is given. It is self giving.

SUNDAY BETWEEN 7 AND 13 AUGUST INCLUSIVE

(Nineteenth Sunday in Ordinary Time)

Genesis 37.1–4, 12–28; I Kings 19.9–18; Romans 10.5–15;
Matthew 14.22–33

Genesis 37.1–4, 12–28

Love is what holds families together, yet in the family we find the strongest hatreds. The majority of murders that are committed in this country are murders within the family. Jacob was born in family strife and in family strife he continues. He has two freeborn wives and two slave wives, and so four sets of children. He also has favourites. This is hardly a recipe for domestic harmony. Joseph is a bit of an upstart. He tells tales about his brothers, and has dreams of grandeur, which he makes no attempt to keep to himself. (The lection omits these.) Even Jacob is embarrassed, but continues to indulge the boy. The 'coat of many colours' which he gave Joseph probably was not anything of the sort, but an ankle length robe with long sleeves. Nobody who expects to do serious work would wear such a garment, and the message, no doubt, was not lost on the brothers. When they get him on his own, out of sight of his father, they take their revenge on Joseph and on his fancy outfit. Their hatred is literally murderous. Reuben, however, persuades them against actual bloodshed. Judah suggests selling him. And this they do.

This is not an edifying tale, but it is only the beginning of a long story and most of the edification comes later. Trust me: there is actually quite a lot of edification. But what can we make of the lection as it stands? It is certainly telling us how human beings insist on making problems for themselves. In a family like Jacob's no doubt tensions were inevitable, but surely he could have managed them better. Joseph, too, must take his share of blame, but youngsters take a while to learn, and perhaps one should not be too hard on him. The brothers cannot be excused. Yes, the provocation was considerable. Little brothers can be extremely aggravating: but murder? To accuse them of over-reacting is to treat them very kindly.

All the characters in this story have a lot to learn. The good news is that before the story ends they do all learn it. It is one of the few stories in the Bible where genuine development of character does take place. But the better news is that this story of Joseph and his brothers is part of the bigger story of the salvation of the people of God, and it demonstrates how God makes things work for good. God's people are saved from famine by going down into Egypt, and Joseph was there in Egypt before them; things which would not have happened if he had not been sold as a slave. Even betrayal and murderous hatred are turned to good account. The purposes of God are worked out all the time through people who are no better than they should be. For this we should be glad.

I Kings 19.9–18

This is yet another reading that will need to be set in context if it is to be understood. Elijah has recently engaged in that dramatic encounter on Mount Carmel with the prophets of Baal, in which he called down fire from heaven upon the altar. This looked like a convincing defeat for the Baal worshippers and a demonstration of the power of Israel's God. Yet since then he has been obliged to flee for his life from the avenging Jezebel, and has made a long journey, much of it through the desert, to the place where Israel had first met God, to Horeb/Sinai. Here, in spite of the victory on Carmel, he talks as if he were the defeated one. Elijah is the great pillar of faith and confidence of his generation. Yet on Horeb his faith is exposed as insufficient. Like Peter, he wants to believe, but when he looks at the magnitude of the forces overwhelming him, he begins to sink.

We might regard our Gospel and this Old Testament lection as studies in the ways in which God comes to us. In our Gospel, Christ comes to his people in the storm. And yet the initial effect of his coming is to heighten the terror. Is this true to life? Are there situations which are difficult enough in themselves without God sticking his nose in with his insatiable demands? To bring in the God factor may bring naught for our comfort, and may actually appear to make things worse. In the long run, no doubt, we cannot leave God out of the reckoning, but initially his entry may look like complicating the issues intolerably. And for the disciples, even when the storm has abated, the awe has not gone away. Again and again the gospels remind us that, in life, Jesus was not a comfortable person to have around.

For Elijah the lessons to be learned are different. He knows about the awe. He has stood on mountains before. He is not afraid of the fire from heaven. He has summoned it. When God spoke on Horeb earlier in history (Exodus 19) he descended on the mountain in fire, and the smoke of it went up like the smoke of a furnace, and the whole mountain quaked greatly. Elijah, too, has experienced the earthquake and the wind that even 'broke in pieces the rocks before the Lord', but this time he learns to find God not in such tumultuous events. His long journey to Horeb was not in fact necessary, for Elijah has taken his problem with him. Elijah is in retreat, his confidence shattered, his view of the future bleak; and he feels himself to be alone. Elijah has entered a cave: a cave of despondency and maybe even of self pity. Now he only knows where God is not. But then Elijah comes to the door of the cave and God speaks to him. And when he speaks, he speaks in silence. We are so fond of words; but when we arrive at true knowledge words are superfluous. The Lord makes little attempt to answer the prophet's repeated objections. God is a good psychologist; he does not bother to argue or persuade. He simply gives Elijah a job to do; several jobs, in fact. What it is not Elijah's job to do is to make analyses of the situation and issue depressing forecasts about the prospects for the work of God. He has turned out not to be very good at this. The Lord's new instructions also head him off from anything too spectacular; no more miracles on mountain tops, just a few routine anointings. Elijah meets the same brusque response as Moses. Moses, too, met God on Horeb and tried to raise theological questions. But God simply handed him a rail ticket back to Egypt and said: 'Get on with it, and leave the theology to me.' God gives his servants support, but they don't always get sympathy.

Romans 10.5–15

This reading is part of the discussion which St Paul introduced in last week's lection, of why the Jews, having received so much from God, have now apparently been rejected. In typical rabbinic fashion he machine guns us with a succession of texts, and hopes we can see what he is driving at. Perhaps we can, though it is easier to do so if we do not confine our attention simply to the lection but look at the argument of chapters 9–11 as a whole. Paul is denying that God has unreasonably rejected his people. They had their chance. They chose to pursue 'the righteousness which is based on the law', but the better righteousness, 'the righteousness based on faith' was on offer all the time. It is there in the scriptures, thinks Paul, and if his countrymen had read them properly they ought to have perceived that. Interestingly, at the beginning of chapter 11 Paul appeals to the episode of Elijah on Horeb to prove his point, insisting that the remnant of seven thousand, of which God speaks to Elijah, is a remnant chosen by grace, not through obedience to the Law.

We may reasonably assume that no Jew would have found these arguments from scripture convincing, unless he was already prepared to be convinced. And we ourselves may find it hard to justify Paul's methods of arguing from texts torn out of their contexts. Paul believes that to attain righteousness through the Law is simply not possible; that it is a dead end. Yet the very passage of Deuteronomy which in our lection he keeps quoting (Deut. 30.11–14) is asserting the very opposite. 'This commandment that I command you this day is not too hard for you'; it is not beyond you. God has not given you a law which is impossible to keep, but one which is entirely within your competence. Paul is using scripture as the church has always used scripture, and as we are still using it, to prove what he thinks he knows already. Perhaps this does not matter, as long as we recognize what we are doing.

Matthew 14.22–33

The story of Jesus walking on the water is told by Matthew, Mark and John, but not by Luke. Only Matthew tells us how Peter tried to walk on the water too. In Matthew this episode follows immediately after the feeding of the five thousand, which, as we saw in last week's reading, followed the breaking of the news of John the Baptist's death. Jesus is still trying to get away by himself, and this time actually succeeds. He not only gets away from the crowd, but from the disciples too. He sends them off in a boat across the lake, telling them he will catch them up later. During the night they are caught in a storm and can make no headway. The placid looking lake can be a dangerous place. The disciples are struggling, but then Jesus appears. And worry turns to terror. An encounter with the divine is rarely a comfortable experience, though it may bring comfort eventually. That is how it is in this case. Only when Jesus speaks does the terror abate. As in the other story of a storm on the lake (Matt. 8.23–27 and parallels), the reaction of the disciples to the whole event is one of awe. They end by acknowledging, 'Truly you are the Son of God.' This is an extraordinary statement, which only Matthew records. It should not be treated as an afterthought.

But what about Peter? St Matthew's story is not just about Jesus walking on water, but about Peter doing so too. The temptation to read this as an account of yet another of Peter's failures is almost irresistible; but this is hardly fair to Peter. Should we really think the worse of a fellow Christian because he can't manage to walk on water, or at least, not for very long? Speaking for myself, I can't walk on water for very long either.

SUNDAY BETWEEN 14 AND 20 AUGUST INCLUSIVE

(Twentieth Sunday in Ordinary Time)

Genesis 45.1–15; Isaiah 56.1, 6–8; Romans 11.1–2a, 29–32;
Matthew 15. (10–20), 21–28

Genesis 45.1–15

A week ago we read the beginning of the story of Joseph and his brothers. Now we read the end, or almost the end. In between, much water has flowed under the bridge. Joseph has had a roller coaster of a career, success following failure and, too often, failure following success. But he has done two things: he has at last risen to be the ruler of Egypt, second only to Pharaoh himself, and he has preserved his integrity. He has also teased his brothers rather heavy handedly, and planted evidence appearing to incriminate his full brother, Benjamin, rendering him liable to the penalty of enslavement. At this point Judah, the one who had originally suggested selling Joseph as a slave, offers himself as a substitute for Benjamin. Joseph's complex plot has succeeded, for he has got Judah at last to acknowledge that he is his brother's keeper.

Joseph, too, has done some learning. The upstart youngster has become the magnanimous mature man. If he wished to take revenge for what he has suffered, he is in an unparalleled position to take it. The brothers plotted his downfall; Joseph himself had laid complicated plots of his own; but the arch-plotter is God. The brothers had sold Joseph, but that is not the way Joseph chooses to see it; that was God, sending him before them to preserve life (v. 5). 'It was not you', he says, 'who sent me here, but God' (v. 8). This makes it sound as if he is absolving the brothers of all responsibility. That is not really the case, or he would hardly have taken the trouble he did to bring home to them their guilt. But without denying human guilt and human responsibility, God still works out his purposes, not in spite of human beings' evil intentions, but by means of them.

For once we have a set of related readings all of which are genuinely related in their subject matter. All three deal with the topic of God's acceptance of gentiles.

Isaiah 56.1, 6–8

On the whole the attitude towards non-Jews expressed in the Old Testament is very tolerant. Apart from a brief period round the time of Ezra and Nehemiah, Israel was a very open society and readily incorporated foreigners into it. But our present reading from Isaiah 56 is more positive than most of the Old Testament in its attitudes. It describes the temple as 'a house of prayer for all peoples', words which Jesus himself is said to have quoted on the occasion of the cleansing of the temple. Interestingly, however, only St Mark records him as using the whole quotation. Matthew and Luke omit the words 'for all peoples'. We do not know what the rules were in Solomon's temple, but in the second temple gentiles were only admitted to the outer court (which was, to be fair, an extremely large area). The prophet is proposing to make them a great deal more welcome than that. He even allows them to make sacrifices. Certainly there are not lacking in the Old Testament texts which welcome non-Jews into the fold of Israel, though our reading for today is one of the most striking. When the church did take the gospel to the gentiles there were plenty of precedents in scripture for so doing.

Romans 11.1–2a, 29–32

Here Paul ends his debate with himself about the rejection of Israel. The argument in these verses of our lection is extremely compressed. It becomes a little clearer if we take into account the whole chapter. Briefly, Paul's conclusion is that God has not rejected the Jews after all. Their rejection is only apparent, or temporary, and has happened in order to facilitate the acceptance of the gentiles. 'The gifts and the call of God are irrevocable' (v. 29), and the ultimate fulfilment of God's plan will be that Israel too will be gathered in.

Matthew 15.(10–20), 21–28

Clearly the intention is that we focus on vv. 21–28, the story of the Syro-Phoenician woman. The optional verses raise again, and in a very sharp way, the quarrel between Jesus and the Pharisees. A faithful Jew, in the eyes of the Pharisees, is recognized by what he eats, and what he refrains from eating. Jesus seems to be saying in v. 11 that what one eats is not a matter of any great significance. If he really means this he is undermining a very large part of Jewish ritual law and we can well understand why the Pharisees were upset. He may not in fact be advocating the total abandonment of Jewish food restrictions. If Jesus had not himself observed Jewish food laws we would certainly have been told. It seems rather that he is saying in a very forceful way that the defilement that really matters is the moral defilement of evil thoughts and evil speech. All this is not altogether irrelevant to the question of the acceptance of gentiles. As the New Testament bears witness in numerous places, the determination of some Christians to adhere to Jewish food laws was felt to be a barrier by some gentiles, and as long as Jewish Christians maintained this adherence it certainly made social intercourse difficult. It was no use Jewish Christians saying to gentiles, 'Yes, we accept you', if they then went on to say, 'But we can't eat with you.' The attitude expressed by Jesus in these verses must surely have influenced the church's eventual decision that, whatever may be said of Jews, Christians were not to be defined by what they ate.

Verses 21–28 describe one of the very few incidents in which Jesus is said to have been appealed to by a gentile. The incident takes place in gentile territory, in the area that we now know as Lebanon. Jesus' behaviour is difficult for us to understand. When the woman makes her first urgent appeal to him he simply ignores her. When the disciples complain that she is a pest and ask him to get rid of her he does not exactly do so, but he does give a very off-putting reply: 'I was sent only to the lost sheep of the house of Israel.' His reply to her second appeal is no more encouraging: 'It is not right to take the children's bread and throw it to the dogs.' This is downright insulting, equating as it does the gentiles with dogs. The woman's reply persuades him to help her at last.

What is going on here? One traditional view is that Jesus is not seriously trying to put the woman off. He is testing her out. But this is not at all Jesus' usual style. The plain meaning of what is said here is that Jesus does not see himself as having any duty towards non-Jews. This fits in with his instructions to the disciples when he sends them off on their mission earlier (Matt. 10.5–6). Unpalatable as it may be, we should probably conclude that the gentile mission was a post-resurrection phenomenon and has few if any roots in the ministry of Jesus. It may be that the incident recorded here was a learning experience for Jesus himself, and did in fact alter his attitude to gentiles.

SUNDAY BETWEEN 21 AND 27 AUGUST INCLUSIVE

(Twenty-first Sunday in Ordinary Time)

Exodus 1.8–2.10; Isaiah 51.1–6; Romans 12.1–8;
Matthew 16.13–20

Exodus 1.8–2.10

At the end of the book of Genesis the family of Jacob had settled in Egypt in order to escape the famine, but it looks as if the settlement had become fairly permanent. The beginning of Exodus tells how the Egyptians began to oppress the Hebrews, and the rest of the book contains the story of how they were delivered and led back towards the land originally promised to Abraham. Today's reading is the story of the birth of Moses. The implication of the story, never explicitly stated, is that Moses was foreordained by God to be the deliverer. It explains how he escaped the danger of being killed at birth; how he was nursed in infancy by his Hebrew mother; and how he was brought up at the Egyptian court, presumably receiving the sort of education appropriate to an upper-class Egyptian boy. It is assumed that we, the readers, are intelligent enough to perceive that all this is part of a divine plan, to make sure that Moses on the one hand knows his origins, and feels solidarity with his own people, but that he also acquires the skills he will later need – skills of management, skills of diplomacy, and many others – to carry out the work God has in mind for him.

Isaiah 51.1–6

This reading relates to the Gospel lection only in the sense that both of them refer to a rock. This is hardly a substantial connection. We could say that in our Gospel the rock is an image of the future. Peter is the rock on which the church will be built. In Isaiah the rock is the rock of the ancestors and therefore the rock of the past. But this is too simplistic. In the Isaiah reading the prophet is certainly referring his audience in the first instance to the past, to the rock from which they were hewn, the quarry from which they were dug. He is talking about Abraham and Sarah their ancestors. But he is referring to the past primarily as grounds for hope in the future. Abraham responded to a call from God, and from that one pair God then brought into being a mighty nation. The moral is: cannot God be trusted to restore his people scattered in exile, disillusioned and apparently without a future? The prophet is saying: If there was a future for Abraham and Sarah, there can surely be a future for us.

Romans 12.1–8

Chapters 9–11 of Romans have been something of an interlude. The subject of the rejection of the Jews was weighing on Paul's mind and he felt bound to say something about it. But at the beginning of chapter 12 he is effectively taking up his train of thought where he left off at the end of chapter 8. He has shown that we are redeemed people, sharing the life of the Spirit, which is the life of Christ. Now he turns to look at what that life consists of, in practical terms. What does it actually mean to live as a Christian; what sort of behaviour is expected of us? The opening verse is double edged. On the one hand, it is horrifyingly demanding, 'That you present your bodies as a living sacrifice'. The demand of Christ is total. There is no room here for compromise. Yet the apostle immediately takes the edge off his apparent literalism by describing this sacrifice as 'Your spiritual worship'. Different versions of the New Testament have differing translations of the phrase, but all make it clear that what Paul is talking about is not a worship centred in the cutting of throats and the shedding of blood, but the worship offered by mind and heart. And this worship is an expression of transformation, of renewal. The Christian is a new person, living a new life which is not like the life of this world. Then Paul begins to go into more detail, and will do so more expansively in the chapters ahead. In our present reading he is making an initial declaration that the ideal of the Christian life is a corporate ideal. It involves for each of us having an accurate understanding of our own place in the community of the people of God and filling with total commitment the role that God has assigned to us. Paul makes a brief use of the image of the body, with its various limbs and organs, which he develops more fully in his first letter to the Corinthians.

Matthew 16.13–20

Peter's confession is a pivotal event in the gospel story. In St Matthew's scheme it is rather oddly positioned in that in 14.33 a whole boatload of disciples have already confessed Jesus to be the Son of God. But that was in a very fraught situation. Here the disciples are being asked for a considered opinion. There were several places named Caesarea. Caesarea Philippi (Philip's Caesarea) was in the far north of the country, close to the sources of the Jordan. It is a beautiful area, with a pagan shrine dedicated to the god Pan. Standing above it is Mount Hermon, snow-capped throughout the year, and the rains and snows of Hermon feed the springs that well up out of the ground. Jesus' first question to the disciples is about popular opinion. He seems to be looking for feedback on the kind of impact his ministry is having. 'What are people saying about me?' The disciples pass on to him the general gossip. The answers only make sense if we appreciate that it was a commonly held view that great figures of the past could be in some way reincarnated. It was widely believed, for instance, that Moses and Elijah would some day return. The answers reported by the disciples assume that Jesus is one of these earlier heroes; the only debate is about which particular one he is. Perhaps this question was just a preliminary. Jesus now asks the big question: 'But who do you say that I am?' In Mark's Gospel the reply from Peter is simply: 'You are the Christ [i.e. messiah].' Luke has 'the Christ of God'. Only Matthew has the full statement that stands in v. 16.

Jesus' response is as significant as Peter's statement. He reacts as if something momentous has been said. He blesses Peter – who of course has never been called 'Peter' until this moment, and seems to promise him a position of prominence and authority. Unexpectedly, Jesus speaks of 'my church'. This is one of only two places in the gospels (the other is Matt 18.17) where the word 'church' appears, and we are bound to ask ourselves whether Matthew is using language here which is anachronistic in the context of the ministry of Jesus.

The final verse of our reading is striking. Jesus has now been recognized as messiah by his own disciples. He immediately tells them not to speak of it to anyone else. The first Christians were convinced that Jesus *was* the promised messiah. They saw his fulfilment of this role as a fulfilment of scripture, and the messiahship of Jesus was a vital strand in the argument when they attempted to enlist fellow-Jews. But the evidence of the gospels suggests that Jesus himself was anything but happy with the title. He may have regarded it as a distraction, and it was certainly open to serious misunderstanding. There was no single, coherent set of beliefs or expectations among the Jews regarding the messiah, and such expectations as there were, were neither as prominent nor as important a part of Jewish thinking as Christians have made them out to be. The label 'messiah' was one which the church found useful in its early mission to Jews, but in Jesus' lifetime it was a label he could probably have done very well without.

SUNDAY BETWEEN 28 AUGUST AND 3 SEPTEMBER INCLUSIVE

(Twenty-second Sunday in Ordinary Time)

Exodus 3.1–15; Jeremiah 15.15–21; Romans 12.9–21;
Matthew 16.21–28

Exodus 3.1–15

Last week we read of the birth of Moses. Since then he has grown up and got into trouble for taking the part of his oppressed people and killing an Egyptian taskmaster. He has fled to the Sinai desert and got a job as a shepherd, and has married the boss's daughter. This experience of desert life, like his earlier Egyptian education, is going to come in handy later.

On Horeb, which he does not yet know is a holy mountain, Moses sees the burning bush. What this phenomenon actually was we do not know, and do not need to know. Was this a religious experience? No. Not yet. What it aroused in Moses was first of all curiosity. There is nothing religious about curiosity. But there is something uncanny about this bush, and the curiosity turns to awe. The experience becomes a religious experience when Moses takes off his shoes. That is the point where he makes a religious response, and the encounter with the bush becomes an encounter with the living God.

Having got Moses' attention, what God does first is to give him a job, and then he makes him a promise. God probably did not need to elaborate on the plight of his people in Egypt, as he does in v. 7. That is already on Moses' mind. God makes it clear that he, God, is going to rescue the people, but he also makes it clear that Moses is to be his agent. This is not an invitation.

Moses' first response is a question: 'Who am I...?' God in answer promises him unconditional support. Moses' next question is: 'Who are you?' God's reply is the mysterious 'I am who I am'. There are two ways we can interpret this, and we are meant to take account of both. On the one hand, we can take it as a profound theological statement, which it is, and spend a long time unpacking it. God is the self-existent, about whom nothing can be said, except that he is. But the statement can also be taken to mean (if we pay due regard to the Hebrew verbal forms) that God is not only the one who is, but the one who causes to be. We might prolong such an exploration at length, but we shall not do so here. On the other hand we may take God's reply as a dismissal. He may be saying: 'Never mind who I am. That's all beyond you anyway. Just get on with the job I have given you.' There *is* a revelation of the name and nature of God in this passage, but it is not simply in the formula, 'I am who I am'. It is in the whole enterprise that God announces here. In the rescue of his people from slavery God reveals himself as a saviour. He reveals himself as the one who is in control of all events; who can manipulate the most powerful nations on the earth, as the God of the universe. He also reveals that if anyone wishes to understand God's nature he can occupy himself better than by asking speculative theological questions on mountainsides. God reveals himself as we do his will, and the unknown God becomes known as we obey his commands and get on with the work he has given us to do.

So the fire goes out, and the bush is still standing there, in the spindly way desert bushes do. And Moses has to turn and look for his shoes.

Jeremiah 15.15–21

This is another of the so called 'confessions' of Jeremiah. Jeremiah, too, faces suffering as a consequence of the work God has given him to do. He has embraced the work: see v. 16. He has been so completely dedicated to it that it has filled his horizon, leaving no time for social life (v. 17). But he has not embraced the pain which the work involves. For this he blames God. 'Be patient in suffering', says St Paul (Rom. 12.12). Jeremiah is anything but. He accuses God of being 'like a deceitful brook', i.e. like a stream that promised to be ever-flowing, even in the dry season, but which turned out to be nothing of the kind. And the prophet's attitude to the people who have given him a hard time is also totally at variance with what we read in St Paul or in the gospels. 'Bless those who persecute you,' says Paul; 'bless and do not curse them' (Rom. 12.14). Jeremiah curses his persecutors, and seems to have no bad conscience about it. Jeremiah is one of the saints of the Old Testament, but today's reading illustrates that what counts as sanctity under the Old Covenant is not the same as sanctity under the New.

God's reply to Jeremiah in v. 19 is surprisingly unsympathetic. Jeremiah has preached repentance, but God calls on the prophet himself to repent. We do not know what lies behind this, but clearly the prophet's work has not in God's eyes been as satisfactory as the prophet thinks. But the reading ends with a promise that if Jeremiah does improve his performance God will defend him and deliver him.

Romans 12.9–21

St Paul continues to explore what it means to live the life of faith. The reading makes an interesting complement to the Gospel lection. Jesus, too, was talking about the life of faith, but looking at the extremes. Christians *may* find themselves faced with demands that threaten their very lives, and those of us who have never been placed in that position can only hope that we would rise to the occasion if the occasion arose. But the majority of us, for most of the time, are not called upon to meet persecution and dire threats to our existence. What, for us, is the way of Christ? Paul, too, knows about the extremes, none better, but here in Romans 12 he addresses a situation more like our own. His description of the Christian life is quite a comprehensive one. It is a mixture of broad principles ('Let love be genuine; hate what is evil') that in particular situations would need more cashing out than he can give them here, and more specific instructions, such as those about offering hospitality and charitable giving. It is interesting to compare Paul's advice here with the Sermon on the Mount. They have a lot in common. The differences between them probably reflect the differences of personality between Jesus and Paul. The Sermon on the Mount is full of hyperbolic statements and instructions so idealistic as to seem quite impractical. But this is not true of Romans 12. Paul, for example, advises us to 'live peaceably with all', but recognizes that in the real world this is not always achievable. 'Live peaceably with all', but 'if it is possible' and 'so far as it depends on you'. But the person who followed Paul's advice and the one who attempted to follow Jesus' would end up living very similar lives.

Matthew 16.21–28

This Gospel reading follows directly on last week's reading. Last week was Peter's high moment, when he recognized Jesus as messiah and received his Lord's almost extravagant commendation. That reading ended with an unexpected command by Jesus not to tell people that he was the messiah. Immediately he goes on to speak of his coming suffering and death and his resurrection. According to the gospel records he had not done this before, and this is what makes Peter's confession such a watershed in the narrative. Clearly this startled the disciples and it throws some light on Jesus' reluctance to let the term 'messiah' be bandied about, since suffering and death were quite incompatible with any messianic expectations circulating at the time. Jesus did not reject the title 'messiah' when Peter offered it, but he seems to be engaged in an urgent campaign to interpret it in a drastically new way. When Peter resists this Jesus gets very angry with him and calls him 'Satan'. This suggests that to take a different way from the way of suffering was for Jesus a very real temptation.

In the succeeding verses (24–26) Jesus makes it clear that the destiny of self-denial, suffering and death is one which he embraces not only for himself, but for his followers. Crucifixions were common in Israel under the Romans and very public. Everyone would be horribly aware of what such a death involved. For us, 'taking up one's cross' has become a cliché. It was no cliché then. When Jesus invited his disciples to 'take up their cross', therefore, even if they heard it as a metaphor, it was a metaphor with a terrifying edge. Here we have another, and very striking, example of the totalitarianism of God. He demands *everything*, even our very lives. Yet with the demand goes a promise, that to give up one's life for God and for his Christ is to find it. To keep one's life and hoard it as one's own property is in fact, says Jesus, a sure recipe for losing it. To read these verses of our lection, and to take them even half seriously is to realize what an incredibly watered-down thing Christianity has become for most of us.

The reading ends with a little apocalyptic appendix. All these things will be sorted out at the last judgement. Our own usual assumption is that any such event is likely to be in the far future, but the final verse (v. 28) implies that it may actually be quite soon. Whose perspective is being represented here? Is this really Jesus himself speaking, and was this his own expectation? Probably so.

SUNDAY BETWEEN 4 AND 10 SEPTEMBER INCLUSIVE

(Twenty-third Sunday in Ordinary Time)

Exodus 12.1–14; Ezekiel 33.7–11; Romans 13.8–14;
Matthew 18.15–20

Exodus 12.1–14

This reading is also prescribed for Maundy Thursday. See the notes at that point, but in its very different present context the preacher may well wish to bring out other aspects of the material.

Since the episode of the bush, which was last week's reading, Moses has been back to Egypt, and God has inflicted on the Egyptians nine of the ten plagues. The tenth is yet to come, but Moses in anticipation is poised to lead his people out of slavery. And here, before it happens, Moses gives instructions about how his people are to mark the victory. Like the institution of the Lord's Supper, the institution of the Passover precedes the event it celebrates. Today it is celebrated as an act of remembrance, but at its inception it was an act of faith. The people who at the first Passover rejoiced in God's salvation took that salvation on trust.

Ezekiel 33.7–11

Ezekiel, like our Gospel reading, is exploring the question of our responsibility for one another and our responsibility to warn if we see things going wrong; but he is not thinking primarily of our duty to warn other individuals who might be in error. He is thinking of the prophet's duty to warn the nation. Ezekiel was convinced, as were several other prophets, that the nation was heading for disaster. To warn was his God-appointed task. But he faced what he saw as a problem. He was also convinced that the nation had gone so far down the wrong road, and that its leaders were so headstrong, that nobody would listen to him anyway. He was bound to ask himself therefore: If I know that no one will listen, why should I put myself to the trouble of uttering the warnings? Why should I face the unpopularity and downright hatred that the message brings upon me, in attempting a hopeless task? I know which side *I* am on and that I have God's approval. Why not be satisfied with that, and leave my contemporaries to stew in the juice of their own invincible ignorance?

The prophet spells out the answer perhaps more clearly in the parallel passage in Ezek. 3.16–21. Basically, the argument is this: the prophet has a duty not only to his contemporaries but to himself. If a watchman sees the enemy approaching and warns his people and they take no notice and are destroyed, the destruction will be their own fault. But if the watchman says to himself: 'Nobody is going to listen anyway, so I won't bother', the result will be exactly the same, the destruction of the people. But this time it will be *his* fault. The job of what nowadays we call a whistle-blower is to blow the whistle. To blow it is something he owes to his own conscience, and, if he is a religious person, to God. To blow the whistle may involve heavy costs to the whistle-blower. But not to blow it makes him an accessory to whatever is going wrong.

Romans 13.8–14

It is sometimes remarked how little explicit reference St Paul makes in his epistles to the teaching of Jesus. It is easy to forget that at least at the beginning of his Christian career he would not have had the opportunity to read a gospel. But here in Rom. 13.8–10 we have what might almost be called a commentary on Matt. 22.34–40 and parallels. Paul does not in fact refer to the first of the two great commandments, but observes that if we keep the second, to love our neighbours, all the other moral commandments will automatically keep themselves. This has the appeal of a huge simplification, though when we get down to the details of what it means to live a moral life some of the simplification turns out to be illusory. We still find ourselves faced with questions like: What, in this particular situation, does the law of love dictate? In some situations the answer is far from straightforward.

In the second half of our lection, vv. 11–14, the apostle points to the urgency of the moral demand. We are not dealing with hypothetical ethical conundrums, to be discussed abstractly, as in a seminar. We are to live our everyday lives in accordance with the moral imperatives which our faith lays upon us, and we must do so in full knowledge that we shall be called to account for what we do, and that quickly. In some earlier lectionaries these verses were prescribed, not inappropriately, for Advent Sunday. Most of us will feel unable to share Paul's perspective exactly, in that few of us anticipate, as he did, that the last judgement will happen soon. But we can share his sense of urgency. Whether the end of the world be far or near, God's judgement on us depends on how we live before him today.

Matthew 18.15–20

We do know of at least one Jewish religious community which was flourishing during the first century AD, namely, the community which produced and preserved the Dead Sea Scrolls. Like the first Christians, they not only had much in common with other forms of Judaism, but they also had distinctive beliefs and principles of their own. We know from their writings that in order to sustain their communal religious life they constructed an elaborate disciplinary code. If the earliest church evolved any such disciplinary codes we are not well informed about them, but Matt. 18.15–20 looks as if it might be a fragment of such a code, giving rules about a dispute procedure. It describes a commonsense procedure with three stages. At the final stage it does not refer the dispute to any authority figure or leader, but to 'the church', which seems to suggest that the final arbiter is the entire local community of Christians. And the ultimate punishment, if the offender is recalcitrant, is expulsion from the community. The way this is expressed, 'Let him be to you as a gentile and a tax collector', is interesting. To use the words 'gentile' and 'tax collector' as derogatory terms does not accord well with the usage of the gospels in general. The power of binding and loosing mentioned in v. 19 seems to be bestowed on the whole church community, as in John 20.23 it is bestowed on all the apostles. This contrasts with Matt. 16.18 where it is apparently given uniquely to Peter. But the procedural details are less important than the underlying assumption that Christians are responsible for each other. We know that we are responsible for each other's welfare; our reading is reminding us that we are also responsible for each other's behaviour. If we see a fellow Christian going astray we have a duty to bring him or her back, even if it involves conversations we find difficult or unpleasant.

SUNDAY BETWEEN 11 AND 17 SEPTEMBER INCLUSIVE

(Twenty-fourth Sunday in Ordinary Time)

Exodus 14.19–31 *or* Genesis 50.15–21; Romans 14.1–12;
Matthew 18.21–35

Exodus 14.19–31

Last week we read how the Israelites celebrated their first Passover in anticipation of a salvation they were yet to receive. But when God fulfils his promises he has a habit of exceeding even the most confident expectations. Salvation they felt sure of, but what a salvation they could hardly have dreamed. They had left Egypt, carrying with them the bones of Joseph, heading for a promised land which none of them had ever seen, but which they were assured was home, and guided by a pillar of cloud by day and a pillar of fire by night. And then they discovered that the Egyptian chariots were pursuing them. The Israelites panicked, but not Moses. This is the point at which our reading begins. The pillar of cloud moves to a position behind the Israelites, coming between them and the Egyptians. 'The cloud of thy protecting love' is what Charles Wesley calls it. 'Then Moses stretched out his hand over the sea.' But Israel was saved not by the hand of Moses, nor by the hand of an angel, nor by the hand of a mediator, but by the Lord himself, in his person and in his Name. So says the Passover *Haggadah*. 'And the waters were divided.' The opening section of the book of Genesis, which we call the story of creation, the Jews call *Havdalah*, 'Dividing', because God operates by making divisions and distinctions. He divides the light from the darkness, the night from the day, the sea from the dry land. But his second great creative act after the making of the light is his dividing of the waters. 'And God said, "Let there be a firmament in the midst of the waters, and let it separate the waters from the waters." And God made the firmament and separated the waters which were under the firmament from the waters which were above the firmament. And it was so' (Gen. 1.6–7). These are the waters which were the waters of chaos, but on which God has imposed his order. And now again at *Yam Suph* he acts in characteristic fashion and orders the waters. As he had divided the waters in order to create, now he divides the waters in order to save.

But this is not the end of the matter. Moses stretches out his hand once more over the sea, and the waters return. In the earliest biblical traditions of the exodus the destruction of the Egyptians is at least as prominent a theme as that of the deliverance of Israel. Salvation for some is at the expense of others. This is bound to raise problems for the Christian interpreter. There is evidence that it raised problems already for at least some Jews. The Song of Miriam, which follows the crossing of the sea, reported in Ex. 15.21, is extremely short. In fact it consists only of a single verse. A Jewish midrash asks: Why is it so short? The answer: the Lord angrily interrupted her. 'My people are drowning', he said, 'and would you rejoice?'

Genesis 50.15–21

This reading is closely parallel to the continuous Old Testament reading for the Twentieth Sunday in Ordinary Time, namely, Gen. 45.1–15. In Genesis 45 Joseph has met his brothers in Egypt, though they do not recognize him. After playing cat and mouse with them for some time, he at last reveals his identity. They are understandably worried, but Joseph is reassuring. He tells them to return home, but then to come back to Egypt, bringing Jacob with them. Under Joseph's protection the family prosper in Egypt. But when our present reading opens Jacob has just died, and for the brothers the whole issue is reopened. They can understand Joseph being concerned for them for their father's sake, while he was still alive, but can they rely on Joseph's magnanimity now that Jacob is dead? Joseph assures them that they can. The reading introduces no new ideas or themes which were not already there in Genesis 45. This Old Testament story complements the Gospel reading very well. The brothers' offence against Joseph was far from trivial, but Joseph is prepared to write off the past, apparently wholeheartedly. One significant thing about the story of Joseph is that the narrator clearly approves of Joseph's behaviour and takes it for granted that the reader also will approve of it. Admiration for magnanimity is not confined to the New Testament; in the Old Testament too it is regarded as a virtue.

Romans 14.1–12

St Paul is here raising a number of associated questions about the keeping of various ritual laws. During the apostle's lifetime there were certainly still unresolved problems in this area. Paul raises two specific sets of questions, one related to food, the other to the obser-vance of special days. Questions about food arose in at least two ways. Some Christians felt obliged to keep Jewish dietary restrictions. This was natural if they were themselves ethnic Jews and had been brought up with such rules, but some gentile Christians seem to have felt the same way. There were also problems, which Paul discusses at length elsewhere, about buying meat on the open market. Much of this meat had been formally offered in sacrifice to pagan gods. Some Christians were squeamish about eating such food. They saw it as somehow contaminated by contact with paganism. Others apparently argued that the offering in sacrifice was a mere technicality. To them it was not a sacrifice, it was just meat. They also observed that since pagan gods did not exist, they could hardly be held to contaminate anything at all. The allusion in v. 2 to the person 'who eats only vegetables' is not a reference to vegetarianism in the modern sense of the word. It was a simple way for squeamish Christians to avoid most of the potential difficulties. There was no problem about idol meat if one abstained from meat altogether, and vegetarians automatically sidestep most of the Jewish food restrictions. The question about the observance of days, which is raised from v. 5 onwards, also relates to Jewish practices, mainly to observance of the sabbath, but probably also other Jewish festivals.

Paul makes no attempt to fudge any of these issues. He is absolutely plain about where he himself stands. In 14.14 he closely echoes the teaching of Jesus as quoted by St Matthew in 15.10–20. But he is adamant that we need to respect each other's feelings, and should not criticize a fellow Christian for scruples which we do not share. In other words, when it comes to the keeping of ritual rules, Christians should live and let live.

In mainstream Christianity there are perhaps few issues today of the kind the apostle is discussing, though some Christian denominations may throw up issues particular to themselves. In some parts of the Christian world there are still disagreements about the keeping of Sunday, which offer a fairly close parallel to the observance of days which Paul discusses, but the question of dietary rules disappeared long ago, largely thanks to the efforts of St Paul himself.

Matthew 18.21–35

In St Matthew's mind vv. 21–22 may be connected with what precedes, the procedure for settling disputes in the church, which constituted last week's Gospel. If this is so, then Peter's question: 'How often shall my brother sin...?' still refers to problems within the Christian community, and the word 'brother' should be taken to mean 'fellow Christian'. But we are not obliged to understand this little interchange in such a narrow way. There is nothing said here which could not apply equally well to relationships with those outside the church. Jesus' answer to Peter is, of course, hyperbolic. He does not mean that we keep a careful count, and on the four hundred and ninety-first occasion say, 'Enough is enough.' The reader is assumed to be familiar with Gen. 4.24, where the antediluvian patriarch Lamech enunciates the law of vengeance as he understands it. What Lamech means is that he takes pride in taking vengeance to the nth degree, even for minor assaults and insults. The man sensitive of his honour takes vengeance without limit. Jesus is saying, by contrast, that forgiveness should be without limit.

The parable which follows (vv. 23–35) is making a parallel point. Again the language is hyperbolic and the story full of deliberate improbabilities. The servant owes his king 10,000 talents. The talent was the sort of unit in which chancellors of the exchequer did their sums, and no individual could ever have run up such a debt. One talent represented about thirty years' earnings for a working man. The servant's protestations that, given time, he would pay off what he owed, are transparently ridiculous, as is the suggestion that the king could recover his money by selling the servant and his family as slaves. (Incidentally, Jewish law would not allow a wife to be enslaved to pay off a debt of her husband's. But the story is set in fairytale land.) The debt of a hundred denarii owed by the second servant to the first is not inconsiderable; a denarius was a day's wage, as the parable of the labourers in the vineyard illustrates. The point is not that the second servant's debt was inconsequential, but that it was finite. The parable is not telling us that what we owe each other, and the offences we commit against each other, are to be shrugged off as insignificant. It is saying that when we consider what we owe to God we see our debts to one another in a different perspective. We should forgive others as God forgives us. As preachers we would like to say that the Christian should forgive as an act of gratitude for the infinitely greater forgiveness extended by God. This is what the New Testament generally does say, e.g., 'We love, because he first loved us' (I John 4.19). But this is not what St Matthew says. The story as he tells it is saying that we should forgive for fear of the consequences; if we do not show mercy, we forfeit our right to the mercy of God.

SUNDAY BETWEEN 18 AND 24 SEPTEMBER INCLUSIVE

(Twenty-fifth Sunday in Ordinary Time)

Exodus 16.2–15 *or* Jonah 3.10–4.11; Philippians 1.21–30;
Matthew 20.1–16

Exodus 16.2–15

Whoever wrote up the story of the exodus, wanderings and conquest
in the Old Testament was clear about one thing, that even from the
very beginning God's people had never shown much gratitude to him
and never really had much faith. At no point had their attitude to their
Saviour been genuinely satisfactory. They were constantly given to
what the older English translations render as 'murmuring'. More
modern ones tend to call it 'complaining', but it is complaining of a
particular kind. Northern readers will understand me if I translate it
as 'chuntering'. Chuntering is the sort of complaining people do on
the back row of a church meeting, when they cannot bring themselves to come straight out with it and state an objection. Chuntering
is a kind of muttered dissent, not openly voiced. It is what people do
when they are unwilling to challenge the leadership directly but will
not give wholehearted support. So 'the people of Israel chuntered
against Moses and Aaron in the wilderness' (16.2). They had groaned
in slavery in Egypt, but now all they can think of is that in Egypt at
least they had enough to eat. Some people will always find something
to complain about, and the people of Israel are like that.

Now these people had not long before been delivered from Egypt
by God, with a strong hand and an outstretched arm. They had been
led, no, were still being led, by a pillar of cloud and fire. They had
come to the sea and witnessed the dividing of the waters, and had
passed through, 'the waters being a wall to them on their right hand
and on their left' (Ex. 14.22). They had seen the Lord's wonders in
the deep. And they had seen their enemies swept away by his torrent
and themselves landed safely on the other side. And they complain
that there are no cornflakes for breakfast.

And God, and Moses, are extraordinarily patient with them. God
provides quails, so that the people have meat. And he provides
a miracle food, in carefully regulated supply, 'bread from heaven'
(v. 4), 'a fine, flake-like thing, fine as hoarfrost on the ground' (v.
14). The people have never seen anything like it before, and do not

know its name. So they call it 'wotsit' *(manna,* in Hebrew) and the name sticks. God has delivered them yet again. And are they pleased? By the time we get to the book of Numbers (11.6) they are complaining about the manna.

Jonah 3.10–4.11

The book of Jonah is a parable, and a parable with a message not very different from that of the parable in our Gospel. The prophet has been sent by God to Nineveh, to threaten its people with divine judgement if they do not repent. Nineveh was the capital of Assyria, at whose hands Israel had suffered grievously. Jonah is reluctant to go, not because he thinks his journey will be a waste of time, but because he is afraid it won't. Jonah is a man of total faith. Although he runs away from the job God has given him to do, he knows from the start that he can't win. When the ship in which he is travelling is overtaken by a dreadful storm and everyone else is terrified, Jonah simply goes below and falls asleep. He knows God has a job for him to do and won't let him drown until he has done it. When the sailors remonstrate with him he acknowledges that the storm is all his fault, because he is running away from God. He says to them complacently: 'You'd better throw me overboard; then it will be quite all right.' So they do, and it is. When he is swallowed by the 'great fish' he is not at all worried. He just sings a song. And when the fish vomits him up on the beach he grumpily says to God: 'OK, you win. I knew you would.' Having got to Nineveh Jonah preaches to the Ninevites the Bible's shortest sermon. It takes up half a verse (Jon. 3.4b). But it does the trick, as Jonah feared it would. The entire nation is converted, from the king on his throne to the cows and sheep in the fields and the cats and dogs in the street. All of them wear sackcloth as an expression of their repentance. And God forgives them, as Jonah knew he would, because that is the way God is and Jonah is his prophet and it is a prophet's business to know these things.

One might have thought that Jonah would be happy at being the most successful evangelist in history, but in fact he is extremely annoyed. 'Didn't I tell you?' he says to God. 'I knew this would happen.' 'For I knew that you are a gracious God, and merciful, slow to anger, and abounding in steadfast love'. Jonah is here quoting a formula which appears, in whole or in part, numerous times in scripture. It is a summary of the divine character, as Israel understands it. But in Jonah's mouth it is an accusation. He *knows* God is merciful – and resents it. He knows about God's undiscriminating love, but objects when it extends to Ninevites. To be undiscriminating is all right up to a point, but there should be limits, thinks Jonah. But now he finds out that in God's mind there are no limits, none at all. Jonah has been preaching about divine mercy all his professional life, but now he has discovered what the labourers in the vineyard discovered, just how offensive to human sensibilities that mercy can be.

Philippians 1.21–30

The lectionary now turns from Romans to Philippians, which is perhaps the most comprehensible and attractive of the Pauline letters. It is basically an extended thank-you letter, written evidently from prison, presumably from Paul's imprisonment in Rome. Philippi is on the Macedonian coast and Paul is clearly on good terms with the people there. If this was his final imprisonment, which it probably was, and Paul is within measurable distance of his execution, then the mood of some parts of the letter would be well explained. It is a mood of what one might call Christian resignation. This is certainly the mood of the opening verses of our lection. Deliverance is of course to be hoped for, but only so that he can do more of the Lord's work. If the outcome is otherwise, Paul will be just as satisfied – no, more than satisfied, for his own desire 'is to depart and be with Christ' (v. 23). Can we detect a certain weariness here? After all Paul had been through it would be entirely understandable. Is there such a thing as apostolic burnout? Maybe not. (Though there is certainly such a thing as prophetic burnout, as the story of Elijah on Horeb demonstrates.)

At v. 27 Paul turns from talking about himself to encouraging his Philippian readers. He knows that they, too, have not had an altogether easy time. He and they are engaged in the same struggle (vv. 29–30). And he has confidence in them, that whether he is able to see them again or not, they will 'stand firm in one spirit' (v. 27).

Matthew 20.1–16

This parable has caused many Christians a great deal of puzzlement, but it is actually very simple and all of a piece with the rest of the teaching of Jesus. The point of the story can be summed up briefly: how God deals with us has nothing to do with what we deserve. The Christian is someone who realizes that this is a good thing, not a bad thing.

In the Sermon on the Mount Jesus notes that our Father in heaven 'makes his sun rise on the evil and on the good, and sends rain on the just and on the unjust' (Matt. 5.45). He does not give good weather to the people who deserve it: we all get the same, just like the labourers in the vineyard.

What makes the parable difficult for us is the setting of the story. It is set in the workplace. And in the setting of the workplace the householder's conduct is totally inappropriate. No trade unionist would tolerate his policy for a moment. There would be a picket line across the vineyard gate next morning. But if we change the setting the problems largely disappear and the message becomes more acceptable. Jesus told another parable, the famous one about the prodigal son. Its message is exactly the same. The father in that parable does not treat his two sons fairly, as the elder of them forcefully points out. He forgives the younger son for his atrocious behaviour and takes the loyalty of his brother for granted. Yet we have much less difficulty with that. Why? Because in the context of family life the father's reaction is much more comprehensible. Why is he so kind to his younger son, in spite of everything? Because he loves him. And we know that in the context of the family no further explanation is needed. Ultimately, the only love we can really depend on is the love we don't have to deserve, and, unless we are very unlucky, within the family we get it.

God deals with us as a parent, not as an employer, and the principles by which he operates are ones of which we all have experience within the context of family life. The overriding principle is that of undiscriminating love. Within the family even we, with all our shortcomings, manage some sort of approximation to that. But in spite of that experience, we still have difficulty in understanding just *how* undiscriminating the love of God is. It is totally, offensively undiscriminating, and the offensiveness is what the parable of the labourers in the vineyard is trying to express.

SUNDAY BETWEEN 25 SEPTEMBER AND 1 OCTOBER INCLUSIVE

(Twenty-sixth Sunday in Ordinary Time)

Exodus 17.1–7; Ezekiel 18.1–4, 25–32; Philippians 2.1–13; Matthew 21.23–32

Exodus 17.1–7

When the Israelites in the wilderness complained about lack of food, God had immediately provided as much as they needed. But the people do not seem to learn from experience. When they lack water, they do not say to themselves: 'God has solved all our problems so far, so we can trust him to sort out this one.' They belligerently assail Moses with demands that he do something. He does, of course, under God's direction, but one is surprised that God is so tolerant of the people's confrontational approach. Their final words in our lection, 'Is the Lord among us or not?' sum up their attitude. In fact they have had plenty of evidence that the Lord is among them, yet they have to be continually wanting more. They seem determined to make their relations with God contentious. In the last resort, faith is an attitude of mind. It depends on what kind of people we are and has very little to do with evidence at all. If we are persons of faith, when we look back on our life so far we can always see that the Lord has been with us. When we look at the world around us, it speaks of his work. The unbeliever looks at the same evidence, but nothing counts. Nothing is allowed to count. They hear the Lord speaking from heaven and say, 'It thundered.' God's hand is invisible to them because they have not learnt to see.

Ezekiel 18.1–4, 25–32

The lectionary makers often have problems condensing long passages of scripture to make them acceptable for use in public worship, but not here. The lection gives us the essence of Ezekiel's very wordy, not to say laboured, argument in his chapter 18. The prophet is dealing with a very real problem. He is prophesying in exile. This exile had been predicted and threatened by prophets over a period of decades, even generations. The prophets had argued that the policies pursued by the country's leaders had been persistently short-sighted, as well as unjust, and were bound to lead to disaster. When that disaster finally happened and the people at last took the prophets' words to heart, one of the conclusions they came to was that they were suffering for a situation not of their making. Previous generations had made the mistakes, they were reaping the consequences. When prophets like Ezekiel, therefore, continued to call for repentance they said: 'What's the point? If we are suffering for our fathers' sins, as you and your colleagues have been persistently telling us, what good will our little bit of repentance do?' For answer, the prophet replies that we are only required to take responsibility for our own mistakes. If we do that, and turn to him in penitence, that will be sufficient for God.

Now there are in fact two sides to this, and Ezekiel is considering only one of them, because he is not only a prophet but a pastor, and sometimes it is a pastor's job to present to people not the whole, balanced truth, but what they most need to hear. We certainly often suffer for each other's mistakes. There is also such a thing as corporate or communal responsibility. Accountability is not always a purely individual matter. Sometimes entire institutions need to be called to account. We see many examples of this in public life. It is likely that if we put it to him Ezekiel would not deny any of this, but it is not the aspect of the matter with which he is concerned here. He is concerned, like Jesus when he tells our Gospel parable, that his hearers take responsibility for their own decisions and their own actions, and on their own account genuinely turn to God.

Philippians 2.1–13

This important passage is also appointed to be read on Palm Sunday. The notes at that point should be consulted. Today's lection is a little longer than the Palm Sunday one and includes more of the context. To read this slightly wider context reinforces some of the remarks made earlier.

Matthew 21.23–32

The context is the beginning of what we call Holy Week. According to St Matthew's account, Jesus had made his triumphal entry the previous day and had gone on to cleanse the temple. After that he had healed people in the temple (21.14). Now on the Monday morning he is teaching in the temple. Jesus is acting very boldly, seizing the initiative in the very centre of religious power. The cleansing of the temple, in particular, was an extremely provocative act. The representatives of that religious power, 'the chief priests and the elders of the people', challenge Jesus. Regulating the temple and its activities is a job for the properly constituted authorities, not for an upstart exorcist from Godforsaken Galilee. When they ask him directly, 'By what authority are you doing these things?' Jesus rather surprisingly begins to talk about John the Baptist. What right had John to do the things he did? Was he acting on God's behalf, or was he an upstart too? The questioners cannot answer that, or are reluctant to. So Jesus refuses to answer the question with which they started. His implication, however, is that if they knew the answer to his question they would know the answer to their own. Jesus is refusing to give a direct reply to the question about authority because for him authority is not really the issue. The real question for 'the chief priests and elders of the people' is, 'Can you recognize the work of God when you see it?'

What follows is a very simple parable. A man had two sons. He asked them both to go and dig his allotment for him. One said 'Yes' very willingly. But he didn't go. The other said, 'Oh Dad, for heaven's sake! This is the one day off I get in the week.' But afterwards he thought better of it and went. It's what you do that matters; not what you say you'll do.

Jesus applies the parable to his questioners. They say they are on God's side, but they don't recognize his work when they see it, so they don't respond to his representatives. 'The tax collectors and the harlots', people whom the self-styled religious despise, may not make a song and dance about keeping the religious law, but when they hear someone like John the Baptist they know what they are listening to and they respond. God will give them credit for that.

SUNDAY BETWEEN 2 AND 8 OCTOBER INCLUSIVE

(Twenty-seventh Sunday in Ordinary Time)

Exodus 20.1–4, 7–9, 12–20; Isaiah 5.1–7; Philippians 3.4b–14; Matthew 21.33–46

Exodus 20.1–4, 7–9, 12–20

Moses had met the Lord first on Horeb, and to Horeb at last he brings his people. He wants to introduce them to the God whom he encountered here and to share with them his experience. In Exodus 19 we have had what one might call the introduction, though that word might seem to suggest something less terrifying and overwhelming than is actually described. But just as Moses, having had his attention caught by the burning bush, was quickly faced with a divine demand, so it is here. The people may have been stunned by 'thunders and lightnings and a thick cloud upon the mountain, and a very loud trumpet blast' (19.16), but the real meat of the encounter is here in chapter 20, when the Lord presents them with his commandments. This is what the long story of the exodus has led up to. God has delivered them from slavery, conducted them across the sea and led them thus far through the wilderness. He has shown himself as their Saviour and proved his good intentions towards them. Now he presents them with the conditions on which his relationship with them will continue. In chapter 24 he will make a covenant with them, but here already he indicates the commitment which the people will have to make if that covenant is to succeed.

God demands first of all total loyalty. There must be no other objects of reverence, nothing to divert his people's attention from their one true worship. Apart from that there are very few strictly religious requirements in this list. Only the command to keep sabbath really comes into this category, for the command not to take the name of the Lord in vain is probably a rule made to safeguard the validity of oaths. The rest are moral demands, and they are moral demands which would have looked quite familiar to most of the people of the Middle East in ancient times, and indeed to most people of most times since. God is not here giving his people a special set of moral rules to keep. God only has one set of rules and he has given us all consciences to know broadly what they are. What God lays on his people is not special rules but a special obligation to keep the rules that everybody knows about.

Isaiah 5.1–7

The opening words of the parable of the Wicked Husbandmen in our Gospel reading echo those of this Song of the Vineyard in Isaiah 5. Jesus deliberately reminds his hearers of it. He is enlisting the authority of his predecessor to confirm that this is the way God's people are and this is the way they have always been. The two parables (for the Song of the Vineyard is a parable too) diverge from each other in the way they develop the imagery. In the gospel parable it is the tenants of the vineyard who fail to honour their obligations; in the prophetic one it is the vineyard itself which fails to respond to the work done on it and the careful maintenance it has been given.

Isaiah's song is actually a very clever construction. We are to imagine him standing up in a public place and singing it, and he has to begin by getting people's attention. He announces it as a love song. This has baffled some translators, ancient and modern, because the poem does not look like a love song; but love song it is, and the prophet's first hearers will have recognized the genre immediately. The image of the vineyard or garden seems to have been part of the erotic imagery of ancient Hebrew literature, as the Song of Songs confirms (4.12–5.1). 'A garden locked is my sister, my bride, a garden locked, a fountain sealed.' The lady replies: 'Awake, O north wind, and come, O south wind. Blow upon my garden, let its fragrance be wafted abroad. Let my beloved come to his garden and eat its choicest fruits.' And then the beloved himself says: 'I have come into my garden, my sister, my bride, I have gathered my myrrh with my spice, I have eaten my honeycomb with my honey, I have drunk my wine with my milk.' So when the prophet announces a love song and begins to sing about a man and his vineyard they recognize that it is to be interpreted on two levels. They know (nudge, nudge, wink, wink) what it is *really* about. It is about a man who had a girl friend. And he did for her everything a man can do and gave her everything a man could give. And she accepted all his attention, and all his gifts, but then she stopped answering his telephone calls and didn't want to know. The audience are waiting pleasurably for the punchline, but when it comes the prophet kicks them in the groin by revealing that the imagery is not, after all, to be read on two levels, but on three. 'For the vineyard of the Lord of hosts is the house of Israel, and the people of Judah are his pleasant planting. He expected justice, but saw bloodshed; righteousness, but heard a cry.' The final couplet in Hebrew is a powerful piece of assonance which no one to my knowledge has ever translated into equally pungent English.

Philippians 3.4b–14

The apostle has just been briefly warning the Philippians against people who will try and persuade them to be circumcised. He uses some rather gross language which the lectionary makers avoid by beginning at v. 4b. Paul denigrates the importance of circumcision because it is transparently a matter of 'the flesh'. 'The flesh' in Paul's vocabulary stands for everything that is opposed to 'spirit'. It is our lower nature. The things of 'the flesh' are the things of this world. To imply that one of the chief requirements of the Jewish law was merely concerned with our lower nature is being very derogatory about Paul's native Judaism. In our lection Paul goes on to say that if he did choose to boast about his 'fleshly' or worldly advantages he certainly has plenty of them. From the Jewish point of view he had every possible asset. But as the NEB finely puts it: 'All such assets [he has] written off because of Christ.'

Once more we notice that though St Paul rarely quotes or echoes directly the words of Christ, he is saying very similar things. Jesus and Paul say similar things about priorities. Jesus insists that if we are to be his followers we must put him absolutely first, before any other calls upon us, even the most pressing. Paul has done exactly that and acknowledged the totality of Christ's demand upon him. Paul's words in this reading might almost be read as a commentary on Matt. 6.33, 'Seek first [God's] kingdom and his righteousness'.

As we read the two final verses of our lection it is worth remembering again where Paul is sitting as he writes this letter and what he faces. But he is still pressing on towards a perfection which he knows he has not yet achieved. 'Achieved' of course is the wrong word. If Christian perfection is to be grasped in this life it is not as an 'achievement' of our own. Paul reminds us that what we can grasp is much less important than the One who has grasped us.

Matthew 21.33–46

With the parable of the Wicked Husbandmen Jesus is building on long and well-understood tradition. The image of the vineyard as representing Israel, and faithless Israel at that, goes back at least to Isaiah 5. But almost equally ancient is the interpretation of Israel's religious history which is implicit in the story. A major part of the story of Israel is covered in the Old Testament by what we call the Deuteronomic History. It is the connected account which runs from Deuteronomy through Joshua, Judges and Samuel and to the end of the book of Kings. Whoever wrote this account saw as one of the connecting threads holding that history together a succession of prophets whom God sent to recall his people to the right way, but who were at best ignored and at worst persecuted. It is a highly stylized reading of history, for the number of prophets known to have been actively persecuted is really very small, but this is unimportant. It was the accepted picture, and given solid scriptural warrant in the Old Testament. The parable takes this picture for granted and slots Jesus into the series as its end and climax. Indeed, he is not merely one of the series, but an exceptional one; not a servant, but the Son. The parable is saying that the people of Israel have not changed their character at all. The present generation are behaving exactly as their ancestors behaved, continuing to resist their Lord's legitimate demands; failing to recognize the messengers he sends and failing to accept their word as the word God wants his people to hear. St Matthew places the parable here because its message follows on logically from what was said in last week's Gospel, about the religious leaders' failure to respond either to John the Baptist or to Jesus himself. But the parable also takes its place as part of the preparation for the passion. It helps to explain why that passion was inevitable.

In v. 43 it is likely that we hear not the voice of Jesus but of the early church. By the time St Matthew wrote his gospel the gentile mission was well established, and he is using the parable to explain its success.

SUNDAY BETWEEN 9 AND 15 OCTOBER INCLUSIVE

(Twenty-eighth Sunday in Ordinary Time)

Exodus 32.1–14 *or* Isaiah 25.1–9; Philippians 4.1–9;
Matthew 22.1–14

Exodus 32.1–14

The Israelites are still at Horeb. Since receiving the ten commandments they have been given sundry other laws and regulations, including instructions about the setting up of the tabernacle and the organization of the priesthood. The laws relating to the priesthood give enormous prominence to Aaron and his sons. A good deal of space is taken up describing how they are to be clothed when they carry out their priestly duties, and describing, too, the elaborate ritual by which they are to be consecrated to the service of the Lord. But now Moses is back up the mountain for a further consultation and the people become impatient. They appeal to Aaron to make them idols of gold to worship, in direct contravention of the first and second commandments. Astonishingly, Aaron agrees.

Our storyteller seems determined to demonstrate, in as thorough-going a way as he knows how, the corruption of his people. Moses cannot count on the loyalty even of his nearest and dearest. But Aaron is not only Moses' brother, a sharer in Moses' labour and a fellow witness with him of all the mighty acts of God. He is, next to Moses himself, a prime figure of the establishment. He is the first priest, first in time and first in rank. He, surely, could be relied on to hold fast to the pure faith so recently delivered to his people and to insist that others did so. But at the first test, he fails, and fails pathetically. His ludicrous excuses, made later in the chapter (vv. 21–24) only emphasize this.

The implications of all this are very radical indeed. We are familiar with the critique of Old Testament institutions offered by the writer to the Hebrews, whose whole case rests on the contention that temple and sacrifices were of little value in themselves, but only as pointers to something more perfect and more efficacious to be revealed later. But here in the Old Testament itself a writer is implying that even in their own terms those institutions were not always to be relied on. Though a religion needs structures and institutions to keep it true to itself, those very structures and institutions cannot be depended upon completely because they themselves can become corrupt, or compliant in corruption. Even the most august and respected authorities of our churches, to which as church members we are all accountable, are themselves accountable and may sometimes be found wanting. This was part of the prophets' role, periodically to call to account the religious institutions of their own nation. And Jesus continues this work, criticizing, sometimes in sharp terms, the religious authorities of his day and challenging them most notably of all by the cleansing of the temple.

This is not the end of the story. God is so angry that he threatens to wipe the people out completely and to start again, raising up a new nation from Moses himself, as he had originally done with Abraham (v. 10). Moses persuades him not to. And Aaron is not forced to resign. The Law stands. The regulations are still in force. The service of the tabernacle goes on, conducted by a priesthood with Aaron and his sons at its head. The institutions may be fallible, and maintained by fallible people, and it does no harm to have that fallibility occasionally demonstrated. But they are still needed, and better a fallible ministry than no ministry at all.

Isaiah 25.1–9

This reading consists of two separate poems, vv. 1–5 and 6–9. Both are what we may broadly call eschatological. The first rejoices in the fall of an unnamed city, which we may guess was the capital of some empire which had oppressed the prophet's people. It is not entirely clear whether the poet is speaking of a fall that has already taken place, or one which is anticipated. It is futile to ask what city he may have had in mind. It may not in fact be any city in particular. Perhaps the poet/prophet is looking to the end of the age and typifying the fate of all proud empires that have oppressed the people of God.

The second poem links with the Gospel reading more directly for it provides an example of the expectation of the eschatological feast. The prophet here envisages God's future good time as a banquet 'on this mountain'. It is a sumptuous banquet and, notably, it is 'for all peoples'. But this seems to be only the preliminary to what God has in store, for 'he will swallow up death for ever, and the Lord God will wipe away tears from all faces'. This is the sort of scriptural passage on which the New Testament writers draw when they attempt to describe the future kingdom of God.

Philippians 4.1–9

We tend to treat the epistles of St Paul as theological treatises and to mine them for Christian doctrine. But they are genuine letters, written to groups of Christians (though Philemon is addressed to an individual) because Paul was interested in them and expected that they would be interested to have news of him. Here at the end of his letter to the Philippians (or near the end – the word 'finally' in v. 8 is not to be taken too seriously) we are reminded how personal his letters really are. Verse 1 expresses heartfelt affection. These are people 'whom I love and long for'. He really misses them. Paul is a good enough friend not to be afraid to tell them off. We do not know what Euodia and Syntyche had been up to, but clearly they had been at odds with one another and Paul is trying to reconcile them. Who the 'true yokefellow' mentioned in v. 3 might be we do not know, but he is clearly someone on the spot who might be able to have a more direct influence on the estranged women than Paul himself could. The two women are people Paul respects. They have worked alongside him and he is grateful for what they have done. All this helps to put in perspective the more general advice given in the rest of the reading. It is very finely expressed, but before we get carried away by the rhetoric it is worth recognizing that life in a community of Christians involves not only listening on Sunday mornings to inspiring scripture readings but cashing out what is said; cashing it out in our common life. That involves friendship with each other; rejoicing in the Lord; not being anxious; keeping on praying; and all the other things Paul mentions. But it also involves making efforts to keep the Euodias and Syntyches on good terms with one another, and making endless cups of tea.

Matthew 22.1–14

St Matthew's version of the parable of the Great Feast is confused and inconsistent. It is much more problematic than Luke's equivalent in 14.15–24. Maybe some in our congregations will not notice the incoherence, but some certainly will, and they will respect our attempts at interpretation more if we are honest with them about the points at which the parable does not make sense. The basic parable is about a man who prepared a banquet and invited his chosen guests. The guests refused to come, so he brought in people off the streets to share the banquet, because he was so determined to have a party. The meaning of the story in this basic form is fairly clear. It links easily with the material of the Gospel readings for the two previous Sundays. The people to whom God's salvation was first made known have refused it. It will now be offered to others. Within the ministry of Jesus the ones who refused the salvation offered would be understood as people like the scribes and Pharisees; those who accepted were the 'publicans and sinners'. The early Christians would doubtless have seen those rejecting as the Jews in general and those who accepted as the gentiles.

As in last week's parable, Jesus is drawing on traditions which would have been familiar to his audience, but are not familiar to us. The expectation that the climax of the messianic age would be a great feast was a well established one. The rabbis even speculated about what would be on the menu. When God created the animals he made two of everything, male and female. But having created leviathan he immediately realized that this was a big mistake. If leviathan began to breed there would not be much future for anybody else. So he killed off one of the pair and salted down the carcass (he had not yet invented refrigeration) to serve as the main course in the messianic banquet. Like many rabbinic stories it sounds silly but has a very serious point. It implies that God created the universe and all that is in it, and created human beings and supervised their turbulent history for all those thousands of years, just so that at the end of it all he could have an enormous party. Jesus' opponents accused him of being too fond of partying. Like Father, like Son?

In Matthew's version the party-giver is a king, and the banquet is a marriage feast for his son. The double invitation was normal and necessary. These people had no clocks. It was no good inviting people for 'Seven for seven-thirty'. The preliminary invitation warned them what day the feast would take place, and on the day the messengers would go round again to say, 'All things are now ready'. Matthew's version gives no prominence to the excuses offered by the guests who did not come. The excuses in Luke's account are meant to remind us of Deut. 20.5–8, where they are the *legitimate* reasons for refusing a call to holy war. His version of the parable is saying that when we are summoned by Christ there are *no* acceptable reasons for refusal. Matthew's statement that the invited guests maltreated the servants sent to invite them seems to be a feature that has crept in from the parable of the Wicked Husbandmen. The feast is ready, the vegetables are nearly done, the joint has already been carved, but when his guests refuse to come the king mobilizes an army and mounts a campaign to punish them and destroy their city. Then he invites other guests and apparently the meal is still there waiting on the hostess trolley. None of this is very plausible. A feature that may well reflect the original parable of Jesus, however, is that the new guests are gathered indiscriminately. The servants 'gathered all whom they found, both bad and good' (v. 10).

Verses 11–14 make a curious appendix to the story. One of those present is not dressed for the occasion. The king is incensed. He does not merely expel the guest, as we might expect, he has him bound hand and foot and cast into outer darkness. But how could someone simply brought in off the street be reasonably expected to be wearing appropriate attire for a wedding? And if he was the only one not properly dressed, as the story implies, where and when did all the others acquire their suitable clothes? There are no answers to these questions. Perhaps St Matthew would say they are not important. The appendix may simply be his way of insisting that notwithstanding the comprehensive nature of Christ's invitation, there is still such a thing as divine judgement and that nothing contained in this parable should delude us into thinking that God has forgotten about it.

SUNDAY BETWEEN 16 AND 22 OCTOBER INCLUSIVE

(Twenty-ninth Sunday in Ordinary Time)

Exodus 33.12–23 *or* Isaiah 45.1–7; I Thessalonians 1.1–10;
Matthew 22.15–22

Exodus 33.12–23

Exodus 33 revolves round two topics which are logically distinct but which the author intertwines. One is the privileged position of Moses as mediator between God and people. The other is the mode of God's presence. In 33.11 (before the lection begins) we have the unique statement that 'the Lord used to speak to Moses face to face, as a man speaks to his friend'. In vv. 17ff. Moses shows himself very conscious of his standing with God and asks for the privilege of seeing his 'glory'. This is a word heavy with meaning in the Old Testament. It is largely a cultic word, often associated with the ark. It is perhaps best understood as signifying the real presence of God. In reply (v. 19) the Lord consents to reveal his 'goodness' and to proclaim his Name. But he says that Moses will not be allowed to see his 'face', because he could not do so and live. These words, 'glory', 'goodness', 'name' and 'face' are interrelated terms for God's presence and being. Moses is being allowed to experience more of the divine essence than any other human person, but there is a limit beyond which even he may not pass. This high theology is eventually expressed in a quaintly childish picture. Moses is to remain hidden while the Lord's glory passes by. He will not be allowed to see the face of God, but may look at his retreating back. Perhaps this is a parable of all human experience of God. To perceive his presence truly would overwhelm us. The utmost that faith can do is to look for signs of where he has been, to detect his footprints. Many of our encounters with God are recognized as such only in retrospect. Like the disciples on the Emmaus road, it is only when he is gone that we realize that our Lord was with us.

The question of God's continued presence with Israel arises because he is still seen primarily as the God of Horeb/Sinai. When Israel left Egypt he was with them in the pillar of cloud and fire. In Ex. 14.19 there is a reference to 'the angel' who accompanies them. God and his angel are in the Old Testament closely identified; the presence of the one is tantamount to the presence of the other. But

God's home seems to be thought of as the mountain; it is to the mountain that the people come to meet him, and that is the place where he speaks with them. The question which this passage answers, but never articulates, is: If they are to go on to the promised land, will he still be there, or will they have to leave him behind in the Sinai? In v. 14 God assures Moses that he will certainly be there. 'My face will go with you.' Most translators render the word 'face' here, quite properly, as 'presence'. In v. 15 Moses presses the point, and is reassured again. Later in Israel's story the presence will make other transitions. The 'glory' will come to reside peculiarly in the temple, and the temple will also be described by God as 'the place where I shall put my Name'. The presence has many forms. The passage is telling us that as we can be aware of that presence in retrospect, so we can trust that it will be there in what lies ahead.

Isaiah 45.1–7

The word 'messiah' is not common in the Old Testament. In Isa. 45.1 it is applied, remarkably, to the pagan ruler of a foreign empire. Cyrus swept to power in the late sixth century BC, overrunning the Babylonian empire and most of the Middle East besides. He was an extraordinary ruler who was highly acclaimed even by people whom he conquered. He established the very effective and well-organized Persian empire. At the time when the prophet wrote the words of our lection Cyrus's conquests were not yet complete, but the prophet anticipates his takeover of Babylon and predicts that he will allow the Jewish exiles to go home. Both these expectations were fulfilled. From the Jewish point of view, therefore, Cyrus was a saviour. The implication of all this is that political and military power is not autonomous. It all falls within the dispensation of God. Cyrus is carrying out the plans of God, for the sake of God's people. His conquests and successes are 'for the sake of my servant Jacob' (v. 4). But Cyrus is not consciously doing the work of the God of Israel. The prophet twice reports God as saying to him, 'you do not know me' (vv. 4 and 5). Cyrus is an agent, or perhaps not even an agent, but a tool, an implement manipulated by the living God. But he and his empire have their proper place within the divine economy. This is the assumption that Jesus seems to be making about Caesar and Rome in his reply to the question about the tribute money in our Gospel reading.

I Thessalonians 1.1–10

Anyone who preaches on today's Gospel and Old Testament reading ought not to ignore Romans 13 and I Peter 2.13–17. However, the lectionary offers us the beginning of the First Letter to the Thessalonians. Thessalonica was an important city, the capital of the Roman province of Macedonia. An account of Paul's visit to the city is given in Acts 17.1–9. His evangelizing displeased the Jews and this led to a riot. So the Thessalonian church had a turbulent start, which is referred to at the beginning of chapter 2. We call this an Epistle of St Paul to the Thessalonians, but if we read v. 1 carefully we find it is attributed not to St Paul alone but to 'Paul, Sylvanus and Timothy', and the letter is written consistently throughout in the first person plural, speaking of 'we', 'us' and 'our'. Not until the penultimate sentence does the writer say 'I', when he asks for the letter to be publicly read out. The writers commend the Thessalonian Christians. The church there is evidently highly regarded throughout the region. This letter seems to have been written very early in Paul's Christian career. The last verse of our reading suggests that Christ was still expected to return quickly. In later Pauline writing this expectation has receded somewhat. But the issue is already felt to be a problem and later in the letter (chapters 4 and 5) the writers address themselves to it.

Matthew 22.15–22

The question about paying taxes to Rome was a much debated issue in first-century Israel. In one sense, of course, it was academic. People had no option but to pay. But it irked nationalistic Jews, for whom payment of the imperial taxes was an acknowledgement of Roman sovereignty. There were religious as well as political dimensions to the issue, for some felt that to acknowledge the sovereignty of Rome was to infringe the sovereignty of God, Israel's only true ruler. Besides, to acknowledge the sovereignty of the empire came unpleasantly close to acknowledging the divinity of its head, Caesar. This last danger was one that Jews were reminded of every time they used a Roman coin. All Roman coins bore the head of Caesar and therefore fell foul of the Jewish law prohibiting images. And the emperor at the time of Jesus' ministry was Tiberius, the inscription on whose coins included his divine title. So it was arguable that one could not pay taxes to Rome without breaking both the first and second commandments. All these issues are very highly specific to the time and place of first-century Israel but they raise a much wider question, which is potentially problematic for all religious people. How do we relate our religious obligations to our obligations to political authority? For most of us, for most of the time, happily there is no tension between the two, but what do we do if a conflict does arise between the two sets of duties? Jesus' answer here is helpful only up to a point. He is not sympathetic to those who want to turn the tax issue into a matter for conflict. His answer implies that the state has a legitimate sphere and that taxation is one of its legitimate demands. Some of the contemporary objections he implicitly rejects as religious nit-picking. Scrupulous religious Jews refused to look at the image of Caesar's head. If obliged to use Roman coins they would distinguish them by feel, like a blind person. Jesus will have no truck with that sort of thing. He asks for a coin and explicitly draws attention to the image on it and the offensive inscription. His common-sense answer is that we acknowledge the realities of political power and let political authority get on with its job, but immediately adds that we should give 'to God the things that are God's'. This is the difficult bit. Jesus is implying that in his judgement there is no irreconcilable conflict between God and Caesar in the situation before him; but what happens when there is? He does not answer this question because he is not asked. It has not yet arisen. It has not arisen for St Paul either, but it has arisen for St John the Divine when he writes the book of Revelation, and it has arisen for Christians in many situations since.

SUNDAY BETWEEN 23 AND 29 OCTOBER INCLUSIVE

(Thirtieth Sunday in Ordinary Time)

Deuteronomy 34.1–12 *or* Leviticus 19.1–2, 15–18;
I Thessalonians 2.1–8; Matthew 22.34–46

Deuteronomy 34.1–12

We have been following the career of Moses through the book of Exodus. For the end of that career we have to turn to Deuteronomy. The high points of Moses' life have all been on mountains. On a mountain he first met God and from it he had to go down to Egypt. To a mountain he brought his people to make their covenant and to hear the commandments of the Lord. But then they had to move on, the presence of the Lord still being with them, towards the promised land. And now Moses has achieved his goal, the goal the Lord had set him, to bring his people upright into his land. And from another mountain he surveys that land. He will not enter it, but takes possession of it with his eyes. And from that last mountain he will not descend.

Some of the traditions in the Pentateuch regard Moses' failure to enter the promised land in person as a punishment for sin. See Deut. 32.48–52 and Num. 20.10–13. The sin is reputed to have something to do with the incident in which Moses struck water from the rock, but all the scriptural writers are extremely hazy about just what the sin was. Perhaps the main reason for insisting that Moses sinned was to assert that even he was not perfect.

Whether the writer intended his words to be so understood or not, it has been common to take v. 5 as meaning that the Lord himself buried Moses. This would explain why the grave of Moses is said to be unknown. The story of the unknown grave led to speculation that Moses did not die at all, but like Elijah and Enoch was assumed bodily into heaven, from where he will return in the last days.

However great the heroes of the faith, none of them is indispensable. A new leader has already been chosen and the people of God go forward into the next phase of the plan God has prepared for them.

Leviticus 19.1–2, 15–18

This reading contains (in v. 18) the famous words of Jesus' second great commandment, but it implicitly acknowledges the first. It begins with the command, 'you shall be holy'. God's holiness provides the motive for our own. 'You shall be holy; for I the Lord your God am holy' (v. 2). And human holiness is always derivative: it is an imitation of the holiness of God. There is no way of acquiring holiness, except by sharing the holiness of God. This talk of holiness seems quite distant from the talk of Jesus, and of Deut. 6.5, about love, but the two are closely connected. Holiness is very difficult to define. In fact, it is impossible to define. The only possible definition is a circular one. God is holy. And 'holy' is what God is. But God's holiness issues in love. Love is what makes holiness comprehensible. And if we wish to share God's holiness (as we would not dare to do, but for the fact that he has said we should) then love is the way in, the way forward.

The author of our reading tries to spell out what he thinks is the way to obey the command, 'You shall be holy'. Most of his attempts to do this fall within vv. 3–14, which the lectionary omits. They are a very mixed bag, containing some high moral commands and some very practical pieces of social legislation, but also (in vv. 5–8) some strange directives about the proper way to offer sacrifices. For our Old Testament author, all this was part of what he understood by holiness. Jesus' summary of the Law gets rid of most of it. Yes, the command to love our neighbours eventually needs spelling out in details of individual conduct and in social legislation, and Jesus elsewhere is not silent on such matters, but if we are to concentrate on basics, which is what his questioner asked about, then let us concentrate on love. That will do for starters.

I Thessalonians 2.1–8

Today's reading from I Thessalonians is a curious piece of self defence on the part of the letter's authors. They assert that their dealings with the church at Thessalonica had not been prompted by 'deceit or impure motives or trickery' (v. 3), that they 'never came with flattery or with a pretext for greed' (v. 5). They made no claim for support by the church, though as apostles they might have been entitled to do so. They also claim that they were 'gentle' in their dealings with the people there. Why should such defence be necessary? It can only be because already in the church (and these were still very early days indeed) there were people who travelled around and did behave in these unseemly ways. The church is full of kindly people and kindly people can sometimes be exploited, and it looks as if, even in apostolic times, there were some ready to exploit them, demanding financial support and behaving in an arrogant and dictatorial manner. Mainstream Christian churches today are organized in ways that make such abuses difficult, if not impossible, but there are nevertheless Christian groups which are exposed to the risk of being taken over by leaders who are less than scrupulous. And leaders in the church, any church, still need to be aware of the need rigorously to observe Christian standards of conduct. All churches have their power structures and some of us enjoy the exercise of power. If we are leaders in the church we often have a choice of roles, a variety of possible ways of serving, and some roles are more comfortable than others and some ways of serving more congenial than others. To be motivated by our own comfort is sometimes tempting. All Christians need to be constantly checking with their role model, which is Christ himself, but Christian leaders need to be more careful than most.

Matthew 22.34–46

Questions like the one put to Jesus in v. 36 were widely discussed in first-century Judaism. The rabbinic teachers, though they greatly elaborated the oral Law and expanded it to cover every area of life and every possible question, were keen to be able to point to simplifying principles which unified the proliferating mass of commandments into a coherent whole. Here Jesus is asked which is the primary, most basic commandment, but for answer he comes up with two. The two commandments indeed cannot be separated, for we cannot love God without doing what God wants us to do, namely, to love each other. The second commandment is an inescapable expression of the first. This might tempt us to reduce the two commandments to one, but significantly, Jesus does not do so. He evidently believes that we still need reminding of our neighbours, so that we do not imagine that being enraptured by the divine will satisfy all that God requires of us. There are Christians who try to reduce the two commandments to one by the opposite means. They argue that the only meaningful way to express our love of God is by loving his children. To love our neighbours is the only way we have to show our love to God. Therefore, in practice, the two commandments amount to the same thing. The argument may be tempting, but Jesus himself treats the two commands as distinct, though interdependent. Love to God is for him primary. Perhaps if we concentrate on loving our neighbour and forget about love to God, there is a danger that sooner or later we forget why we are doing it. Jesus keeps telling us that real love has no limits. The only love without limits is the love inspired by the Limitless.

ALL SAINTS DAY
Revelation 7.9–17; I John 3.1–3; Matthew 5.1–12

Revelation 7.9–17

Protestants tend not to pay much attention to the saints, but All Saints Day is an important festival because of what it tells us about the nature of the church. The realities of church life for many of us are for much of the time not uplifting. More often than not our corporate worship fails to satisfy us, and simply to keep the organization going can be something of a labour. But All Saints Day is a reminder that the church does not belong only to the here and now. We are the people of God, and the people of God have had their high moments and their low moments but they stretch back in unbroken succession to Abraham and beyond. Their grasp of the things of God has not always been perfect but they, or rather we, have remained witnesses to the conviction that God is real, that he can meet us when we do not look for him, and that he can change us and change our world. The message of All Saints Day is that we belong to this 'bright succession' which extends not just into the far past but into the eternal future. Rightly appreciated, All Saints Day changes our day-to-day perspective of our Christian community.

And it is a celebration of *All* Saints. We do not only honour those of exceptional faith or virtue or Christian achievement, the ones whose names people have heard of. The saints we honour are the vast army of believers, and half-believers, whose faith was no better than it needed to be. These are the ones with whom most of us can identify.

Some of this St John the Divine is trying to express in the resounding phrases and powerful imagery of our reading. The ones he particularly honours are in fact the martyrs, the ones 'who have come out of the great tribulation'. And the message he particularly wants us to grasp is that there is a goal to the great march of the people of God. We are going somewhere, not just soldiering on. In so far as the Christian life involves struggle, as for the martyrs it certainly did, there is an end to that struggle. In so far as it involves doubt, or at best faltering faith, there will be an end to that too. We need to have faith that faith is not for ever, and that eventually we shall no longer believe, but know.

I John 3.1–3

St John, too, is thinking about the goal to which we are moving. There is much that is, and must remain, unclear, but some important things that can be said. First, we know where we stand in the present. 'We are God's children now.' Like children in any family, we are sometimes disagreeable and even downright rebellious, but our status is not in doubt. Doubts or rebellions aside, it is in this family, the family of God, that we know we belong. What we shall become eventually cannot be defined. That is a matter of trust. But we do know some things about it. Our goal is defined by Christ. What we shall be is defined by what he is. Ultimately we are to be like him. That does not mean that we shall cease to be ourselves. It does not mean that we shall all be the same. It does mean that his character will grow in us until we attain a maturity 'measured by nothing less than the full stature of Christ' (Eph. 4.13). How much of this maturing we can expect to take place here, and how much in the world to come, St John does not discuss. He does tell us that the climax of the process is bound up with the revealing of the Son of God. As with his colleague who wrote the book of Revelation, his perspective takes him, and us, beyond the here and now.

Matthew 5.1–12

This Gospel reading has already been set for the Fourth Sunday in Ordinary Time. See the notes at that point. In the context of All Saints Day we cannot help noticing how much of the passage is about rewards. Some seem to be rewards in this world, some in the next. Christians do not serve God for any reward, and have often been very wary of using the word, but the New Testament is not. Both Jesus and his apostles promise us that the rewards are there. Not all is hard labour. There is also fulfilment in the Christian life.

SUNDAY BETWEEN 30 OCTOBER AND 5 NOVEMBER INCLUSIVE

(Thirty-first Sunday in Ordinary Time)

Joshua 3.7–17; Micah 3.5–12; I Thessalonians 2.9–13;
Matthew 23.1–12

Joshua 3.7–17

Moses is dead, Joshua has taken over. The story of the crossing of the Jordan establishes that he too is able to divide the waters. But the event takes place not merely to establish the credentials of Joshua; it is intended as a demonstration to the Israelites that the Lord is still with them, and that he who can divide the waters is able to ensure that they will defeat their opponents and take possession of the land.

Moses held back the waters by waving his staff. For Joshua it is the priests bearing the ark who actually initiate the miracle. Joshua is asking a lot of those priests. They are to remain there, in the middle of the river bed, until all the people have passed over. They are the men who stand nowhere. Behind them are the great days of the Red Sea and the wilderness, of Sinai and its thunders and the giving of the Law. Behind them the manna and the water from the rock. Ahead (or so they are promised) are the great days of conquest, of king-making, of temple building, of the making of another holy mountain to match the one they have left. But they have not yet come to mount Zion, or the city of the living God. They are up to their ankles in mud and casting anxious glances upstream. These things are a parable. For the people of God the great days are usually yesterday and tomorrow. The priests no doubt complained to Joshua: 'Can't you get us out of this? We want to get ashore and get on with the job.' To which he will have replied; 'For the time being, standing still *is* your job. Do it.'

All the same, by the time they got their feet washed, the crossing of the Jordan was already part of the story of salvation.

Micah 3.5–12

Jesus' criticism of the religious leaders of his day, illustrated in today's Gospel, is well in line with Old Testament tradition. The prophets saw it as one of their chief functions to call to account the leaders of their people, and this included religious leaders as well as political. Micah takes to task first of all other prophets, along with seers and diviners. All of these he accuses of prophesying for money. But his strictures also include the priests and the political rulers (v. 11). Any healthy society has to include within its structures some provision for self criticism. In modern societies some of this provision is institutionalized in the form of the press and the parliamentary opposition and a democratic constitution. In ancient Israel it was institutionalized in the form of the prophetic movement. But no society can rely on these institutions alone, because the institutions themselves may become corrupt. There has to be a place for the freelance critic. The prophetic movement occasionally threw up such freelances, who were not afraid to attack the movement itself. Micah is one such. Jesus is another, for he is a religious teacher calling to account religious teachers.

I Thessalonians 2.9–13

For once the Epistle connects neatly with our other readings, or at least acts as a foil to them. This is pure chance, but is worth noting and taking advantage of. Old Testament and Gospel are telling us about the bad shepherds (though neither uses those words). Our Epistle is telling us about good shepherds, Paul and his companions, who not only, as the genuine prophets did, proclaimed the true word of God, but have been true pastors, binding their converts into the family of Christ, suffering alongside them when suffering came their way, and feeling for them a profound affection.

Matthew 23.1–12

Jesus is extremely condemnatory of the scribes and Pharisees. He does not mince his words at all. In this passage the main thrust of his criticism is that they are hypocrites, though at this point he does not actually use that word. His quarrel is not with their teaching. He says (v. 3), 'Practise and observe whatever they tell you'. His objection to them is that they do not live up to their teaching. It is difficult to know who Jesus had in mind here, for his strictures do not apply to the Pharisaic movement as a whole. If we read the writings of the Pharisees themselves we can hardly fail to respect them. They can certainly be pedantic about minute matters of the oral Law, and one wonders at times whether they might be failing to see the wood for the trees, but much of their teaching is very fine indeed and they themselves are very hard on hypocrisy. The person they condemn most heartily is the one who makes a great point of studying the Law but then does not live by it. Rabbi Eleazar b. Azaryah used to say: 'He whose wisdom exceeds his deeds, what is he like? He is like a tree whose branches are many, but whose roots are few; and the wind comes and plucks it up and overturns it upon its face.'

Jesus also accuses the Pharisees of being too interested in making a display of their religion. In a religious society, this is always a temptation.

Our lection brings home to us just how selective our reading of the teaching of Jesus usually is. Jesus here and elsewhere says some sharp things about styles and titles, which only the Quakers have ever attempted to take seriously. Christians have tacit agreements among themselves about which elements in the teaching of Jesus need to be taken literally and which not. The distinction is in many cases arbitrary. The titles Jesus rules out are of course ones current in his own time, but one wonders whether he would think any more highly of the ones we use today. Would he really approve of his followers calling themselves 'Reverend', or 'doctor'? Even more startling is his rejection of the title 'father'. 'Call no man your father on earth, for you have one Father, who is in heaven' (v. 9). It is true that in the Jewish society of Jesus' day (and in the Middle East generally, even now) 'father' is not just a name people call their dads. It is a frequently used title of respect. But Jesus' words here do not seem to distinguish between the two usages. We are used to the idea that Jesus was a religious radical, but if we did take his words seriously, all of them, we might discover that he is far more of a social radical than we generally realize.

SUNDAY BETWEEN 6 AND 12 NOVEMBER INCLUSIVE

(Thirty-second Sunday in Ordinary Time)

Joshua 24.1–3a, 14–25; Wisdom of Solomon 6.12–16 *or*
Amos 5.18–24; I Thessalonians 4.13–18; Matthew 25.1–13

This is an interesting week, in that there is a choice of related Old
Testament readings. Wisdom 6 relates to the theme of the Gospel,
Amos 5 to that of the Epistle.

Joshua 24.1–3a, 14–25

If a covenant is to be effective, it needs periodically to be remem-
bered and reaffirmed. Since we last encountered Joshua, crossing the
Jordan, he has gone on to lead Israel in conquering the land and
dividing it up among the tribes. Now he brings those tribes together
at Shechem, in the centre of the country, to re-enact their covenant
with God. Joshua begins with a brief history lesson, most of which
the lection omits. He goes back to the time of their ancestors, even
before Abraham, reminding them of how the Lord has led them and
what he has done for them. Curiously, though he speaks of the work
of Moses, he does not mention the earlier covenant-making on Sinai.
In the light of all this, Joshua faces his people with a choice and challenges them to commit themselves firmly to the worship of the God
who has saved them, and to reject all other gods. They respond
decisively. But then we get a surprise. We are used to the fact that in
the Old Testament, as well as in the New, God is a God of love: 'a
God merciful and gracious, slow to anger and abounding in steadfast
love'. Here Joshua asserts the opposite. He warns his people not to
commit themselves lightly, for the Lord is not to be trifled with. 'He
is a holy God, a jealous God; *he will not forgive…*' (v. 19). Once they
sign up to this covenant they will be held to it, and if they let the Lord
down it will be worse than if they had never engaged with him in the
first place. All this of course is prophetic, because the rest of the Old
Testament is the story of how God's people failed consistently to
keep the covenant, and suffered a dreadful judgement. Like our
Gospel parable, this reading reminds us that though God is love,
nothing is so demanding as love. It is the people who love us most
who expect the most of us.

Wisdom of Solomon 6.12–16

This little passage is typical of Old Testament wisdom writing. There *is* a tradition in the Old Testament about the hiddenness of wisdom, and the difficulty of finding it. This is exemplified in Job 28, for instance. But it is a minority tradition. The usual emphasis, as here, is on wisdom's availability. She does not hide herself. She is 'radiant and unfading' and 'easily discerned'. All you have to do is to want her, and there she is (vv. 12c-13). The desire for wisdom is itself a sign of wisdom. She herself goes out of her way looking for devotees (v. 16). So there can be no excuses. Though the passage does not say so, the corollary of all this is obvious; only the wilful fail to find her, and thus bring about their own loss.

Amos 5.18–24

Traditionally these words of Amos about the 'Day of the Lord' are taken to refer to the day of judgement. That may not be what Amos meant. We can just as accurately translate the phrase as 'The Lord's Day', and for an English reader transform the meaning. This makes very good sense of vv. 21–24, where the prophet goes on to condemn sacrifices and hymn-singing. But whether we think that Amos's audience are complacently assuming that in the day of judgement they will be exonerated, or whether they imagine they are doing God favours by offering him expensive sacrifices and rich, musical worship, the prophet's point is exactly the same: they are in for a nasty shock. The prophets in the Old Testament, and Jesus and the apostles in the New, tell us about lots of people who claim to be on God's side, and who think that what they are doing pleases him, but who have in fact got it badly wrong. We may be confident in God's mercy, but would be wise not to be too sure of ourselves.

I Thessalonians 4.13–18

It is still early enough in the history of the church for the Thessalonians to have some rather naïve questions about the last times. They are answered seriously. The Thessalonians had been led to believe that the Lord would return quickly, and take the believers to himself. But now some have already died. Have they missed out on the full benefits of salvation because they will no longer be around when the Lord comes? Far from it, say the apostles. When it comes to the resurrection, those who have already died will actually be at the front of the queue. The imagery in which the authors describe the coming of the Lord suggests that naïve eschatology is not confined to the Thessalonians. What is surprising is not that the apostles and the other first Christians began with a simplistic eschatology but how quickly they moved on and worked out more refined and sophisticated ones.

Matthew 25.1–13

Like several of the parables peculiar to St Matthew, that of the Ten Virgins is a strange and rather problematical one. It is a story about a wedding, but an eccentric one in which the focus is entirely on the bridesmaids, and the bride never gets a mention. Perhaps we would understand it better if we knew more about the details of first-century Jewish wedding customs. It has been allegorized in at least a dozen different ways – the bridegroom is the messiah, the bridesmaids the church, and so on – but is it meant to be an allegory at all? Perhaps we should concentrate simply on those one or two things that can be said about it with a reasonable degree of certainty. It is surely a parable of judgement. Whether we see its context as the ministry of Jesus, and the judgement as being embodied in the coming and presence of Jesus himself, or whether we see it in the setting of the earliest Christian church, who would readily have interpreted it as referring to the coming of Christ in glory, the emphasis does seem to be on preparedness. However we envisage the judgement, what matters is that we are ready for it. And however we envisage the judgement, in the parable it is represented as totally uncompromising. The error of the foolish, letting themselves run out of oil, we may see as easily pardonable. But it is not pardoned. No allowances are made and no second chances given. Yet it is worth noting what is *not* there in this parable. The five unfortunate young ladies are not cast into outer darkness. There is no gnashing of teeth. They simply miss out on the party. They are just left outside. Or rather, they leave themselves out by not being ready at the crucial moment. Perhaps for us soft-centred modern Christians this is a more acceptable image of judgement than the fires of hell. Heaven is the soul's feast with God for all eternity. Hell is simply not being there.

But we must not let the sharp and unforgiving climax of the story distract us from its beginning, and forget that it is about wisdom and foolishness. It draws on a tradition going back deep into the Old Testament. Wisdom in the Old Testament is not something abstruse and intellectual. It is highly practical. It is about common-sense things, like knowing that if one is building a house it is better to build its foundations on rock rather than sand. And it is freely available. Wisdom offers herself, readily, to those who seek her. So there can be no excuses for remaining a fool. Everybody knows that a lampful of oil won't last all night.

SUNDAY BETWEEN 13 AND 19 NOVEMBER INCLUSIVE

(Thirty-third Sunday in Ordinary Time)

Judges 4.1–7; Zephaniah 1.7, 12–18; I Thessalonians 5.1–11;
Matthew 25.14–30

As is fitting as we approach the Advent season, all three related readings focus on aspects of accountability.

Judges 4.1–7

The lectionary has briefly allowed us a glimpse of Joshua crossing the Jordan, conquering the land, remaking the covenant. Now we move on. The promised land was no place for the people of Israel to rest on their laurels. Having moved in and taken over the country, they faced a series of challenges from other people who wanted to do exactly the same thing. The book of Judges explains that these other people were only allowed by the Lord to make serious trouble when Israel was untrue to him. When a faithful leader brought them back to their proper God they were able to expel their enemies and live in peace – until next time. It is a very simplistic reading of history, but it is the one that scripture offers us. Today's lection is merely a sample of one occasion on which Israel is oppressed by a powerful enemy (not, this time, from outside, but from within the land). When the people appeal to the Lord he raises up for them a saviour. On this particular occasion it is in fact two saviours, Deborah and Barak. Deborah is the inspired one, a prophet. She already has a great deal of prestige as a community leader (v. 5) and she is the one who takes the initiative, summoning Barak and giving him orders. The lectionary deprives us of the rest of this exciting, albeit bloodthirsty, story. But even as far as it goes, there are some important lessons here. We are often told that Old Testament society was a patriarchal society and that the Old Testament is a male-dominated book. Up to a point this is quite true, but not entirely so. The story shows that there was a place for women's leadership in Israel. A completely different aspect of the story is that it should prompt us to think harder about where our problems lie. Israel in Deborah's time perceived herself as having a problem with the Canaanites. She did have a problem with the Canaanites. There they were, with all their iron chariots. There was no denying they were real. The judges demonstrate that, notwithstanding the chariots, the real problem is not outside but inside. If only Israel would get her priorities right, put God at the centre of her life, the problems of the world outside might be made to look quite different. The judges begin with faith, proceed to faithfulness, and only then prepare to take on the world.

Zephaniah 1.7, 12–18

The prophet Zephaniah was apparently a contemporary of Jeremiah. He is looking towards the imminent disaster of conquest and destruction which he sees to be hanging over the nation. The language is dramatic and threatening. The text of our reading forms the substance of the *Dies Irae*, which has traditionally formed part of the requiem mass. In the context of today's lections the key verse is v. 12. The leaders of the nation are conscious of no threat. They see no problem of divine judgement. 'They say in their hearts, "The Lord will not do good, nor will he do ill".' In short, God can be ignored. Our other readings are about having confidence in the face of judgement. But this is not confidence, it is complacency.

I Thessalonians 5.1–11

The judgement of God is something to be taken seriously, not something to worry about. It looks as if the Thessalonians have been worrying. One thing they have been worrying about is when it will happen. The apostles remind them gently in vv. 1–2 that they know the answer to this question already. We have been told no date. There will be no warning, other than the warning we have already been given. Any hour can be the hour of judgement, and every hour we need to be prepared to be called to account for what we do. But this is not meant to be scary. Christian people, behaving as children of the light, which is what they are, and trusting God, which is what they normally do, have no need to worry. God is on our side. We know that. What the apostles are saying to the Thessalonians is: 'Go on being what you are; and be confident in God.'

Matthew 25.14–30

It is hard not to be sorry for the one-talent man. Most readers feel: 'That might be me.' That's what we are meant to feel – and to be warned. God is no egalitarian. The way the master shares out the money suggests that he knew before he started who was likely to make the best use of it. But what did the one-talent man get wrong? He kept his master's money secure. Wasn't that the first requirement? Evidently not. The sin of the one-talent man was to play safe. God doesn't like people who play safe. The story of the Bible is the story of a God who himself never plays safe. The one-talent man ends up gnashing his teeth in outer darkness (St Matthew's favourite repository for life's failures). This seems cruel, but when you think about it, not playing safe has a lot to do with faith. Faith is what the one-talent man lacks, faith and confidence. Some of it is self-confidence. Again, one sympathizes. Risking your own money is one thing, risking very large sums of somebody else's is quite another. But it isn't only self-confidence he is short of, it is confidence in his master. He actually gets the character of the master quite wrong. 'I knew', he says, 'that you are a hard man.' But God is not a hard man. God *expects* his servants to take risks on his behalf; demands it, even. He trusts them to do their best with what he has committed to them, and expects them to trust him as to the outcome. (The parable does not tell us, however, what would have happened if one of the servants had speculated in futures and broken the bank.) There is plenty of room for humility in the Christian life, but none for timidity. Advent approaches, when we remember that we are all accountable to God; all will eventually face judgement. But the person of true faith is not afraid of judgement. We may 'with confidence draw near the throne of grace' (Heb. 4.16), not because we are sure of ourselves, but because we are sure of our Lord.

SUNDAY BEFORE ADVENT

Ezekiel 34.11–16, 20–24; Ephesians 1.15–23; Matthew 25.31–46

The Methodist Worship Book does not mention that the theme for this Sunday is 'Christ the King', though some other service books do so and the theme is certainly reflected in the first of the two collects for today. In the readings themselves the figure of the shepherd is at least as prominent as that of king, and the two motifs are intertwined, as indeed they frequently are in scripture.

Ezekiel 34.11–16, 20–24

The chapter begins with some fierce strictures on 'the shepherds of Israel', the leaders of the nation who have failed to look after their flock. (This is in vv. 1–10, before the lection starts.) God's answer to the problem is that he will take over the job himself. 'I myself will be the shepherd of my sheep', he says (v. 15). In the translation before me the divine pronoun 'I' occurs fifteen times in six verses, emphasizing that the Lord himself is taking personal responsibility. Verses 11–16 set out in detail the ways in which he will care for his hitherto neglected flock. But in the second half of our reading there is an abrupt change of perspective. No longer are the criticisms directed at the bad shepherds. It is the sheep themselves who are being condemned for offences against one another. The shepherd is here transformed, as it were, into the judge. Before the lection ends we have another unexpected twist, in vv. 23–24, when the Lord reverts to his role as God and the good shepherd becomes an earthly ruler. But this is a ruler superior to the bad shepherds dismissed earlier, 'my servant David'. By this the prophet means a king from the ancient royal house. Ezekiel is prophesying at the time of the exile, and in fact no such king of the house of David ever was restored to the throne of Israel. That prophecy had to await its strange fulfilment in the person of Jesus Christ.

Ephesians 1.15–23

The Epistle does not use shepherd language, but the language of kingship alone. The reading begins, however, not with Christ but with Christians. The apostle is sketching, in glowing colours, the bounteousness of the Christian hope and 'the riches of [God's] glorious inheritance'. But he quickly passes on, for any glory in store for

Christians is contingent upon the glory of their Lord. The authority of Christ is expounded in uncompromising terms. In v. 20 the resurrection becomes almost a minor prelude to the main action, for 'God raised him [Christ] from the dead and made him sit at his right hand in heavenly places, far above all rule and authority and power and dominion, and above every name that is named'. The rest of the description could hardly be more exalted. The authority which is claimed for Christ is not only the highest conceivable, it is the most comprehensive conceivable, 'the fullness of him who fills all in all' (v. 23).

Matthew 25.31–46

This is such a familiar passage that it is easy to overlook the fact that at its heart is an oddity. It is a judgement scene, with the Son of man enthroned as king and judge. Yet what is being judged is a flock. Those in front of him are being separated into sheep and goats, as a shepherd sorts out those under his charge. We are accustomed in scripture to seeing the shepherd represented as a carer, but as Ezekiel reminds us, there is also a threatening side to his activities. He is the one who sorts out the bullies from the flock (Ezek. 34.20–22).

The parable draws on the widespread tradition of the divine visitor who appears incognito. 'The King' (v. 40) has appeared to all these people, and they have not known him. It is interesting that both parties, the sheep and the goats, are surprised at the judgement. Both ask the same question: 'Lord, *when* did we see you hungry etc?' (vv. 37 and 44). Both are judged, but neither is aware of the basis on which judgement has been made. There are many salutary conclusions that could be drawn from this parable, but one of the most salutary is that when the Son of man comes in his glory, and all his angels with him, we are likely to be judged not by the great moral decisions over which we agonized, but by the ones we took in a fit of absence of mind.